Against the Odds, Given up for Dead

The Life Saving Work of Dr. Al Plechner

David Spangenburg

and Dr. Alfred Plechner DVM

Against the Odds, Given up for Dead –
The Life Saving Work of Dr. Al Plechner DVM

Published by
The Opinion Sector, Publishing
5601 9th Ave N,
St Petersburg, FL 33710

ISBN-13: 978-0615684154
ISBN-10: 0615684157

Book Cover Designed by B. William Design, Walnut, CA
Cover Photo of Jayden Plechner and Jack, by Shelly Plechner

The medical information contained in this book is intended for informational and educational purposes only. It reflects the thoughts and opinions of the authors and Dr. Al Plechner's clients and supporters. We hope it will make a difference in you, your family and pet's health and well-being. Please contact your own health care professional for specific recommendations and treatment. Health care professionals interested in further information about Dr. Al's clinical studies and medical suggestions are welcome to consult his website...

http://www.drplechner.com

On line, in depth consultations are also available through the Consultation Page on his website.

Dedications

This Book is dedicated to my most devoted and loyal readers, my dear sister and brother, Pat and John Nappi. Always there with encouragement, support, coffee and happy talk.

To Ray and Kit (Spangenburg & Moser) who set the bar high through their; dedication to the craft, prolific writing and their hundreds of books that have made science, technology, engineering and literature more "interesting" and accessible to young readers, around the world.

And of course, to my most trusted partner, my closest and dearest friend and loving wife, Kate, you make my world turn and hold my heart as a happy captive.

Last but not least, I would like to raise a cup to the amazing Dr. Al, for his decades of work at the "end of the line". Due to his clinical research and deep love for all creatures, great and small, he was able to save the lives over 200,000 animals, which were given up for dead by the very vets who berated him and refused to follow his incredibly important medical findings. Here's to you, my dear friend and partner.

David Spangenburg

I would like to dedicate the book to my son, Jay Louis Plechner. Several years back, disappointed, angry and frustrated with the closed mindedness of many of my peers, I quit my practice and went into retirement. Jay knew that I live for my work and could never turn my back on my people and their animals. If it were not for his devotion and loyalty to me and my work, I would not be in practice today and would never have worked on this book with David. I also dedicate the book to, Gary Tavernetti. From our first encounter, he adopted me as his older brother and I adopted him as my little brother and we have been dear friends ever since. Through all these years he has continued to believe in me and has always been tremendously supportive of my studies and other endeavors.

I am also thankful that David believed in my studies and findings enough to write the wonderful words that you will read in this book. I applaud my son for getting me back into the healing world that I love so much, Gary for his friendship and support and David for bringing my findings to the world in such a thoughtful and entertaining way.

Al Plechner

Author's Note

A funny thing happened on the way to publication, this book became the second of two books being written and published about Dr. Al Plechner DVM. Almost three years ago, I was asked by an acquaintance to write an article about his veterinarian. The story he told me about Doctor Alfred Plechner; his remarkable practice and amazing clinical research findings, really peaked my interest and after quite a bit of research I wrote a very opinionated but complimentary article called *Medical Ice Age!?* . It was published, Thursday May 14, 2009 simultaneously, on my Blog, **The Opinion Sector.com** and on the popular progressive news and opinion website, **OpEdNews.com.**

A somewhat negative comment, left by one of **OpEdNews** editors, generated such a protective outpouring from Plechner's clients; it compelled me to do a follow-up article on both sites. The follow-up, *Medical Ice Age, Revisited* was actually created as a vehicle to give voice to these dedicated, enthusiastic and devoted Plechner "people", whose beloved pets had been saved by this "plain wrapped" unassuming healer. Their dramatic true stories of life and death touched my heart and convinced me that the story of Dr. Al's amazing clinical findings and how they changed these people's lives needed to be told. And so, *Against the Odds, Given up for Dead* was conceived.

Al was very enthusiastic about the idea, even though he was already involved in a long term project with client and close friend of ten years, Kirk E. Nims. Kirk was editing Al's biographical writings, helping to create Al's autobiography, *Fifty Years of Healing.* As Al and I worked on *Against the Odds...* certain biographical excerpts were drawn from the original historical materials that Al provided to Kirk. So, those of you who read both books about Dr. Al Plechner and his work you now know how the small bit of similarity between a few of those biographical passages innocently came to be. For those of you who haven't read *50 Years of Healing* please do so with the knowledge that it is a more complete "biography" and (outside of those few passages) is a completely different book in content, attitude and technique. Kirk, as an editor, endeavored to maintain Dr. Al's manner and style of writing. I, on the other hand, being an author use my own distinct "voice" when I write. A lot of this book is *partner* written. Al providing the medical genius and scientific and biographical facts which I, in turn, would lay out in an engaging, plain spoken and hopefully entertaining and somewhat witty kind of way.

D. S.

CONTENTS

VOLUME ONE

The Man and his Medicine

CHAPTER ONE

Doctor Al Plechner DVM
Healer, Conservationist, Animal Activist

CHAPTER TWO

The Plechner Syndrome and Protocol

CHAPTER THREE

Second Opinions
Peer Support

CHAPTER FOUR

The Human Factor
Health in the New Millennium

CHAPTER FIVE

His People Speak
True Stories of Life and Death, Courage and Commitment

VOLUME TWO

The Healthfully Yours Handbook For Whole Animal Health

Volume One

The Man and his Medicine

Introduction

"Large numbers of pets and people die or become sick before their time despite the best efforts of healthcare professionals. In order to change this, there must be a realization that we are in a, 'Medical Ice Age'."
  - Dr. Alfred J. Plechner DVM

How would you feel if you found out that they've discovered a cure for cancer but they're not going to let anyone know about it? I'm sure you're all responding to this question by attacking it. "Why would they do that?" "That makes no sense!" "What about the money they could make?"

I could answer all of your objections by stating a single fact. The profits that a cancer cure would accrue wouldn't even come close to the profits made by all of the cancer treatment drugs and the associated services involved in treating cancer. Sad to say, the treatment of cancer has proven itself to be, a tremendously successful revenue builder. Why wouldn't you keep a possible cure under wraps?

But of course, this is purely a hypothetical question. We couldn't possibly believe that our medical institutions could be callously driven by the pursuit of profit. Why, they're as ethical as our great financial institutions are and look at how successful they've been.

The frightening fact is that a cancer cure could prove to be financially disastrous to the pharmaceutical and all of the other dependent medical industries. The key word in the preceding sentence is *industries*. In our corporately constructed society, the medical profession has become, an industry directed more by profits than by principal.

The 'hands on' noble vocation of healing the sick seems to have become just another job. Controlled and limited by corporate officers and regulatory agencies like the AMA and the FDA, medicine is driven by the cold hard facts of student loans and malpractice insurance. The current corporate medical paradigm's methodology seems to be based on the principle that "there is more profit in treatment than there is in cure".

Has the Hippocratic Oath become a semantic punch line by the juxtaposition of a single letter? The sad reality is that our medical and pharmacological institutions have become far more financially successful by treating maladies than they would be by actually curing them. More importantly, they seem to see no reason to upset the "status quo".

How can you argue with success? Well that depends on what your primary goals are and how loyal you are to your principals. Not to mention any concern you might have for improving the human condition. Or the animal condition as the case may be.

Doctor Alfred J. Plechner is a Veterinarian who is concerned with both. He stands at the opposite end of the spectrum. He is the consummate medical professional whose devotion to duty reflects a true 'calling to vocation'. People who have sought his healing hands to help "end of the line animals" have called him, "the doctor who never stops caring."

He began his practice in 1966 in Los Angeles, A young but dedicated practitioner he soon became frustrated by the fact that many of his patients weren't responding to standard treatments. As he puts it,

"Large numbers of pets and people die or become sick before their time despite the best efforts of healthcare professionals. I believe much of this has to do with hormonal imbalances that have possibly deregulated (lowered) animal and human immune systems, and thereby has undermined their natural protection against illness and disease."

Refusing to, just accept the inevitable. He decided to find another way to treat them. He has researched (on his own time and his own dime) for over 40 years. That clinical research, led to his discovery of an "Endocrine - Immune Imbalance", the *Plechner Syndrome*. It involves a defect in the middle layer of the adrenal glands, which are pair of ductless glands that sit astride the kidneys in the lower back.

The defect keeps the glands from manufacturing enough cortical hormone (helps the body fight stress and infections) and can cause the cortisol to bind up (become inactive). In turn, too much adrenal estrogen can be produced and not enough thyroid hormones, causing an imbalanced immune system. Dr. Plechner believes,

"...this creates a ripple effect throughout the body's physiology, making them susceptible to conditions ranging from, Autoimmune Diseases, Cancer, Common Allergies, and Reproductive Failure."

Dr. Plechner developed a simple treatment procedure to minister this defect. The *Plechner Protocol* is a series of physiological (low dosage) injections (or oral medication) of cortisone to boost up the adrenal glands. He also found it necessary to give low doses of thyroid hormone to 90% of his dogs and 10% of his cats. Once the endocrine system is back in balance, the immune system kicks in and all the disease symptoms disappear. Commonly, this protocol of low dose oral hormone replacement must continue for the rest of the animal's life.

This ongoing usage of cortisol, a known steroid, has lead Dr. Plechner's findings to be met with disapproval, reproach, and some downright condemnation. Many of his veterinarian peers have refused pet owner's requests to initiate the *Plechner Protocol* testing and treatment. They refused to try a successful therapy, even when they themselves had no alternatives. They ignored the pet owner's demands and actually offered euthanasia, as the only compassionate recourse.

Two other "reasons" for the condemnation he has faced were that he had not conducted "controlled" double blind studies using split groups of patients along with placebos and the ever present, asinine, statement "I never read that in medical school!".

These are pretty weak arguments when you consider that Dr. Plechner's successful treatment program has "saved", well over

3

200,000 dogs, cats, horses and even humans who were literally "given up for dead". Dr. Plechner firmly believes that as a veterinary clinician, he not only has the right, he has a moral obligation to do all he possibly can, to heal his patients. He will do everything within his power to prevent them from becoming one of the numerous sad statistics that are euthanized by confused veterinarians every day. Many veterinarians are; victims of reactionary, "inside the box" educational curriculums and intimidated by the professionally provincial and insular environment of the medical community that constrains many vet's approach to their practice.

The Animal and Human Protocols that. Dr. Plechner has developed to treat *Plechner's Syndrome* have been extremely effective, throughout the world. They produce remarkable, almost miraculous, results, even in the most desperately ill and diseased animals and humans, when continued, as directed, on a long-term basis by healthcare professionals.

As you will see, later on in this book, Dr. Plechner's findings have been more readily embraced by medical doctors than by veterinarians. Dr. Plechner has consulted with numerous MDs who have patients that are plagued by Endocrine/Immune maladies which are caused by *Plechner's Syndrome*.

Dr. Plechner's *Protocol* has had a very pronounced effect on FIV, feline immunodeficiency virus. With a remarkable recovery rate of over 70%, it's no wonder that *Plechner's Protocol* has already been utilized by medical doctors in their fight against human HIV (AIDS). Every animal that Dr. Plechner has treated for cancer, has also had *Plechner's Syndrome*. Once his healing *Protocol* has balanced the patient's immune system, the advance of the cancer has slowed dramatically and in numerous cases went into a lengthy if not permanent remission.

Given the fact that almost every one of his cancer patients has shown positive improvement, is it possible that we might be able to cure or perhaps even prevent cancer? Could we find a way to STOP this insidious killer by studying Dr. Al Plechner's clinical research into this "adrenal defect"? These are questions that continue to be asked, due to the advanced stages of "status quo"

4

which has so grievously afflicted the corporate medical establishment.

Due to "over-whelming request", Dr. Plechner has come out of retirement and is currently in practice at **Center Sinai Animal Hospital** in Los Angeles, California. He still continues to offer consultations for the general public as well as for healthcare professionals interested in exploring the possible role of *Plechner's Syndrome* in various diseases.

Dr. Plechner has published three books and has compiled a Compendium of Articles written for medical journals. Even so, what you hold in your hands is the first book to take an *intimate and personal look* at the Doctor and allows his people to tell their own dramatic, true accounts of life, death, courage and commitment. It is our hope that this book will mainstream Dr. Plechner's findings, to pet owners and medical professionals around the world.

We encourage the Schools of Veterinary Medicine to give Dr. Plechner's successful findings, very close scrutiny. Many medical professionals, in both animal and human health, continue to seek out his counsel on a broad range of topics. This professional interest grows exponentially as the tally of efficacious cases grows. Perhaps it's time to review and amend your standard and traditional but limited and somewhat antiquated curriculums.

More importantly, we'd like to offer a personal challenge to all you young vets, just starting up your practice. Keep your minds open to all the "possibilities in healing", even those not taught in the classrooms. Always remember, that you are the *future* of Whole Animal Health, not the *past*.

David Spangenburg
St Petersburg, FL, 5/2012

Prologue

It was sweltering in southern California. The Santa Ana winds, blasting hot, dry desert air through the canyons, pushed any hopes of a cooling sea breeze back out over the Pacific. The late afternoon traffic seemed denser than usual and the heat and Santa Ana "brain static" were adding to the mix. Tension layered the air, thick as the smog that was beginning to color the western sky.

In between the abundant stop lights along Sepulveda Blvd, traffic was humming like an intermittent live wire. Inpatient drivers were leapfrogging and hop-scotching through as many lights as possible. Squealing brakes sounded, counterpoint to repeated horn honks as obscenities highlighted this angry urban fugue

It was a deadly obstacle course for Judy Flerman and her yellow Lab, Haven as they made their way on foot through this chaotic scene. She was tired, troubled and just wanted to get home. Her main concern was for Haven. She knew that her dog was feeling even worse than she was.

The young Lab had been victim to numerous health problems ever since she came into Judy's life. They had made the rounds of the local vets and after spending money and time that Judy _did_ not have to spare. Haven seemed sicker than ever.

Judy knew this was their crossing even though Haven seemed hesitant. As they started across the street Haven seemed to falter and after a slight stumble she lay down and try as she might Judy could not get her to stand. As she crouched to encourage the exhausted dog, Judy could sense the energy mounting. The street light was about to change.

She commanded Haven to rise and walk but her words were swallowed by the increasing chorus of horns. Knowing that Haven was not going to stand on her own, Judy struggled to pick her up. As she rose with the trembling dog in her arms, Judy lost track of the direction they were traveling.

Standing in the middle of the stalled roadway holding her disabled Guide Dog, Judy felt totally exposed. Horns and angry insults filled the air as the sightless Judy blindly waded through the threatening traffic, not sure at all which way led to safety.

* * *

When he first heard this story, Dr. Alfred Plechner was amazed by Judy Flerman's quiet courage not by the veracity of her words. Having had a Veterinarian practice in Southern California for many years he'd had more than his share of work with debilitated line bred "champions"

He knew that service dog breeders, like most professional breeders, utilize a reproductive technique called line breeding -- mating slightly removed family members such as nephew to aunt, grandsire to granddaughter - to hopefully pass on certain skills that the sire and dame have been taught. These matings sometimes pass these learned behaviors on to their offspring genetically, which in a number of cases is a good thing.

Line breeding is, basically, a type of inbreeding; a restrained form but inbreeding nonetheless. The breed registries, or Studbooks regulations demand the use of registry animals only, thereby creating a closed gene pool. They do this to "insure" offspring with consistent *breed specific* regularities. While they are seeking "consistent excellence" through the creation of a homozygosis type of excellence, this type of breeding often passes on deleterious genes as well.

Some of the service animals, Al has encountered, were so genetically defective there was no possible way that they could handle the responsibilities required of a guide dog. It's a shame that these physically disabled owners give their love to an animal that requires more care than they can realistically offer and whose life span is shortened by these defects. A number of the animals never last the good eight to ten years that they should.

Some time ago, Dr. Plechner contacted the guide dog school and offered his services, free of charge, to help them deal with these potential medical problems. He had developed special hormone specific blood tests which would determine possible deficiencies and a protocol to follow to eliminate these deficiencies. Al still feels that it's not enough to uncover just the obvious clean hips and clean elbows.

"These animals need to be clean and fully functioning inside as well as out. They need certification for normal adrenal cortex function and normal antibody response. The guide dog schools should make every effort to ensure that their animals can serve the handicapped owners without the guide dogs becoming handicapped themselves."

Even though Al assured the Guide Dog School that they could be totally certain that they were providing only healthy, sound and happy dogs for the sight challenged. The school was not interested. It did not see the need to pay the lab for these "extra" tests.

"They hide behind their good intentions." Judy Flerman once said to Al, *"What's the use of all the good intentions if the dogs bring more burden than benefits? The one thing we do not need is more burdens."*

8

CHAPTER ONE

Doctor Al Plechner DVM
Healer, Conservationist, Animal Activist

Plechner at a Glance

1938 was quite a year. They found oil in Saudi Arabia, Bugs Bunny made his first screen appearance as (what else?) the hare and ***Times*** magazine named Adolph Hitler their 'Man of the Year'. Not one of the most historic years but interesting none the less.

There was also a minor happening in '38 that didn't register on the Richter scale of notable events but still has proven to be relatively historic. Alfred J. Plechner was born in an area called "Three Tree Point" on the Puget Sound in the state of Washington on April 4th of that year.

Now I know some of you are saying, "Who's Alfred J. Plechner?", and rightly so because Al didn't find the oil in Saudi Arabia, hasn't graced the cover of ***Times*** and though he has spent quality time with some rabbits it was never immortalized on the silver screen. Not yet anyway. However, there are still a lot of you out there who have quiet prayers on their lips blessing this quiet, unassuming, rebel *with* a cause.

Those of you who chanced upon him in an hour of traumatic need and desperate urgency, it's more likely than not, that he surely delivered you and your loved ones from an almost hopeless time. A time when others' said there was nothing they could do. The odds were against you. It was the end of the line.

You were frantic. You couldn't just give up on a family member even if they were of the furry persuasion. There must be someone who could help. Second opinions; echoed the first and it seemed that there was no one who had the answer you were hoping for. Reality flaunted her bona fides and you felt helplessly trapped by the inevitable.

Those of you, who were lucky enough to find Doctor Alfred Plechner, DVM, found a man who spent a lot of his time at the end of the line, a man who had faced the *inevitable* many times and, through many years of research by clinical trials had discovered a way to beat the odds and not only prolong the inevitable but fill that extension with a number of more happy, healthy, quality years. You made the call, witnessed a miracle and asked yourselves, "Is this real?"

Reality, it has been claimed, is *what is real or existent* the *real nature of a thing*. Reality however is also highly subjective. The true nature of things is always determined by the mind of the beholder. One person's reality is often another's fantasy. We would all love to live our fantasies but, more often than not, reality calls the shots and can be a harsh mistress. The lessons she teaches can make or break a person.

It was reality that schooled Al's early years. The reality was that his fisherman father's extreme allergies and severe asthma caused him to become somewhat bedridden and the family was forced to leave the quiet beauty of the Sound and move into town. Reality was that his 4 year old sister was run over by a car and the nearest hospital proved to be too busy to see her, despite her massive head trauma, so by the time they reached the next she had died. Al was just 7 years old at the time but old enough to remember the reality of the incident and, ponder years later, the true meaning of the "Hippocratic" Oath.

Reality smiled on Al once again when he was but 11 years old. Returning from school one day, he was told that his Dad had a severe asthma attack and had gone to the hospital for an injection of a bronchodilator, called Aminophyline, Instead of the expected relief, his father had a terrible reaction and died within minutes. Reality was batting a thousand. Al was three and 0.

These brushes with reality convinced Al to go into medicine. At the end of his first year in medical school, Al developed some gastrointestinal problems.

The Dean of Men blamed Al's medical problems on freshman nerves so a two week course of Paregoric and bed rest was prescribed. However, after losing 40 pounds, and a lot of his hair, Al thought that he might just die.

He flew home and presented such a sight that his Mother and Grandmother immediately took him to the family physician who, after gauging Al's clinical symptoms with serum titers and using a practioner's thoroughly inquisitive and medically driven diagnostic skills, announced that Al had typhoid fever.

Reality barely contained her chuckles, a 3rd world disease misdiagnosed in a student at such a highly rated medical school! The medical school's Dean was amazed at the serious diagnosis, and mumbled something about people being too close to the picture. He suggested that Al rest up then come back next year, and join the February class.

While Al was recuperating and considering his next course of action he took the family's English bulldog, Moose, to see his veterinarian. While there, he admitted that medical school was like getting a PhD in a basic science and he that he always wanted to be a clinician. The vet suggested that he drive up and speak to the Dean of the Veterinary School at the University of California at Davis. Something clicked in Al that day. Something told him to take a chance and he agreed.

The next day, he drove up to Davis and it turned out that the Dean was doing similar research studies as he was. The Dean asked Al, if he would like to join his fall class. After thinking about it for two weeks Al called and accepted his offer. He started Veterinary school the fall of 1962 and graduated in August of 1966.

During his sophomore year at UC Davis, reality once again upset Al's world, He came home for the Christmas holidays and discovered that his Mother had a lump in her left breast. She was 52 years old with no family history of any kind of cancer. Her left breast and axillary lymph node were removed and revealed the presence of a malignant mammary tumor.

The surgeons took out both adrenal glands and irradiated both ovaries to reduce the risk of an "estrogenic effect," which not only caused the original tumor, but could also cause it to spread._ Al watched closely and made note of the fact that after replacing the two types of adrenal hormone, glucocorticoid and mineral corticoid, she did well for four years.

Even so, his mother began to seriously decalcify, any cough or sneeze, would fracture the bones in her spine and ribs. It was a tough time for Al but it encouraged his further hormonal research. He began working on the cortisol, thyroid, and estrogen connection. He was already aware that a thyroid imbalance often, if not always, accompanies a cortisol-estrogen imbalance.

He soon deduced that the thyroid hormone was bound (blocked from the receptors) and each time the daily dose of steroids was given; there remained a residue of cortisol. So after a number of days, the regulatory amounts of the controlling cortisol went from a physiological (low) dose level to a harmful, pharmacological (high) overdose.

Besides the pathological fractures she continued to sustain, his mother was cold all the time and began to lose her hair. Her axillary temperatures were subnormal, even though her thyroid hormones were normal and she continued to de-calcify. Al suggested thyroid hormone replacement to her physician who agreed that it could not hurt. His mom felt better immediately upon receiving the thyroid hormone. Her temperature started to rise and the decalcification stopped and eventually she began to recalcify. Mom Plechner lived for another 36 years on the adrenal thyroid replacements and just "went to sleep" one day during her 88th year.

The truth is that reality, as harsh a mistress as she may be, actually became a muse for Al. Her cruel lessons textured his life, directed him to a medical career and drove him in the clinical researches that lead to his discovery of an endocrine-immune system imbalance, *Plechner Syndrome,* and his subsequent development of the *Plechner Protocol.*

Even though these phenomenal findings have not become a part of mainstream medical practice, as of yet, their benefits have touched the lives of over 200,000 animals and their people and offered possible answers to many serious medical questions that continue to plague modern man.

Senior Project

Al's, senior research paper at UC Davis was to show, what the veterinary academics called osteogenesis imperfecta (brittle bone disease) was actually a completely different syndrome specific to animals. Al reached these conclusions while working on his senior project.

His senior project found him working with a young mountain lion in Oakland, California. A 4 month old, male named, Tigger. Whenever Tigger jumped off, even a low chair or mattress, he would fracture his bones in a manner which is referred to as pathological fractures. This was due to the fact that the cortices of his long bones were tissue thin, along with all the other bones in his body.

The general opinion, at the time, was that he was suffering from; osteogenesis imperfecta which, in humans, is a genetic disorder that leads to the same kind of pathological fractures that Tigger was suffering. However, after analyzing Tigger's diet, Al found that he was being fed only meat, which has 20 parts of phosphorus to 1 part calcium. Al determined that Tigger, actually did not have osteogenesis imperfecta, but rather was suffering from a serious nutritional imbalance.

Every day, as Tigger ingested his 'total meat diet', the 20 to 1 ration of phosphorus to calcium was his true nemesis. His body needed to keep a 1 to 1 or 1 to 2 ratio between phosphorus and calcium. To meet these requirements, his body factory was being forced to remove calcium from its own bones. To create this normal ratio, it was releasing an excess of parathyroid hormone (PTH) and by doing so, his bones became much weaker and fractured on their own.

In the wilds this did not happen because the wild felines ate most of their prey including bones and skin which contained the needed calcium. Al had the pet owner add calcium and bones to Tigger's diet and in the weeks that followed his skeletal system began to re-calcify. Al's senior paper detailed how Tigger's disorder was not, in fact, osteogenesis imperfecta but rather a nutritional hyperparathyroidism.

A few years later, it was decided that all the big cats in zoos and other captive sites also needed to be fed bones with their meat, to avoid similar problems. Years later, after Al created his first commercial non-meat balanced food product with calcium and phosphorus, he was pleased that it was quickly adopted for use in zoos. They called it *Zoopreme*.

Years of Practice, Life Saving Discoveries and Controversy

Al, graduated from the University of California, Davis, School of Veterinary Medicine in 1966 (*his sons say 1866*). After graduation, Dr. Alfred Plechner DVM was hired into an established practice. Young and raw, he was jokingly referred to as the "smart ass from UC Davis"; a nick name that Al admits was pretty close to true. Fueled by the fervor for his vocation, he was proud, idealistic and full of himself. Even so, he had a way with the clients and his furry, scaled and feathered patients all yielded to his healing ministrations. They could feel his love and dedicated concern, through the sure touch of his hands.

As time progressed, Al's numerous cases increased his interests in allergy, auto immunity and catastrophic diseases. These on-the-job experiences, along with the vivid memories of his mother's battle with breast cancer and the hormonal replacement therapy that restored her health, confirmed to Al, that he had made a critical discovery. All of these conditions appeared to be connected to a major dysfunction that seemed to be caused by a cortisol imbalance, originating in the middle layer adrenal cortex. This imbalance caused a domino like chain reaction among the other hormones which quickly lead to a breakdown within the immune system.

This made sense to Al. It also explained why cortisone injections were so common and so successful. Besides being an effective anti-inflammatory agent, they were also, unknowingly, restoring hormonal balance to the immune system. After 11 years in practice, controlling many successful cases, Al was very anxious to share his findings with his peers. He was excited to offer them, a valuable tool to use in their practice, to better serve their patients.

Innocently, he wrote an article called, "*Immune Complex Diseases*". *Modern Veterinary Practice*, interested in his work, published this paper in November of 1976. The "smart ass" finally had his first paper published and, knowing the ways of academia, quietly waited for its "educational gears" to add their thoughts to his findings! Little did Al know, he had backed into a 'veterinary academy band saw'! The academy read his work and assigned one of their more sardonic members to, anonymously, critique the article. The following excerpt offers a hint of the general demeanor of the critique...

"The first paragraph gives one an indication of what one is in for when the author apparently equates immune complex disease with autoimmunity. The rest of the paper varies from scientific to absurd and gives the appearance that alternate paragraphs were written by a scientist and a 10th grader with a fascination for science fiction".

After 2 pages of this veterinary academy review (assassination?), the critic delivered the coup de grace with this quote...

"I have to conclude that the extensive decontamination process which was carried out on the astronauts return was not in fact successful and that this accounts for this rash of new diseases in the canine population".

This review created quite an uproar. The overwhelming opinion being that, whether the information was correct or not, the "review" was a highly abusive and unprofessional "attack" and should never have happened. We now know, the information in Al's first article was innovative, ground breaking and completely correct and even though Al was shocked by the attack and the outrage that followed, the hullabaloo just encouraged the "smart ass" to continue his clinical studies, which lead to many more significant findings.

As Al continued to write about his findings, he continued to discover that it was very difficult to reference an "original discovery" to the liking of his peer reviewed veterinary journals. This, however, did not seem to be the case with the Medical Doctors. Many MDs found Al's findings quite convincing and soon his papers were being published in numerous MD and PHD journals including; *Medical Hypothesis, Journal of Toxicology* and the *Townsend Letter*. A Compendium, containing a collection of his articles from around the world, has been published and is available on **Amazon**.

Not all of his peers discount his work. **The American Holistic Veterinary Medical Association** has published one of his articles and a number of their members and members of other veterinary organizations are utilizing the findings of Al's forty years of clinical research and are having great successes with their patients. It was these "on the job" successes that led to Al's true support base, the tens of thousands of clients that have benefited from Al's dedicated work to heal their deeply loved animals.

Most of the criticism of his findings was due to the fact that they weren't subjected to double blind studies and other costly and time consuming procedures to confirm what had already been proven, time and time again. Al did all his clinical research on the job and "on his own dime". He didn't have the access, the money or the time. He was too busy saving a continuous procession of dogs, cats and horses from the euthanasia needle suggested by many of his puzzled peers, who didn't have a clue, what to do.

It were these "real life" results that led to the publication of two very popular books, which Al coauthored with Martin Zucker. According to, Dr. Albert J. Simpson DVM, the first, *Pet Allergies, Remedies for an Epidemic,*

"...offered valuable information not taught in Veterinarian school nor mentioned in Veterinary Journals..."

Dr. Simpson continued his observation about the Endocrine - Immune Imbalance, the *Plechner Syndrome* and the *Plechner Protocol* that Al had developed to treat it.

"This indeed appeared to be a major discovery. I felt that somebody had given me the missing pieces to a jigsaw puzzle I had been trying to solve for years."

The second book, **Pets at Risk**, was praised again by Dr. Simpson

"This book is an eye opener. For Veterinarians it fills a big knowledge gap and opens a broad avenue into effective prevention and healing. This information is decades ahead of mainstream veterinary medicine."

...and also commended by Medical Doctor, Dr. David Brownstein MD...

"Al Plechner's revelations from years of clinical practice have connected the dots between unrecognized hormonal defects and immune system disorders. As a medical doctor, I find that his work explains many of the chronic problems I see among my patients. This book shows how safe and effective hormone treatments can be used to rebuild the immune system."

Currently, besides this volume that you're reading, there is another in-depth biographical book that is available on **Amazon.com** called *Fifty Years of Healing*. This concerted effort to further mainstream Dr. Plechner's contributions and continuing work; illustrates the love and admiration for this man of medicine. He is, truly, the consummate healer personified. His efforts have provided us with, not only, the map to chart our course to whole animal health but the keys to unlock the cures to many of the catastrophic diseases that threaten all creatures on this planet. His astute findings should take their rightful place in the curriculum of all schools of veterinary medicine. It is imperative to world health that his work is carried on by new generations of healers.

Currently, in his early seventies, Al is not wiling away his time on some golf course, getting fat and lazy in retirement. He is still in active practice at **Center-Sinai Animal Hospital** in Los Angeles, California, healing ailments and offering more than just hope.

At night, after long days in the clinic, he is still at work, consulting over the phone (and computer) with thousands of frightened pet lovers and their questioning vets. He is still saving the lives of animals that were given up for dead by the very peers who criticize his findings. All of "Plechner's People" have seen the "miracles" and demand notice. It is time that our medical professions offer more than just treatments. It is time to take the keys in hand and unlock the CURES.

In Search of a Healthful Diet

During his early years in practice, Dr. Al Plechner, became well educated in the various allergic conditions that were threatening our pet population. He knew that these allergies were roused by the various allergens within each of the afflicted animals' environments. Knowing that he could not control all the environmental stimulants like pollens, room fragrances cleaning products and other environmental inhalants, he decided to look at the primary thing all of these animals had in common...food

In the late 60's, most of pets in the US had a major thing in common. They were eating commercial pet foods. You didn't have to be Sherlock Holmes, to deduce that many of the allergies affecting our pet population were due to food allergies or food sensitivities. Al decided to take a long hard look at ingredients of these commercial pet food products to determine what they were actually ingesting.

What Al found, upon researching many commercial foods, was truly alarming.* The '60's pet food market was more or less an extension of the grain-based livestock feed business. Dry pet foods utilized vegetable and soy proteins in place of meat, and canned foods were made of meat byproducts, which were high in fat and dubious in quality.

Al soon determined that the majority of the popular brands contained a number of nonfood products and other questionable sources of protein, fat and carbohydrate. These products could definitely adversely affect a pet, whether through allergy or just bad formulation. He also saw, quite clearly, that the choice of ingredients for these commercial foods, was not really based on nutrition and pet health but instead was heavily influenced by the bottom line; the cost of the ingredients versus the company's profit.

** You can read more about the history and horror of commercial pet foods, in the **Healthfully Yours**, section of this book.*

"When I looked really close, the first thing I realized was, what appeared on the label, might not be what was really in the can or bag. I knew that if I was going to determine what percentage of food allergies really occurred in pets, I would need to design my own diet. Having absolutely no experience with formulating diets, I decided to keep it simple. I knew, in this situation, less was better than more."

Al took a long look at the Asian populations. They have survived in a healthful manner for thousands of years, eating their simple and healthy basics; soybeans, rice and vegetables. He sent away for a hand book on the "composition of foods", put out by the **United States Department of Agriculture**. Al spent many hours reading about ingredients and trying to formulate a diet that was "Asian healthy" and tasty. Al's original formulation included soybeans, brown rice, carrots and celery.

He sent his formulation to Mark Morris, senior, who had created the Hill's Prescription and Science Diets. Dr. Morris informed Al that he always considered him "the holistic veterinarian of California". His one suggestion was that calcium be added to Al's formula to balance out the amount of phosphorus in the soybeans. Al added the needed calcium and decided to share his healthy diet with his clients.

"I printed out copies of my recipe and passed them out to my clients to try and low and behold, many of their pet's signs of allergy completely disappeared. I had so many people peeling carrots, chopping up celery and cooking all the ingredients together that I could not believe it. It looked like I was on my way.

Late one evening when I was still at the animal hospital, I had an irate husband call me saying that "I am standing in my kitchen with a 5 foot stack of carrots, and if you don't find a better way to provide our pets diet, I'll come down to the hospital and shoot you". Though I knew he was exaggerating, I also realized that I had to find a way to provide this diet in a more accommodating way."

Al knew that the time was right to create some kind of commercial non-allergenic pet food but how could he mass produce a natural, non- allergenic commercial pet food and, more importantly, safely preserve it? Freezing seemed to be the easiest and most natural process. Once the food was prepared, he would preserve it with clean, purified water and then freeze it into a frozen loaf. He might be able to produce enough loaves for his clients but if he wanted to offer this healthy new diet to all the thousands of allergy stricken pets he'd need to find someone with the facilities to mass produce.

Al researched frozen pet food loaf manufacturers and decided to call **Breeders Choice**. He spoke to the owner, Hal Taylor, who scheduled a meeting the next day. Hal and his sons knew there was a growing market for non-allergenic pet foods. They liked Al and his idea and knew it was a no-brainer to mass produce and market his formula for the very first, non-meat, commercial food ever created for pets. The diet was called, **Naturally Yours** and soon thereafter was also available as a naturally baked kibble. Dr. Al, had become, Chef Al.

"The response was remarkable. It seemed that people were excited the fact that their family pets were eating a pet food in which all the ingredients were fit for human consumption. It worked so well, that there were numerous instances when a husband would come home late from a card game or from bowling, and while raiding the refrigerator, they would spot the loaf and eat the entire thing, with crackers. The next morning the wife would open the refrigerator wondering what happened to her pet's food!"

This initial success just made Dr. Al more determined to provide his natural and healthy animal diets to pet populations around the world. His next opportunity came by way of a near tragedy. The son of one of his clients contacted Al, stating that he had a "horseback riding foundation" for physically challenged children. It seems that the commercial pellets that were delivered to feed all his 26 horses were; actually *cattle* feed that contained a *weight enhancing chemical* called Monensin (Rumensin). Monensin's toxic dose in horses is the same as a toxic dose of cyanide

He told Al that someone had suggested that he give his horses the natural, trace mineral clay, called calcium montmorillinite. Al agreed heartily and recommended dosages. Most of the horses survived and in lieu of payment, Al suggested that he help produce a full line of natural canned and dry pet foods using Al's wholesome, non-allergenic recipes. So it came to pass, one extra sunny afternoon, **Nature's Recipe** was created.

"It was an exciting time. After studying Dr. Albert Rowe's books on Food Allergies, especially his pediatric diets and his food elimination diet for children and drawing from my own creations and further research, I was able to do the formulations and the first Lamb and Rice diet was created. This was the very first time a lamb and rice formula had ever been offered to the world commercially."

This diet became so popular that other pet food manufacturers, created and sold their own lamb and rice diets. However many of the formulations were less nutritious than others and because profit always seems to trump quality; the cuts of lamb soon became lamb byproducts and the brown rice became brown rice hulls.

What happened then, Dr. Al?

"More and more, allergy prone canines seemed to build up a tolerance to the diet. Sadly, after 10 years, many of the pets developed an allergic reaction to the lamb and rice diet.

As I know now, food sensitivities develop, not from the foods themselves but because allergic pets actually have an endocrine–immune imbalance that has accompanied them from birth due to disastrous 'inbreeding practices'. This imbalance, the Plechner Syndrome, causes allergies, and other ailments, including numerous catastrophic diseases. It is covered in-depth throughout this book.

So it was back to the Drawing board to design a new, non-reactive food that these food allergy pets could again eat. I began to realize, that the fewer ingredients in the new pet food the less chance of reaction. So I thought, why not use a very limited ingredient diet that would only have one protein and one carbohydrate. This diet was called, **Innovative Veterinary Diets (IVD)**, which I formulated for **Nature's Recipe** in the '80s.

It was offered as both a canned and dry food, using only one protein source either of venison, duck, rabbit or fish. The carbohydrate source was white potatoes. I also instructed pet owners to change to a different **IVD** every 3 months to help stop the production of anti-antibodies to the **IVD** diet that they were currently feeding.

When **Nature's Recipe,** was purchased by **H.J. Heinz Company** in 1996, the carbohydrate source in the **IVD** feline diet was changed from potatoes to peas because peas were considered to be tastier. This might be so but what was more important was the fact that many cats simply can't tolerate peas and this lead to diarrhea and vomiting.

At the time I suggested that my clients feed their cats, the canine diet instead and to be sure to supplement their cats, daily, with 800 milligrams of taurine, an essential amino acid. I still use **IVD** in my practice but I'm no longer involved in their formulation and cannot guarantee that **IVD** or any other manufactured food will be tolerated by all pets."

In this new millennium, we are also faced with brand new dangers in our pet foods. We now have to worry about individual ingredients that come from foreign countries which may be contaminated with chemicals, pesticides and other un-scrutinized leftovers that are certainly unhealthy and possibly deadly.

Also, some of our "organic" pet food ingredients are being produced from "genetically modified" seeds that can lead to catastrophic diseases and even death in people and animals. Not to mention, the danger they poise for the other "natural flora" of our planet.

"I have developed a tremendous amount knowledge regarding pet foods over the years and, even though, years ago it was considered a no, no to feed your pet, scraps from the table. That practice might be safer in this world of today. When you consider all of the invisible dangers that surround us in this corrupted environment that "industrial civilization" has created; if you are feeding your family correctly, you may just want to offer the same cuisine to your pet."

Bighorn Sheep Project

In the early 80's, Al heard a report that was issued out of the Chicago Zoo. It involved a Bighorn ewe giving birth to a sickly lamb. The lamb had pneumonia and was not responding to the routine course of treatment being given to it by the Zoo's medical staff. An important point of interest to Al was that the antibody level in the lamb's lungs was IgA deficient.

He began to wonder if it the endocrine/immune imbalance syndrome was at work. Line breeding can prove to be a dangerous thing. When family ties become too tight, Mother Nature usually throws the penalty flag.

Containment is an important factor in the development of the syndrome. Whether by enclosure walls, fences or highways, limiting a herd animal's movements leads to continuous procreation by the dominant male or his sons. This incessant inbreeding will taint the herd's gene pool and eventually cause the development of defects within individual herd member's immune systems.

Al wondered if the *Plechner Syndrome* was also effecting the wild sheep population. It seemed highly probable, considering that highways, fences etc. limited their wild migrations insuring that the dominant male and his male decedents controlled the breeding, thereby limiting the lineage of the herd and assisting the development of the *Syndrome*.

This possibility led Al to volunteer to be the immunologist for a research group being created by the **Bighorn Sheep Society of Southern California**. Jim De Forge performed the administrative functions of the group while Charley Jenner rounded out the group as the other veterinarian. Their duties included; determining population density, setting up water systems and springs for the sheep, and trying to discourage the wild burros from contaminating the water that the sheep drank and also stopping the burros from chasing the sheep out of the grazing lands Due to environmental pressures and the endangered habitat, they considered the best solution was the capture and relocation of the chosen sheep to a safer and healthier habitat.

They began by 'taking a census' to determine the current number of Bighorn Sheep in the highlands of southern California. Criss-crossing the beautiful San Gabriel Mountain range in helicopters, they counted and logged the various herds of sheep that populated the area. Yeah, it was a tough job but somebody had to do it.

The herds appeared to have good numbers and they seemed to be healthy, so the group's next task was to create a study group. Using apple butter baits they were able to net 16 lambs and ewes and they relocated the chosen animals to Independence, California. Then, with the aid of a helicopter and a tranquillizer gun, they safely captured and transported two very large rams. To assure genetic diversity, all of the study group animals were gathered from separate herds in different locations throughout the range. Al took blood samples from all the sheep to make sure they did not have *Plechner's Syndrome*. A & E laboratories ran his endocrine-immune panels on all the sheep at no cost to the group.

The results of Al's "*Syndrome* studies" indicated that there were enough genetic differences between the individual animals that this group of sheep would be a very compatible and healthy herd and, except for interference by predators and people, showed a potentially high survival rate. The transplant was a success.

Capture and relocation of wild sheep is extremely difficult and can be very dangerous to the sheep because they are very susceptible to "capture myopathy". They are very skittish and, due to their extremely sensitive cardiovascular systems, the slightest fear or excitement can cause their blood pressure to sky rocket, rupturing blood vessels and causing the death of the animal. The *Sierra Nevada Bighorn Sheep Captive Breeding Contingency Plan* states emphatically...

"*Avoid chasing bighorn sheep for more than 5 minutes to reduce the risk of death and injury from capture myopathy and fractures.*"[1]

There was a heartbreaking incident in the years following the California Study, at the **Lava Bed Sheep Preserve** in Oregon, a relocation mission that ended in tragedy. Due to the previous relocation successes in California, the **Oregon Department of**

27

Fish and Game decided to use a capture-relocation as a media event. The sensitive relocation maneuver became a carnival occasion with dozens of newspaper, magazine and radio reporters and several television crews who were there to *capture* the capture for posterity.

With all the noise and commotion, the frightened sheep would not go under the nets. So all of those involved, experts and media alike, over reacted and formed a force line press to move the sheep with helicopter assistance. They joined hands and drove the herd back into some caves. The less experienced drovers, not realizing the danger, became caught up in their duties grew louder and more boisterous causing the cornered herd to become extremely and tragically agitated. The helicopter hovered over the animals and, on several occasions, used its siren in an effort to get the sheep moving again. The disorganized chaos and pandemonium so terrified the sheep that over half of the relocated sheep ended up dying from *capture myopathy*. They were literally scared to death.

To reduce the possibility of future calamities like this, Charlie Jenner and Al, flew up to the University of California at Davis, to work with Jim De Forge in establishing a PHD program which would address the dangers involved with Bighorn Sheep capture-relocation programs and to create a set protocol to follow to reduce the possibility of this tragedy reoccurring. .

{1} *UC Davis Sierra Sheep Capture Plan*

(http://www.vetmed.ucdavis.edu/vgl/wildlife/pdfs/SierraSheepCaptivePlan.pdf)

The Battle of Stonewood Meadows

There have been various versions quoted, of what went down at **Stonewood Meadows** so I thought, for this volume; we should use an unbiased account that came out in 1983. It was reported by Jack Stevens in the September/ October Edition of the *California Viewpoint*, a bi-monthly South Californian periodical. Stevens edited *California Viewpoint* during the 1980s and has had editorials and columns published in the San Francisco Chronicle, the Sacramento Bee, and Sacramento Union. His reporting on **Stonewood Meadows** is reprinted here in its entirety.

******

Wildlife Savior's Incredible War with the California Coastal Commission

Al Plechner and the Battle for Stonewood Meadows

By Jack Stevens.
CALIFORNIA VIEWPOINT,
September/October 1983

When Dr. Alfred Jay Plechner, now 45-years old, purchased 20 acres of property in the rugged Cold Creek area of the Santa Monica Mountains near Calabasas ten years ago, he had no idea that his land would become the focus of a Wild-West-style range war and a bitter, protracted struggle with the California Coastal Commission.

All the Los Angeles veterinarian and immunologist *w*anted to do was build a house and treatment barn, set up a wildlife preserve and plant crops whose sale would fund the care of injured wild animals.

29

" I saw it as an ideal place to relocate wildlife specimens that people bring to me at the California Animal Hospital." explains Plechner, "I fix them up and nurse them back to health and when they're strong enough to have a chance to survive in the wild on their own, I bring them here. It's sort of a halfway house for them, before they go back on up into the mountains."

Working alone, he cleared thick brush and chaparral and planted multitudes of almond, apricot, and eucalyptus trees. Within hours of surveying his land, he spotted baby cougars. Ringtail cats, a herd of deer and rare wild birds, raccoons, rabbits. fox, bobcats, and golden eagles (an endangered species) abound.

"Here, near a population of ten million people, I found a last refuge of the animal kingdom." marvels Plechner as he points out the lush vegetation and towering bluffs of the place he named Stonewood Meadow.

He deepened Cold Creek and established numerous water holes for thirsty wildlife. With his sons, Jay, now 12, and A.J. now 8, he nurtured a bee colony.

The wildlife preserve, which he registered with the state Fish and Game and Agriculture department, gradually began to take shape. Citizens, wildlife organizations, animal control facilities, and the Los Angeles Zoo brought frightened or maimed wildlife, otherwise destined for the gas chamber, to Stonewood Meadows. Plechner treated them at his own expense.

Ministering to hundreds of wild animals, he has improvised with fiberglass to repair turtle shells, treated rabbits for glaucoma, pinned a broken bone on a seagull and even performed a hysterectomy on a ferret.

Officials of the Santa Monica Animal Shelter call him a "uniquely selfless individual, an animal lover in the truest sense," and he has received public praise from the U.S. Department of the Interior. the L.A. Department of Animal Control. the Elsa Wild Animal Appeal. the Committee for the Preservation of the Tule Elk. and the Society for the Conservation of the Big Horn Sheep.

Trouble in Eden

But, Stonewood Meadows was almost too much of a good thing, trespassers hiking in or on horseback, trampled his planted soil cut fences, slashed irrigation lines and harassed recuperating animals.

A hint of troubles to come occurred one day when a woman on horseback rode into the sanctuary and told Plechner. "Get out. This area is for horses and houses only. Take your animals somewhere else."

A group of horsemen, described by his neighbor, as an adult and two youngsters later ripped out a whole vineyard. Three riders with four dogs chased down a young fawn that the veterinarian had recently saved. Before anyone could stop the dogs, they tore the fawn apart. In a separate incident, a local game official found a 12-week-old raccoon on the property that had been shot out of a tree and left to die.

Ten beehives were vandalized, cornmeal was poured into the gas tanks of all of Plechner's farm machinery, and groups with chainsaws cut down live trees as well as dead ones.

Finally, on the suggestion of the United States Department of Agriculture, Plechner erected a boulder-and-earth barrier at each end of Stonewood Meadows to isolate it from marauders.

What Property Rights?

As local equestrian groups accustomed to invading land belonging to others loudly protested the barrier. Plechner soon discovered that the property rights he thought were guaranteed him under the state and federal constitutions were callously ignored by the very government charged with preserving them.

A number of trail and "environmental" groups, more concerned with their leisure class recreational activities than private property rights or the well-being of wild animals, angrily alleged that Plechner had blocked public access to a well-worn lateral feeder trail to the Santa Monica Mountain's crest and coalesced to halt Plechner's farm and wildlife relocation.

Some hotheads talked of renting bulldozers to "unseal" Stonewood Meadows. Tipped off by one of Plechner's neighbors, then-Supervisor Baxter Ward alerted the Malibu Sheriff's office, while some 40 of the doctor's neighbors contacted all of the local equipment rental firms and admonished them not to allow bulldozers in the Cold Creek area. The raid never materialized.

When Plechner's adversaries couldn't succeed by force, they turned to a host of land use control agencies that might be able to trip up Plechner on one permit technicality or another. First on their list was the California Coastal Commission.

Located four and one-half miles inland and behind a major ridgeline, Stonewood Meadows is not within sight, earshot, or smell of the ocean. But, in one of the stranger legislative twists of 1976, the Coastal Commission was granted regulatory authority over areas up to five miles east of the sea. Not until July 1977, did the Commission get around to issuing maps showing which areas fell under their newly-expanded purview.

The Coastal Commission is dedicated to protecting the environment and preserving wildlife-right? Wrong.

In October of 1977, it issued Plechner a violation, alleging that he did not have a permit for the improvements on his property completed during the prior ten months. He later found out that the Commission was anxious to push a trail through his land and that several commissioners themselves were former trail association and equestrian group leaders.

Plechner, an ardent conservationist, applied for an exemption. Since he had done substantial work, incurred a large financial stake in the project and proceeded in good faith upon certification from the United States Department of Agriculture, the doctor was granted a "vested right" exemption by the Regional Coastal Commission. But that was only the beginning.

Under a weird provision of the Coastal Act which allowed regional decisions to be appealed -by anyone -and heard de novo (from start to finish again) by the State Coastal Commission in San Francisco. Plechner's adversaries appealed the local decision.

The veterinarian had some inkling that he would not be getting a fair hearing when the person assigned to write the Commission staff report on his case was revealed to be a past president of the Santa Monica Trail Council, a close personal friend of two of the equestrian groups' leaders and the architect of the trail proposed for the Cold Creek area.

The Commission's legal aide advised Plechner to apply for a coastal development permit and avoid the need for further hearings over the "vested right" issue. "I told her I'd be happy to." remembers Plechner. "but then I asked her, 'If I go for a permit, won't you turn right around and ask me for public trails through my property'!' She told me -'There's a very good chance.' So I told her, 'I don't want to talk to you then.'"

Insiders warned the doctor that the Commission was scheming to gain public access through the stream bottom at the southern end of his property -in the precise spot where he released wildlife - and along the northern border, where he planned to build a treatment barn.

At the same time, the enemies of Stonewood Meadows mounted a campaign against Plechner's personal credibility; claiming that he was a "phony" and the animal sanctuary merely an elaborate "ruse for large-scale land development." Two "environmental activists" charged that Plechner had bulldozed Cold Creek into oblivion, turning it into an "arid desert."

Allegations flew so thickly that the Los Angeles Times eventually entered the fray, publishing an article on September 5, 1978 that sympathized with Plechner and displayed a photograph of him squatting knee-deep in the full, vibrant streambed he was alleged to have covered with dirt.

Plechner finally won a permit from the Regional Coastal Commission in January 1979. only to see the decision appealed once more to the State Commission.

But this time, the doctor came better prepared. He recognized that the outcome of his appeal depended more on politics than upon any objective interpretation of the Coastal Act the Commission had proven incapable of rendering.

Plechner mobilized support from local politicians and Wildlife organizations. The Department of Fish and Game filed reports that contradicted the claim that the veterinarian was harming the area's riparian environment. Local residents, some of whom had lived as long as 40 years in the Cold Creek region, submitted affidavits emphasizing that natural trail corridors had never existed through Stonewood Meadows.

Represented at the hearing by Pacific Legal Foundation the Sacramento-based, conservative, public interest firm, Plechner overwhelmed his opponents, who were unable to establish "substantial cause" for a reversal of the regional decision.

A Dramatic Protest

Though at long last Plechner had been awarded a development permit for the wildlife sanctuary, he encountered new headaches when he approached the Commission for permission to install a well to be used as a watering hole for the animals. Predictably, members of the local horse set showed up at the Regional Commission hearing questioning the need for such "development". Rather than brook continued harassment. Plechner withdrew his application and hooked up water through the Las Virgenes Water District.

Wearied of having to seek bureaucratic approval for improvements to his property that landowners outside the Coastal Zone perform routinely without government oversight; Plechner decided to defy the Commission and. at the time, protest its deprivation of his constitutional liberties. He and his two sons erected a large pole and raised the stars-and stripes over Stonewood Meadows, dedicating it to the preservation of Wildlife in the Santa Monica Mountains and daring Commission bureaucrats to take it down.

Absent a coastal development permit, the flag-raising violated seven state laws, but the Commission backed off from prosecuting Plechner likely out of fear of a public relations debacle.

The Final Round

In order to complete the last phase of his project, the veterinarian still needed the Commission's permission to build a home and treatment barn so that he could provide 24-hour care to injured animals. The Commission's staff let it be known that they had no problem with Plechner's request -upon the condition that he surrender, without compensation, a 10 to 20-foot-wide easement through Stonewood Meadows for hiking and equestrian use.

"It's a chess game.' Plechner realized. "If you want to build on your property, you have to give them land or money." The agency's extortion was even more confounding in view of the fact that a trail through Plechner's property would be superfluous - one already existed on an established roadway just west of Stonewood Meadows,

But the doctor was not about to give in. "The hikers and horse owners have a choice." he pointed out. "They can take alternative trails that already exist. For the wildlife, there is NO alternative. The animals are in such a stressful state that it doesn't take much - a dog, a horse, or voices - for them to bolt. They can then jump into the well and break a leg, further injuring themselves to the point where you can't relocate them because they can't survive."

Again, letters and telegrams poured into the Commission from scores of individuals and animal protection organizations irate over the agency's treatment of Plechner.

On January 13, 1982, Supervisor Mike Antonovich wrote the Commission: "Trails anywhere on this property would force Dr. Plechner to close down and the County would then be deprived of our only wildlife treatment center. We would then have no alternative but to destroy all of our injured wildlife."

Wilting under public pressure, the Commission backed off from the most extreme of its demands but still took its pound of flesh. At Plechner's final encounter with the "protectors of the coast" in January 1983, he was granted a permit in return for (1) a 100-foot open space easement on the north side of Cold Creek; (2) 12 out of 20 acres of the farm based wildlife preserve; and (3) a trail easement the full length of Cold Creek (effective when and if the veterinarian ever stopped treating wild animals.)

His neighbors agreed to donate easements on nearby roads and trails circumscribing Plechner's property so that the Commission's proposed easement - within five feet of the treatment barn - would not be necessary. Bureaucrats had gobbled up a one half mile easement as compared to the 660·foot proposed trail through Stonewood Meadows. They had succeeded - at least in terms of their expansionist objectives.

He'd Do It Again Today,

With the concrete foundations for his barn already poured. Plechner displays a remarkable lack of bitterness about his experiences with California's coastal "commissars." By the doctor's estimate, the Commission's refusal to allow construction of his wildlife treatment facility for 5 1/2 years cost the lives of some 15 to 30 deer.

"Without a treatment barn, the County had no choice but to destroy deer with fractured legs." explains Plechner, "The shame of it is that we might have been able to save them."

Looking back, Plechner says that he would do it all again, despite the frustration, heartache, and expense. "The Coastal Act and the Coastal Commission are two different things," he stresses. "We were In support of the Coastal Act. We believed in it. But there is no justification for the Commission. Why did innocent animals have to suffer?"

Recently Plechner was awarded one of the federal government's few eagle rehabilitation permits. His wine crop produced and bottled by Calabasas Cellars in Clarksburg, California, bears a colorful wildlife label. As soon as the treatment barn is completed, it will show off a beautiful, 5 -foot high stained glass window designed by Rena McKenzie of Santa Monica. It displays, brilliantly and lovingly, the flora and fauna of Stonewood Meadows - wild flowers, trees. grapes, coyotes, cougars, quail and deer. But, at its center is the American eagle grasping in its talons, the California Coastal Commission.

Jack Stevens.

California Viewpoint,
September/October 1983

Doctor Al Plechner's, Eulogy for Stonewood Meadows

In the mid 1900's we were all just beginning to realize the negative effects of human expansion throughout the world. The Endangered Species Act, signed into law by President Richard Nixon on December 28, 1973, was a wake-up call for our planet. The startling fact that entire species of wildlife were becoming extinct brought into focus the true scope of this ongoing disaster. It was a cry to arms for naturalists and animal advocates everywhere. Thinking back, Al reflects on his battle for those injured animals rights...

"I knew that I had to lead the way locally. We had provided a safe haven for the damaged wildlife creatures in our own "backyard". Stonewood Meadows started as a Dream, but it became a microcosm of the continuing crisis. Each and every one who joined me in the fight for the preserve realized just how critical our actions were. No matter who our adversaries were, no matter what they threw at us, I knew we must persevere because there was too much at stake to give up the fight.

Good land use allows us to protect and enjoy what nature has provided for all of us. There is room for hiking and horse trails even room for off road vehicles but first and foremost, we must respect and preserve our natural surroundings. The wonderful riparian habitats, the grassland and forest environments that remain, sadly are, few and far between so we need to act now to insure that our wildlife has habitation for them inhabit.

I think the biggest legacy my battles for Stonewood Meadows created was that they set an important precedence for "wildlife over recreation". Each Commission skirmish, every PR confrontation, every victory and even every setback gave other prospective wildlife and treatment rehabilitations centers a 'template for action' and the hope and the ability to fight the good fight. As I have told many people, "As hard as it is to die for what you believe in, it is a hell of a lot harder to 'live' for what you believe in".

A short post script to this story, CBS had a script written which depicted my battle of Stonewood Meadows. They were going to shoot it for a movie of the week, but decided not to because the legal department was concerned that it might offend the Sierra Club which in turn was concerned about their "recreational environmentalist" members.

Dan Haggerty, (TV's Grizzly Adams) wanted to do a TV series based on Stonewood Meadows. Unfortunately his Drug arrest, jail time and a motorcycle crash ended the project before it even began."

After Al finished his battle with the **California Coastal Commission**, the **California Department of Fish and Game** asked him to join a new organization. It seems that they were starting a coalition called the **Wildlife Alliance**. The main idea of this organization was to consolidate all the experience, passion and commitment of those individuals and organizations that were already making great strides in wildlife treatment, rehabilitation and relocation.

Martine Collette, a friend of Al's, was also asked to join. Her compound, **The Wildlife Way Station**, is still in operation today. Through the **Alliance**'s efforts, a number of free treatment and rehabilitation centers were established throughout the state of California. Even more importantly, this organization set the blue print for others around the world to follow. Many interested people visited **Stonewood Meadows** to seek Al's advice and assistance so that he could show them what they needed to do to enhance their habitats for the wildlife species that they were relocating.

Life and Death

It's a horrible decision, that no one should have to make but when you look into the eyes of a suffering animal with no hope of recovery, you'll know you have no choice but to help them by putting an end to their agony. In Al's long career as a healer, he has had to make those decisions, each and every one justified. Still, Al told me about a specific instance that continues to "haunt" him.

As Al remembered it, it was a bleak fall day, when a young coyote tried to cross a narrow highway winding its way through Lake Arrowhead, California. Sadly the highway was occupied by sparse but speeding traffic and the unaware and tragically unlucky coyote was critically struck by a vehicle. Al didn't witness the incident; actually, he was not even aware that it had happened.

At that time, he had a small lake house in the area and many of the residents knew he was a veterinarian. A neighbor witnessed the accident and saw the poor coyote drag itself down towards the lake. It appeared to him, that the coyote could not use its rear legs. He called the sheriff and soon after the Sheriff picked him up, they were both standing at Al's door. They quickly explained what had happened and asked for Al's help.

It didn't take them long to reach the area where the coyote was last seen. They split up to search for the injured animal. Al was the first to discover his poor drag marks and found it huddled behind a sodden tree stump that had made its way to shore. As the sheriff and neighbor watched Al from above, he moved slowly towards the badly damaged animal. The frightened coyote whimpered softly and crawled towards the water. Watching its tortured movements, Al knew immediately that it had a fatally broken back. It moved slowly through the water and upon reaching the first floating dock it just disappeared.

The neighbor and the Sheriff called out to Al. Their first thought was that the coyote had drowned. Al's thoughts were much darker. Past experiences had shown him just how strong the survival instincts of wild animals were.

39

His concern was that the coyote may have gone under the dock float and was hanging on, quietly suffering in the air space beneath it. The water was cold and definitely not inviting, but the thought of the suffering coyote was enough to force Al's next actions.

To the shock of the Sheriff and the neighbor he moved quickly into the water and swam towards the dock. When he came up into the airspace beneath it, the poor little coyote, barely hanging on, bared its teeth in silent defiance.

It wasn't fear that forced Al to leave the airspace and swim towards the shore. What drove him was concern. He feared that the terrified coyote would try to move on, where the only hope of ending his pain would be through the terror of a slow drowning. Al quickly made it to shore. With a grim face he took the neighbors old rifle and quickly swam back to end the poor little coyotes fear and suffering.

When Al told me this sad story he said that his heart is always heavy whenever he thinks about this little coyote, but he knows that his solution was justified. The coyote was mortally damaged and suffering, ending his life swiftly was the only course of action. He hopes that no one will ever have to experience a day like the one that he had to experience but he knows, as we all do, that "death" is always the final act of "life".

Junior, the Red Tail Hawk

Al was also licensed by the **California Fish and Game and Commission** and the **U.S. Fish and Wildlife Service** to create a bird of prey center at the Stonewood Meadows preserve. He received many birds for their relocation use and also offered care, at his hospital, to many damaged or young birds that had either been abandoned or had fallen out of their nests.

One day, the **Department of Fish and Game** brought in a proud, young red tail hawk with a fractured right wing. Normally this would be an easy medical fix; however the break was close to the elbow which often makes flight impossible. Al didn't want to amputate the wing and see this lovely symbol of freedom spend the rest of his life in a cage. He set the wing and hoped that motility would return to his wing and euthanasia would not be the hawk's final act.

Al named him Junior and did everything he could to help him to live. Feeding him chunks of meat and chicken to stoke the engines of healing. Junior was also doing his part to return to normal. Keeping active each day and carefully climbing the stairs to the veranda at sunset where he would spend each night. Feeding time would bring a smile to Al's lips. Junior reminded him of a little old Rabbi as he made his way to the food. As soon as Junior realized he could use his healed wing a bit. He worked very hard at flexing and moving it. Soon his broken bone healed and he regained use of his elbow. He found he could still fly but not very well.

As Junior regained his "air force wings", other more territorial red tail hawks began to chase him. Al knew it was good exercise but would always leave the garage door open, so junior would have a safe haven. Slowly but surely he became his own hawk. Every dinner time Al would whistle and hold a lamb heart in the air and junior would swoop down and pluck it from his hand. His near vision was not quite as good as the far and Al still has scars to prove it. It was a long hard road but eventually Junior managed to become, king of the hill.

41

Junior became one of the family. On windy days when Al's sons would fly their kites, Junior would drop down from 10,000 feet and knuckle their kites. Each day when the boys would walk up the farm road to catch their school bus, Junior would follow close behind, perch on the telephone pole while they waited and then fly back as the school bus left.

Then one day, **Fish and Game** brought out a large, female, red tailed hawk. Al called her Bianca. She had flashing eyes and an independent manner and it did not take her long to capture Junior's fancy. They set up housekeeping in a huge eucalyptus tree at the end of the canyon. Each day, they would soar the thermals together returning to their nest each evening as the sun painted the western sky.

One day Al noticed that Junior was flying solo. Concerned, he visited the tree at the end of the canyon. Bianca was there, seriously redoing the nest. One afternoon, while one of the occasional parties Al hosted on the veranda was in full swing, Bianca flew by to show Al what was on the menu for the baby. A 6 foot long gopher snake. As fall fell, Al found that his favorite hawks had vacated their nest. He was a bit sad but not too concerned for almost all of the 150 to 200 birds, Al had rehabilitated, were migratory. This year Junior, Bianca and their young one gave in to the urge and joined the migration.

The next Valentine's Day was a grey day, the morning heavy with rain. Al happened to glance out at the railing and there perched Junior, wet but still proud, his familiar blue sear visible on his beak.

As Al looked beyond him to the large split rock at the back side of the preserve, he saw Bianca and their young one and was, unexpectantly, caught up in his emotions. They had come home to Dad! It was raining so hard that there was nothing for them to catch so...they came home to Dad.

Al quickly got some chicken breasts out of fridge and held one out to Junior. He took it smooth and easy. Old habits are hard to break. The others he flew back to his mate and the young one.
Al watched from a distance as they shared the catch under the dense grey sky.

Soon the rain let up and the family moved on but to this day, whenever Al hears the scream of a hawk, He looks to the heavens hoping that it might be *his* Junior, stopping by for a visit.

` *The Inhumane Practices of Puppy Mills*

Through the years, Al has consistently tried to educate the general public on where to look, and what to look for, when they want a new puppy. He always explains to them the dangers of buying puppies that might come from a puppy mill. Whether they're the backyard, one breed variety, or a factory farm, churning out hundreds of "pure" (?) breed varieties and crating them off to pet shops around the country.

Locked in cages, these poor little creatures are products of constant and careless breeding all destined to suffer from serious genetic flaws. Most will fall victim to debilitating allergies and diseases. They will die young and before their time, their lives filled with affliction and pain.

Serious breeders care about their pups. They want them healthy and happy and ready for a long, vigorous life with their new families. Puppy mill owners are "flesh peddlers", concerned only with the profits from their cash crop. They have no emotion for the animals they breed; the pups are merely "product", produced as cheaply and quickly as possible. If an animal is sick or damaged and stops producing puppies they are quickly killed in the most cost efficient manner, usually by shooting them.

I am sorry to be so blunt but my Rat Terrier, Skipper, was rescued from one in Georgia. Just 4 weeks old and covered with demodectic mange, she was saved by a Rescue group and brought to Florida where I was lucky enough to adopt her. If anything brings out the ire in me, its puppy mills and Doctor Al feels the same way.

"I learned early on in my practice, the pain and heart break that puppy mills cause. Seeing a small child holding in his arms, a sick puppy mill puppy while he and his entire family, are pleading with me to do the impossible, to save his poor puppy. Test results had told me what my heart already knew. The boy's puppy was so badly damaged genetically; there was no way in nature that it would live. Its life would be a series of ailments leading to its demise. It tore my heart apart to deliver the bad

44

news and I made a vow, there and then to do something to stop these "birthing camps". Little did I know, it was just the beginning of a lifelong mission.

I contacted the local news in Los Angeles, ABC, Channel 7, I believe it was. I spoke with Paul Moyer, and Paul suggested that we to do a series of special reports, 5 nights of investigation into the horror of puppy mills. That series so shocked the viewers, it created a citizen's crusade."

(Do you remember back when everyday citizens had the power of numbers to actually change things that needed changing? Back when the world was less apathetic...and made more sense.)

"We were able to get laws passed in the state of California, ruling that a puppy had to be 8 weeks or older, with teeth, to be allowed to be shipped into the state. The law also demanded that the pet shops who sold a puppy, would be held responsible for all health problems that puppy might have for a specific amount of time following the purchase. This allowed the new owners to have their own health check done, so that they would know the condition of the animal before emotional ties, truly developed. Veterinarians were encouraged to offer low cost "puppy checks" to assist in the crusade.

Within my own practice, I offered all new puppy owners, a free health exam and if I found any problems I'd inform the puppy's owner about their rights and encourage them to hold the pet shop responsible for any possible medical costs."

Al actually flew to New York and did the **Geraldo Show**, with some of his clients, "who had dogs in this fight" dogs that were genetically damaged and afflicted with terminal diseases. Geraldo was sympathetic to the cause. The owners gained a lot of support. With their damaged pups, at their side, they spoke directly to the cameras about the pets they had grown to love and could not give up on. Al knew, that everyone that had tuned in, could see how much the owners were suffering, right along with their dogs.

"The puppy mill owners, of course, protested all the way. As I looked into the eyes of these "flesh peddlers" and listened to how many "heads" of dogs and cats' that they sell, I could see no compassion...and not even an ounce, of regret. It was apparent to anyone with a heart, that dogs that wind up as part of a puppy mill operation, are definitely Gods most unluckiest and certainly the unhappiest animals in the world."

Though Al's efforts did put a dent in the puppy mill's profits in California and made pet shops shoulder more responsibility for the puppies they sold, the problem never truly went away. Frankly, on a national level, it is as bad today as it was when Al first began his efforts. Considering the environmental damage our species has wrought on our planet, today, here in the "shiny", new millennium...it is many times worse.

Now, there is far more sinister side to puppy mills. The over production of their "product" has created a population explosion. Shelters and rescue centers are over flowing with the results of puppy mill greed.

A large majority of these dogs are medical catastrophes just waiting to happen because of their "assembly line" breeding methods. They are in this, only for the money and don't really care if the animals they produce are prone to cancer, allergies, seizures, and more. As long as the puppies are cute, there are pet store owners, ready and willing to move their product.

"The battle of the puppy mill continues. The governmental agency that oversees them is understaffed, underfunded and many times their staff just doesn't care. It is up to us to "financially" shut these people down, by boycotting pet stores that buy from non-certified breeders. This boycott should also include our backyard, local puppy mills. Even though these micro-breeders work on a smaller scale, some are breeding puppies for the same motive and under the same squalid conditions as the larger scale puppy mills.

Here is what you can do:

Never accept a puppy that does not have a 72 hour return policy at the very least. Have a veterinarian examine the puppy. Make sure that you have a written agreement that guarantees you'll receive "full compensation" if the puppy is returned for health reasons. Do not accept a replacement, (who may also be damaged).

If you buy your puppy from a local breeder, you not only need to have the same written agreement but also make sure you meet the parents of the puppy. This will give you a good idea of what your puppy will be like in adulthood.

With our overpopulation problem, we should follow Oprah's impassioned recommendation. Rather than buying a puppy from a pet store go to your local animal shelter or rescue center to adopt. Her researchers informed her that 99% of all puppies sold in pet stores come from puppy mill.

Once you have an animal, unless you are planning on breeding it, have it spayed or neutered so that you are not accidentally contributing to the overpopulation of pets that wind up in shelters having to be euthanized because of pet overpopulation."

Doctor to the Star's...Pets!

In one of our early email exchanges, I was pleasantly surprised to find out that Al was once considered to be the "Doctor to the Star's...pets". I playfully asked Al to list a few of the celebrity owners of many of his patients. This was his response...

"I had many of Hollywood's artists, personalities and luminaries as clients, primarily because of my devotion to animal health and the success I had in maintaining my patient's healthiness and wellbeing.

This reputation developed quickly by word of mouth. I was told I was known as someone who could be trusted, one who would never take advantage of their celebrity status. Even more importantly I was known to treat all of my patients with the same loving care as if they were my own pets.

When I first began practice, I had the honor of treating the family pet of Nat King Cole and his twins, Still dog lovers to this day, identical twins, Timolin and Casey Cole, the youngest daughters of the late great crooner, pamper their 3-year-old pet Labs, Treble and King Cole, by playing the dogs their dad's records.

Sam Goldwyn would board his wonderful, huge Irish Wolf Hound Adam at the hospital where I first practiced. When Adam was brought to the hospital for boarding, they always sent along a large, white, English Bone China dish full of cooked and seasoned pieces of chateaubriand steak. I can remember sitting in a large double cage with Adam when I was on call, making sure he never had to eat alone.

It was very tasty steak!

Over the years I did care for a number of other famous Hollywood people's pets. Merle Oberon would fly in from Aspen to see me. Marsha Mason was a client, Dandy Don Meridith, could not stand the sight of blood so if his Irish setter, Amigo, got hurt, his wife or his secretary would bring the dog in.

Glen Close, Lilly Tomlin, Joanne Worley, Dom De Luise, Edgar Bergen and his daughter, Candice with their beagle and Ringo Star and his wife, Barbara Bock. I saw singers like Della Reese, Patty Page and Jackie DeShannon (who wrote "Bette Davis Eyes") with her husband Randy Edelman.

The famous producer Norman Lear was a client of mine for many years. Isaac Tigrett, founder of Hard Rock Café and House of Blues. He married Maureen Cox Starkey, Ringo's first wife, who unfortunately died of Leukemia. Maureen was a wonderful person. I remember their daughter, Augusta, coming into my lobby with a young male cat that was brownish orange. She was probably 8 years old at the time. Someone in the lobby asked this little girl what she called her kitten. Unbelievably, she announced to the people that his name was "Rusty Nuts". Go figure. I guess she called it the way she saw it.

I was the Vet for a number of Television News Anchors and Reporters in the Los Angeles area, such as, Tawny Little, (Miss America 1976, KABC-TV Reporter) Kathy Vara (KNBC Morning News Anchor) and Jerry Dunphy (Evening News Anchor at KABC-TV, LA's top rated TVstation) I had given Jerry and his wife Sandra a wirehaired terrier that I had rescued. Unfortunately, they could not keep him, so I kept him with me in a cage in my treatment room. His cage was always open so that he could go in and out as he pleased. At the time, I also had a lovely teacher as a client. Irene had just lost her wirehair to a catastrophic disease. I waited a short time before I called her and said ", I may have a super surprise for you. She was very happy to have another wirehaired and the dog felt the same way about her. Every time Irene brought her "new dog" back to my hospital, he would excitedly run back into the treatment room and climb back into his cage. Pretty neat stuff!

There were so many wonderful clients with their pets that I was so privileged to see over the years including Brooke Shields, Gilda Radner, Mike Nichols, Robert Goulett, Gary Coleman and his Mom and Dad, Richard Prior, Richard Simmons, Ester Williams, Gabe Kaplan, Michael Nouri. James Worthy, the Laker basketball player and his wife, would bring in their two boxers named Bossy and Hammer. Nancy Wilson, Jean Claude Van Damme, Steven Siegel, Eddy Fisher and his wife Debbie Reynolds and daughter, Carrie, who played Princess Lea and the Everly brothers who brought in their turtles.

Last but not least was Jan Berry from the 'Surf Rock' Duo Jan and Dean. When Jan became a client, it was after he had a near-fatal automobile accident and had suffered severe motor and speech trauma. The light of his life was his white German Shepherd called Queeny. Jan boarded Queeny at my hospital without letting my staff know she was an escape artist! Unfortunately when Queeny was in an outside run to get some fresh air while getting exercise and eating, she somehow scaled the 10 foot high wall of the outside kennel and took off.

I immediately called Jan and relayed to him what had occurred and asked him to meet me at the front of the hospital to help me canvas the neighborhood looking for her. When Jan arrived, I was waiting in front for him and as he pulled in, I noticed something funny in his back seat. I yelled for him to look in his rear view mirror, and all he could see was Queeny sitting in the back seat of his car.

Apparently Queeny went home and jumped in and laid down in the back seat of Jan's car and he was in such a rush to meet me that he never noticed her. It was probably a good thing that Queeny decided not to drive!

Even though it's true that I had many clients that were "stars", their pets, my patients, were all just really, 'down to earth'."

The Shatner Story

Let me preface this vignette with a little background (and personal admission) first. I suffer from an Essential Tremor in my hands and arms which makes it extremely difficult to write or print legibly and my typing skills are sadly 'two finger limited'. That being the case, when I first started researching this project, I wrote and requested that all of Dr. Al's people who were submitting their 'Plechner' stories to please do so in writing. That is all but one, a very special one.

The Introduction in Dr. Plechner's book, *Pet Allergies*, was written by William Shatner. Yes, that William Shatner...Captain James Tiberius Kirk...Denny Crane...the Priceline guy. I was very impressed. Actually, it was somewhere between spellbound and awestruck. William Shatner has always been a personal favorite of mine. I remember the first time I saw him perform on TV. It was before the original **Star Trek** TV Series, about three years before. It was 1963, I was a sophomore in high school, a serious Drama student and acappela group member...that's right a GLEEK, and desperately in need of heroes.

My brain began reeling off his performance in that ***Twilight Zone*** episode, *"Nightmare at 20,000 Feet"*. Shatner played, Mr. Robert Wilson... ah, I can still hear the honey rich, sardonic voice of Rod Serling...

"A salesman on sick leave, Mr. Wilson has just been discharged from a sanitarium where he spent the last six months recovering from a nervous breakdown, the onset of which took place on an evening not dissimilar to this one, on an airliner very much like the one in which Mr. Wilson is about to be flown home."

I was so impressed by his performance. His portrayal of fear...the intensity...the fervidness...the passion, all the things he will be lampooned for, years later, by impressionists, jealous peers and finally (with real relish) by himself. William Shatner!

Captain Kirk! The consummate HERO figure! A talented and successful author himself, I needed to have him write his "Plechner" story for our book.

I put together a very compelling email, explaining our project to mainstream Dr. Al with the book. Roz Wheelock (who also provided her story for this book) was very helpful in obtaining an email address for Shatner's office. As a "healthful" Doberman breeder she's had a number of friendly dealings with him in the past.

Following a couple of email volleys between Shatner's extremely friendly and highly efficient assistant, Chris Carley and myself, I was told that Mr. Shatner was currently traveling but would be home and could provide some time the day before or following Thanksgiving day. I immediately started to prepare my most important request to date, to ask William Shatner, actor, writer, extraordinaire to pen his personal "Plechner story" for *my* book.

On the Tuesday just preceding Thanksgiving, Chris sent me an email asking me if I would you have some time to talk to Mr. Shatner tomorrow (Wednesday) at 3:00 pm PST, 6:00 pm my time? I wrote back that I would and began immediately to type down my "script", the spoken presentation I would use to 'encourage' William Shatner to write his story for the book.

The next day, at 2:59 pm PST, 5:59 pm my time I was a nervous wreck. I was calling...William Shatner! I believe I was actually starting to vibrate, and it wasn't my Tremor

"Hello", Chris Carley quietly answered the phone.

"...er...hello..." tumbled out of my mouth. *"...Hi Chris? This is David...uh...Spangenburg. Is Mr. Shatner, there?"*

"Your phone is very quiet, can you increase the volume"? Chris asked.

I was at a loss. My phone was too quiet? How do I increase the volume? Maybe use the other one...the extension phone?

"Yeah, hold on I'll try."

I ran for the extension phone in the bedroom I picked it up and as I clicked it on...DIALTONE...it shut down both phones...I immediately dropped the first phone and ran back to my office checked the number and punched it into the second phone. It seemed like an eternity but soon...

"...are you there?" Chris's voice seemed slightly annoyed. *"Hello, David..."*

"Yeah, Chris..." I spoke quickly. *"... sorry but I lost you for a moment."*

"Can you turn your volume up some?"

Damn, all that for nothing. I adjusted the phone against my face spoke right into the receiver and raised my voice just short of yelling.

"Is this better?" I asked hopefully.

"It's better." Chris said tentatively. *"Hold on David, I'll get Mr. Shatner."*

"Hello?" The quiet voice of William Shatner filled my ears.

This is it. My one shot to get Bill Shatner to add his story to my book. My brain told my mouth to get it together...then went totally blank...

You're talking to William Shatner and he's on he's only got a few minutes of his Priceline time for you... say something, you idiot...!

53

"Hi, Mr. Shatner,,, um...can I call you Bill? Is it alright I mean...?"

"Yes, please do." his voice had a smile in it.

This is it, just be sincere, honest and really sell it.

"I'm David Spangenburg? I sent you an email about the book that I'm writing about Dr. Plechner? We're basically trying to mainstream Dr. Plechner and his work and..."

"Yes..." Bill quietly interrupted. *"I think what you're doing for Dr. Plechner is an admirable thing. He's saved my dogs. Dr. Plechner is an amazing Vet...it's alright to call him Al, right?"*

"Yeh, sure..." I quickly said. *"Al's called you a couple of things too..."*

"What?" Bill sounded a bit leery all of a sudden.

"No..." I went on quickly. *"...I mean Captain Kirk...Bill... William..."*

"Oh..." Bill continued a bit less hesitant. *"Al is an amazing Vet and a great human being. He really cares for animals. It's more than just a job for him. It's like... whoa, I'm getting a head of myself. How do you want to do this?"*

This is it! He wants to write his story for the book! I'll just have to explain that he should put some drama into it. That it should be factual but he should write it like a heartfelt drama. Maybe with a little...

"Are you going to tape this or just take notes?" Shatner's quiet question put a quick lump in my throat.

"Huh?" A lump I couldn't quite dislodge.

"The interview, are you going to record it or just take notes?" Bill enquired further.

"Um...notes? Yeah...I'll...take notes."

As I spoke those fateful words my tremor started trembling, slightly at first but as my mind began to absorb the fact that I was actually interviewing William Shatner over the phone *and* I had to take *NOTES*, my tremor started to rock and roll like Mick Jagger on 100 proof adrenaline with a"red bull" chaser,,.

"Are you ready to go?"

"Let me get a...pen..."

As I reached for my pen jar the only thing there was a medium sharpie. As I picked up some scrap paper, my brain sat my arm and my ear down and spoke straight from the heart.

Relax, we can do this! You, just listen closely and absorb each word. You, write down the words he emphasizes and the ones that you feel are important to the story. Me, I'll just open up and let it all flow in and then, for god's sake, we can't let it get out!

******

One Saturday, many years ago, due to a simple twist of fate, Al Plechner met William Shatner. As Bill remembers it, he had taken his car into 4 Day Tire, which was just south of the animal hospital where Al was in practice.

"I was killing time and my Doberman had come along for the ride so we went for a walk while I waited for my car to be fixed." Bill explained to me.

"I had been spending a lot of time with my dog because he had huge tumor that was growing in his armpit. We had been to a number of vets and they all agreed that it was a Lipoma which is basically a tumor composed of adipose tissue (body fat). All of the vets we had seen were afraid to surgically remove it.

The mass had invaded most of the nerves in the armpit and it was so intertwined they all felt it would be impossible to remove it without causing permanent paralysis of that front leg.

It wasn't cancer but it was inhibiting my dog's movement and even worse, it was still growing. I knew that something had to be done; I just couldn't find someone to do it.

Well, it so happened, that day the universe called to me. I don't mean that in a...mystical way. Let me say, I feel that intuition is not mystical; it's more like a combination of experience...and a leap of fate! Whereas, whatever you experience, causes you to store up all sorts of information that you aren't even aware of. You have the information and by osmosis you seem to be able to draw up knowledge that you didn't even realize you had in the first place. Somehow I chanced to wander into Al's office. I had no idea who Al was I just had been worrying about my dog and I seemed to end up there."

Al chuckled as he remembered his first encounter with Bill...

"In comes Captain Kirk with his Doberman. He had no idea who I was, but he came in anyway. He said something about waiting for his new tires but it was obvious he had more on his mind than tires. He told me that his dog had a huge tumor beneath his armpit and none of the Vets he had seen would remove it.

It was a Lipoma, which is a huge fat deposit that can envelop structures. All of the vets had said that since the mass had invaded all the nerves in the surrounding area, (the brachial nerve plexus) it could cause paralysis if they tried to remove it. I had a total discussion with Mr. Shatner and said I would carefully dissect out the mass and reduce its bulk as much as possible, trying obviously not to sever any nerves. Bill said, "Do it", and to my surprise he said he wanted to be present with me in surgery.

Obviously, no one says no to Captain Kirk." Al recounted with a chuckle. "He stood back and observed as I did the anesthesia and surgery. I could feel his deep concern as he looked on and I kept saying to myself 'make this work'. Bill did a lot better than I would have, considering it was his own dog.

Fortunately the mass had a number of invasive processes that could be slowly untwined from the brachial nerve plexus and the entire mass was removed leaving all nerves intact. Captain Kirk was really pleased with my success and this ended up being just the beginning of my long veterinary journey with William Shatner and his animals."

There after Bill *and* his family became more than friends and Al looked after their animals for many years. Al introduced Bill to Roz Wheelock, who provided Bill with many huge, happy and healthy Dobermans.

Bill continued his reminiscences...

"I've always loved dogs, especially Dobermans. I've bred them, showed them and assumed that I knew everything there was to know about them, which proved to be a false assumption. I had a beautiful and spirited, female Doberman named Heidi, she was a very alert and healthy. I lived in a smaller house then, which had a pool in the back and Heidi loved to lie on a carpet beside the pool. Whenever, Marcy or I came into the area she would leap up and bound over and greet us in that special way that all dogs do.

One Saturday, as I made my entrance, Heidi did not react as playful as she usually did. She just looked up at me and I could tell that something was wrong. It was difficult for her to stand; she seemed to be having problems with her back legs. We took her into an emergency animal hospital and they took x-rays but they were inconclusive. All the vets there seemed to have their own theories; possibly Wobblers...possibly a back injury... the only thing they seemed to agree on was...it was a lost cause and she'd never walk again. Putting her down was the only solution.

We said no to euthanasia, we just felt we should wait and take here to see Al on Monday. Throughout the weekend she was getting weaker and weaker and was losing the ability to move her back legs. The whole family was sick with worry. We were certain that that she was dying, which caused us all to start grieving her loss before her time.

The first thing, Monday morning we took her and the X-rays into see Al. After looking at her x-rays he threw them down in disgust and he gave her a thorough examination. When he was done he looked at me with a smile, and said that 'the rumors of her demise were greatly exaggerated'. He also said that it certainly wasn't Wobbler. To my amazement he said the problem was her diet and that he could help her if she stayed with him at the hospital for a few days. I was still very worried but the look in Al's eyes, convinced me that everything was going to be alright.

We followed his recommendations and in a couple of weeks the dog was much better. Soon she was perfectly normal again and she stayed that way, a very healthy dog, until she died at age 14. Heidi's problem, of all things, was a beef allergy that severely affected her hind legs.

Al remembers that day very clearly...

"I helped Bill and his 2nd wife, Marcy, with their red Doberman, Heidi. It was the weekend, and Heidi was taken into the hospital because she could not walk and was dragging her rear feet. They were told by the emergency hospital vets that it might be Wobbler disease or she might have ruptured a disc and there was no guarantee that she would walk again. Bill and Marcy refused the offer of euthanasia and chose to wait until my return on Monday.

Upon examination, I could see that there was no Wobbler and no apparent injury. After palpating her lower body, I determined that she was suffering from a horrible gas build up in her abdomen. *What is not realized is that, abdominal pain can be transferred to the rear legs, not unlike how a person with a heart problem feels pain and stiffness in their left arm.*

Heidi had been on beef etc., so I designed a quick diet change and formulated a special diet for her, involving, brown rice, soybean, carrots and celery. By removing the ingredients that her body was reacting adversely to, her signs (symptoms) began to diminish almost immediately. In short order the gas dissipated and as the pressure weakened and she regained her strength, her movement returned to normal. I eventually called this the **Heidi Diet**.

As Bill related his version of this 'miracle' to me, I could hear the emotion in his voice...

"We were ecstatic. Those other vets had us scared to death, saying that we were going to lose Heidi. They suggested, 'euthanasia' (!) and all the time it was a food allergy. Al knew right away, what the problem was and he created a special diet for Heidi. She was healthier than ever. We were so glad to have such a fantastic Veterinarian and such a dedicated friend."

Al added an interesting post script, to this already, fascinating story.

"Marcy was a dancer. Soon after we began the Heidi diet, at a follow-up exam, Marcy mentioned that she could not dance because she had knee problems. As I remember, I told her she might have a gluten-sensitive enteropathy and suggested that she stop eating foods with wheat. Soon thereafter her knees were fine and she was able to dance again. Over the years I have helped the Shatner's with a bunch of neat Dobies."

And that, in a nutshell, is William Shatner's 'Plechner Story". My apologies, Bill, if I left anything out but there's no Rosetta stone for my scribbling.

Chapter Two

The Plechner Syndrome and Protocol

The Mystery Unravels

Back in the late '60's, in the early years of his practice as a Vet, Dr. Al realized early on that standard veterinarian practice was not having a lot of effect in its dealings with catastrophic diseases. The Status Quo at that time was that certain diseases inevitably lead to certain outcomes...death, in most cases, by euthanasia. Once the prognosis was determined to be lethal, treatment for the most part was considered to be useless. It was common practice to cut your losses early and accept the inevitable and put the animal down before they began to suffer.

Dr. Al didn't really subscribe to that school of thought. He felt that giving up was certainly not in the patient's main interest. Of course, eventually, there could come a time when the pain and the illness became too much for the patient to bear, however, until that time Dr. Al felt if they could speak they would argue that if any extra time was available and it was still quality time, well...he would continue his research.

He had begun to realize that any problem not solved, left a trail of loose strings behind. The more he studied these loose strings; he began to discern that they seemed to be weaving a faint pattern. As he observed this pattern an idea began to loom in his mind. A certain, common denominator was at work amongst these many and varied patients. Even though they were affected by different fatal disorders, they all seem to be linked by common threads. If not the diseases themselves perhaps it was similar weaknesses within the bodies of those afflicted.

He started to look closer at the body's defenses against disease. HQ for these stalwart defenders of the body was the immune system. He felt if he could determine that common factor they shared he might be close to discovering a possible treatment for these varying catastrophic diseases. Up until then and even still today, for the most part, even though most research has turned up effective treatments for dealing with the signs and symptoms none have actually addressed the causes in a preventative sense.

During the course of his clinical work, he became aware of a major hormone based, immune system deficiency. This defect initiates in the adrenal glands and continues to spiral out, disrupting many critical points in the body's physiology. The conditions Al encountered ranged from conventional allergies and reproductive failures to catastrophic auto immune diseases and even cancers.

Throughout the years, Al's clinical work enabled him to identify and correct this endocrine system based deficit, the *Plechner Syndrome*, allowing him to develop an extremely successful diagnostic and treatment protocol which has helped thousands of patients not only in his own clinic but also in many other veterinary clinics and hospitals throughout the world.

The Endocrine-Immune imbalances he has seen result from an unsuspected deficiency, defect or binding of cortisol. Whether due to genetics, environmental toxicity, stress, aging, or any combination possible, He has found that many animals lack sufficient active cortisol. Not only is the average pet owner not even aware that they and their animals absolutely must produce a certain amount of natural cortisone to be able to function and live. There is a general lack of medical knowledge on how to administer a cortisol replacement safely, in order to regain the natural physiological level required for good health.

Many medical practitioners are apprehensive due to a predetermined and unfairly prejudiced opinion of ongoing cortisol therapy. Most of the owners whom Al consults with, who are desperately seeking treatment for their seriously ill pets, have been told basically, "This was not taught to us in veterinary school." by their own, bewildered veterinarians. Through the years, Al has found that many professionals...

"Focus only on the trees directly in front of them, therefore (unfortunately) miss the overall view of the forest."

When animals (and people) require long term use of a cortisol replacement, it is essential that thyroid hormone also be administered, to guarantee that the cortisol is properly metabolized and is not allowed to accumulate in the system. Al corrects the cortisol deficiency by using very low (physiological as opposed to therapeutic) doses of a cortisol replacement, which is the pharmaceutical equivalent of the body's naturally occurring cortisol, along with thyroid hormone depending on the species he is working with. Personal communications and clinical experience support his not using the natural forms or cortisol.

As a clinician, treating his patients has always been his primary concern. For this reason, he has not had the time or the funds to conduct "controlled studies" where one group of patients receives proper therapy and the other group receives a placebo. Even so, a success rate of over 200,000 seriously ill patients, worldwide, seems to be a strong confirmation of Al's findings and validation of his techniques. As Al put's it...

"My hormonal replacement treatment, the Plechner Protocol, has been extremely safe and effective when followed, as directed, on a long-term basis by pet owners. When the identification and proper replacement protocol is carefully followed, this program has rapidly and significantly improved the health status of even animals being recommended for euthanasia by other Vets. It is also an approach that has shown significant potential for the treatment of human illnesses, even catastrophic diseases.

I am a "plain wrapped" working Veterinarian who has never denied proper treatment to a suffering patient. Forty plus years of clinical work has proven to me that solid medical practice is a blend of Eastern and Western medicine and includes a regimen of proper nutrition, supplementation, exercise, stress reducers and sleep. This then is what I like to call "Wholistic" medicine because it involves whole animal health; body, mind and spirit."

Clinical Impressions of a
Plain Wrapped Veterinarian

Nearly fifty years of clinical inquiries have convinced me that the quintessential apex of thriving, healthy life comes from a harmonic ratio between total estrogen and active cortisol. These findings have proven to me that the endocrine system regulates the immune system and although these 'facts' may not be easily accepted by all those within our medical professional circles, their veracity may be easily determined by a careful measurement of the levels of cortisol, total estrogen T3, T4, and IGA, IGG and IGM within the blood

The results of an **E-I – Human** blood panel will indicate whether there is a proper balance between the cortisol and total estrogen levels and a functioning immune system. These results will further indicate whether the hormones are deficient, defective, bound or in excess, for even if your patient's hormone levels fall within normal limits, you cannot automatically assume the hormones are actually available to fulfill the needs within the body. This is why it is essential to compare the hormone levels to the immune levels.

If the test reveals that the level of cortisol and the total estrogen level are both elevated, this result indicates defective or bound cortisol. This outcome does not indicate a true *Cushing Syndrome*, this is instead indicative of an atypical cortisol imbalance syndrome commonly referred to as *Plechner Syndrome*.

If the antibody levels are low, what may actually be occurring is that the defective cortisol is not being recognized by the pituitary gland and the negative feedback between the hypothalamic-pituitary-adrenal axis, is impaired. In response, the anterior pituitary gland begins to secrete Adrenocorticotropic which stimulates the inner layer adrenal cortex to produce an excess of adrenal estrogen and androgen.

This excess estrogen causes the creation of a reverse T3, which binds the receptor sites of the thyroid hormones, deregulates the B and T cell and suppresses Immunoglobulin production. This imbalance may also cause rapid weight gain which then may lead to excess aromatase, the enzyme in the fatty tissue which turns testosterone and androgen into more estrogen. And so, round and round it goes, this vicious cycle continues.

If, at this point, you provide the patient with an active cortisol replacement you will be reversing the negative feedback to the pituitary gland, reducing the amounts of defective cortisol, adrenal estrogen and androgen. Furthermore, , the protection by the B and T cells will return and the immunoglobulin levels will normalize.

As this transpires, in humans and canines, thyroid replacement is critical to correct the reverse T_3 while the estrogen levels return to normal. Continuation of the thyroid hormone replacement ensures that the physiological level of active cortisol replacement is broken down by the liver and excreted by the kidneys within 24 hours. This will prevent residue build up, which would generate pharmacologic levels of the cortisol replacement causing undesirable side effects.

I have observed that the possible hazards of long term steroid use are due to the absence of thyroid hormone replacement during the cortisol replacement protocol. In humans a T_3, T_4 supplement is warranted whereas only a T_4 is needed in canines. The normal daily production of cortisol from the middle layer of the adrenal cortex in humans and animals is approximately 30 to 35 units daily.

The amount of active cortisol and thyroid hormone needed in each individual patient is based upon the normalization of the immunoglobulins. When the active cortisol replacement is too high, the immunoglobulins will be suppressed. If the cortisol replacement is not high enough, the elevated level of adrenal estrogen will also cause a suppression of the immunoglobulins. Though the balance between active cortisol and total estrogen will vary with each patient, normalization of the immunoglobulins will always dictate when the correct amount of hormone replacement is attained.

It is important for me to note that when the level of IGA drops below a certain point oral administration for hormone replacement will not be absorbed through the inflamed gut. When this occurs an injection of a steroid will be needed to bypass the gut and reach the circulatory system to directly affect the pituitary production of ACTH and reduce the excess estrogen so that the IGA level can rise and allow for oral absorption to occur. Based upon measurable levels of IGA, it may take more than one injection to accomplish this. For further information, please go to www.townsendletter.com and look for an article entitled "*The Importance of IGA*".

Earlier I mentioned total estrogen. Estrogen is thought to be produced mainly by the ovaries, but what about adrenal estrogen? Total estrogen is the sum you derive when you add the ovarian estrogen level and the adrenal estrogen level. Women produce estradiol, estrone and estriole. Males are thought to produce only estradiol. Many medical professionals measure just the ovarian estrogen. My clinical findings have demonstrated to myself and many others that total estrogen produced in excessive amounts is proving to be a major source of concern in the development of many catastrophic diseases.

To prove this, take a blood test for estrogen in a menstruating female human on the 7th day of her menstrual cycle when the least ovarian estrogen is being produced. Then, once again later in her cycle, when ovarian estrogen production is at its highest. I know you will be surprised, to see how much adrenal estrogen has been included in the laboratory normals, especially in their extreme ranges for the various stages of the ovarian cycle.

Although it has been shown that a decrease in ovarian estrogen promotes the inflammation of the endothelial cells of all arteries in the body including the cerebral arteries and research has shown that many females may have migraine headaches and epileptic seizures just after their ovarian estrogen has decreased, further studies are needed. This is due to the important fact that none of these studies have been completed based on the sum of total estrogen, including the adrenal_estrogen, actually present during this time.

Every epileptic animal I have tested, over several thousand patients in the last 45 years of practice (female and male) have all had elevated levels of total estrogen. These seriously high levels were due to cortisol deficiency or imbalance and/or from eating estrogen rich foods which also augment the possibility of estrogen dominance.

Currently, inflammation of the cerebral arteries is also thought to be a concern for Alzheimer patients. More information is available, on my website, www.drplechner.com about foods that contain natural estrogen and foods that contain estrogen inhibitors

You can see how birth control pills containing estrogen might be problematic for a patient that is adrenal estrogen prominent. This might also further explain why woman with in vitro fertilization cannot implant even when the procedure is performed during the lowest period of ovarian estrogen production.

One last thought about the dangers of elevated total estrogen levels. When you consider the inflammation of the endothelial cells that line the arteries throughout the body, you begin to recognize the possibility that this might initiate the fibrin lay down that paves the way to atherosclerosis, arteriosclerosis, and on down the line to coronary occlusion, strokes and other deadly cardiovascular diseases.

I personally believe that it is time for the medical professions to recognize...

- There is more estrogen being produced in the body then is being determined by the presently accepted standard estrogen testing procedures.
- Testing should be expanded to identify and measure adrenal estrogen levels and more effort should be put forth to understand the importance it plays in total estrogen prominence.
- It must be perceived and accepted that the endocrine system does indeed regulate the immune system.

- Even if normal amounts of measurable hormones appear to be present, this does not automatically mean that those hormones can actually be used by the body.
- When your patients exhibit any of the aforementioned maladies and many others, as you are running standard tests, draw some blood for a simple **E-I Human** blood panel to test for the *Plechner Syndrome*. If it's present, you'll have, at the very least, some new facts to base your therapy upon.

My thinking may be "outside of the box", but when you're dealing with serious and sometimes catastrophic diseases you need to do everything in your power to heal your patient before you offer euthanasia. It is a simple test and it could make a great difference in the outcome.

Healthfully Yours
Dr. Al Plechner DVM & David Spangenburg

Endocrine – Immune Blood Panel Animal Test

Plechner Syndrome, can be easily measured. Once your Vet draws the blood, serum samples need to be spun down immediately and refrigerated.

- **If the sample reaches room temperature or higher, the test results will be incorrect and the actual cause of the disease missed.**
- **They need to be sent to the lab by a refrigerated, overnight delivery service.**
- **A temperature strip should accompany the sample from the hospital to the laboratory, to insure the proper temperature has been maintained.**

Currently there is only one Laboratory that is doing this testing...

National Veterinary Diagnostic Services, LLC
4221 Pecan Bend Drive
Richmond, TX 77406-8601
Phone: 281-661-4292
Fax: 877-349-8217
E-Mail: info@national-vet.com

Its website is located here, http://www.national-vet.com/. New Client Packets and sample submission forms are available here, http://nationaldiagnosticservices.com/

You should request the
ENDOCRINE-IMMUNE BLOOD PANEL ANIMAL TEST (E-I-1 ANIMAL).

Once your Vet has the results they can initiate the *Plechner Protocol* for proper hormone replacement. If your Vet has any questions or concerns they can contact Dr. Al Plechner. Information is available on the
Consultation page at...
http://www.drplechner.com

Hyperadrenal Cortisism

Hyperadrenal Corti:

Much of the controversy regarding the
triggered by two factors; fear and educated
of health care professionals are hesitant to initiate
cortisol replacement therapy, even if a cortisol imbalance has been
identified.

Their formal education has limited their thinking to "inside the box" standards. These standards tell them that the continued use of cortisol (a steroid) is bad, even though it has been proven that cortisol is a natural hormonal secretion that is vital for maintaining good health. Cortisol is actually produced every day from the middle layer of the adrenal cortex in all normal and regulated people and animals. If this cortisol production becomes deregulated it causes an atypical cortisol imbalance in the immune system, which has become known as, *Plechner Syndrome.*

Once this *Syndrome* is identified and *Plechner's Protocol* started, there is a chance that the cortisol production might possibly return to normal, even though this is rare. Routine testing of all the comparative levels can determine if the cortisol supplement can be stopped or at least reduced. Once the immune system is balanced, minimal maintenance dosing is usually continued, to sustain the proper balance.

There are some medical professionals that make the supposition that cortisol supplementation might cause diabetes mellitus. Even so, diabetes mellitus is more often considered to be an autoimmune disease in which the deregulated immune cell is binding (blocking) the insulin, the cell membrane or the cells that actually produce the insulin.

If a diabetic state does occur, the hormone supplementation is normally continued along with an addition of insulin to control the problem. For those health care professionals that are concerned with the possibility of diabetes mellitus, fructosamine can be added to the routine **E - I blood test**. Any increase in fructosamine can be determined before a state of diabetes actually occurs.

is important to remember; *Plechner's Syndrome* is stealthy
ι requires an **E - I** blood test to be discovered. This explains the
ιfficulty in diagnosing. Patients that suffer from this cortisol
imbalance are very complex and may exhibit various symptoms.
Plechner's Syndrome, carries the potential for a myriad of possible
maladies, many of which can possibly prove to be catastrophic.

Fighting the Good Fight

Dr. Plechner once had a consultation client, who called him one evening. She sounded desperate. It seems that her vet refused to do the blood draw and to send it in to **National Veterinary Diagnostic Services** lab for **EI** testing. As it happens, he'd never heard of the *Plechner Syndrome*. They didn't cover it in the Veterinarian School that he'd attended. Nor was it in any text book he had read.

"*Besides...*" her vet said, "*...it's dangerous to use cortisone* (a steroid) *as an ongoing maintenance treatment!*"

She had showed him her copy of Al's book, Pets at Risk and though he said that he'd read it, he would not change his mind. He told her there was no hope for her stricken Terrier; it would be better to...put the dog down.

Can you imagine that? This 'medical professional' had no answer for her Terrier's illness but he still refused to step 'out of the box' and try an unfamiliar and "unorthodox" treatment to save this woman's dog from death's door. It sounds like a bad drama doesn't it? It isn't! It has happened hundreds, if not thousands of times throughout Dr. Al's lengthy career.

Throughout those years, Al has fought the good fight but, a lot of the time; it felt like he was fighting his way upstream.

You know what I mean? Well, maybe not.

If not, consider this.

You're a medical professional, in practice for close to half a century. Throughout those many years of practice and clinical research, you uncover a defect within the endocrine system. You find a hormonal imbalance that causes an immune system breakdown. This discovery led you to develop a treatment protocol that has been proven successful time and time again.

You would think that your fellow medical professionals would at least have the professional "curiosity" to determine if this defect really does exist. And, if it does, will the protocol really fix it? You'd think they'd at least consider the benefits that it offers. The potential it shows, to find cures for many catastrophic diseases. I know that it wasn't taught at veterinary school and that it's not in any textbook. I also realize that there haven't been any double blind tests and it's considered "outside the box" but remember penicillin was once considered to be just a *mold* that grew on bread and fruit.

One vivid example was a consultation client Al helped in Canada. Al suggested a course of action that she and her vet might implement to help her seriously ill pet. The next day, Al received an irate phone call from his client's local vet telling him that she was reporting him to his state board in California for suggesting dangerous and erroneous information that would only hurt the animal in question. The vet was licensed not only in Canada but also in California. Al calmly told the vet that he had only made suggestions and asked the vet, point blank, why a simple **E -I ANIMAL** blood test can't be included with the other blood tests done at the same time.

Al has never asked a professional to act upon the test results. It is always the choice of the vet and the pet owner, however, if *Plechner's Syndrome* shows positive, then then Al will make treatment suggestions, and if there is no interest, it's time for him to move on.

In this case the owner insisted that the Vet do the E1-1 test and the puzzled vet conceded, realizing that she didn't have to act upon the results. Interestingly, AL once again heard from the vet, with a different attitude this time. The test had proved positive and so Al made some suggestions which the vet implemented and the patient did a whole lot better.

He's had his share of "converts". Throughout the years a number of medical professionals have grudgingly realized that there are times when you *do* step outside the box. Those times have been, for the most part, when their patients were at deaths door and they had no other answers to give. Their patient's owners, having more to lose than just a revenue source, were not willing to give up. They demanded action, no matter how unfamiliar or unusual it appeared and to the vets amazement it worked!

Some, made excuses, said a remission had happened and the replacement hormone therapy was not involved in the least. There were dedicated others though, who cared enough to see the true potential of hormonal replacement therapies. Even though, over 950 veterinary hospitals in the US and Canada have done Dr. Al's tests, the labs have confided to him that not all the hospitals are "friendly" to the cause. Friendly or not the *Plechner Protocol* has saved the lives of over 200,000 dogs, cats, horses...and humans too.

Some of Al's biggest supporters have been medical doctors. Dr. David Brownstein M.D. has used hormonal replacement therapies to, as he puts it, *"...rebuild the immune system."* of many of his chronically ill patients. Dr. William Jefferies M.D., a clinical professor emeritus of internal medicine at the **University of Virginia, Medical School**, has effectively used cortisone medication, without harm, for numerous human illnesses involving, what he calls, *"adrenal cortical deficiency"*. Dr. John R. Lee M.D. admits that Al has *"a different spin on the problem"* that he has with humans but he calls Al *"a much needed pioneering clinician in veterinary medicine"*. Another thing that Doctor Al Plechner DVM has in common with these gifted M.D.s is the potential they all see in the effective use of hormonal replacement therapies in finally defeating many catastrophic diseases including allergies, cancer and AIDS.

As Al sees it, there are two types of health care professionals and as a pet owner or as a patient, it is up to you to determine which you will choose to use.

One who accepts their job as their calling and will try anything, within reason, which might help those in their care. The kind of healer that will help their patients even if it means using new information and techniques which others might consider unusual, outside the box, or possibly even dangerous. If it means it might save or even just "healthfully extend" their patient's life.

Or, will you pick

One who chose the field of medicine because it offered a financially secure lifestyle and is driven by a business model and not the "passion to heal". One who is afraid to trust anything not learned in the classroom or read in a textbook and feels it's easier and more profitable, to treat the symptoms than it is to cure the cause. It's always safer to maintain mediocrity then it is to challenge the status quo.

Remember, if your pet is facing a life threatening situation, there is no logical reason not to determine if *Plechner Syndrome* is present. Have the **E-I** blood panel run. If they test positive, there still may be a good chance to change their prognosis. If it's a matter of life or death, you *must* be your pets advocate. Have your vet try the hormonal replacement protocol. There is information available throughout this book and on Dr. Al's website, http://www.drplechner.com , which will assist you. You must also remember that, while you are controlling the imbalances found in the syndrome, a healthy diet, nutritional supplements and enzymes are all important in this complete "wholistic" approach.

From a support standpoint, many veterinarians from Al's generation have retired. Not all are gluttons for punishment like he is. The younger professionals they sell their practices to, are programmed with a different methodology. Some of them also seem to be less dedicated to their work. They treat their practice as if it were just a *job*. You really can't blame them; it's a sign of the times. This world today has become very "shallow" Our "techno" society appears too caught up with gadgets, social networks and reality television programming. Many seem to have forgotten about vocation, truth and genuine commitment. More importantly, as our environment worsens and more food allergies plague our pet's lives, their immune systems are under direct attack which makes them vulnerable to many life threatening diseases. Dr. Al is very concerned about the future of healthcare.

"This old vet won't last forever, someone must see that my work is understood and continued. That's why David and I wrote this book. Even though you might find more "technical" information in my other books Pets at Risk, Pet Allergies: Remedies for an Epidemic, The Endocrine Immune Imbalances and Human Health Implications and Fifty Years of Healing. This book was written, from the heart. It highlights some fascinating

episodes from my life and_allows some people I've helped to tell their own dramatic, true accounts of life, death, courage and commitment." , it also contains a comprehensive collection of thoughtful, therapeutic information. The Healthfully Yours Handbook, is an engaging, proactive guide for
Whole Animal Health."

This book was written as a personal appeal to all animal lovers and you "just plain" humans too. You all can make a difference in this world but first you need to understand three simple facts...

- The Endocrine-Immune Imbalance does exist.
- The Hormonal Replacement Protocol is the only treatment that can correct it.
- This information should be included in the curriculum of all the Schools of Veterinary Medicine.

It's up to you to comprehend the "all too real" dangers of the *Plechner Syndrome* and the amazing benefits of the *Plechner Protocol*. You can change the world. All you have to do is to make your healthcare professional aware of this <u>proven</u> information we have given you and suggest that they include this testing and treatment in their practice.

If they don't, then find one that will.

Healthcare professionals must address all of the needs of their patients and respect the opinion of all of their clients. The more professionals who experience the remarkable results, the more that will influence academic change within the medical profession, the day that happens will be the day we finally win the "good fight".

Chapter Three

Second Opinions
Peer Support for Dr. Al Plechner's, Research and Findings

FR: Albert Simpson, DVM.

In today's veterinary medicine, changes in treatment, diagnosis, and pathophysiology usually comes from research at our universities and schools of veterinary medicine. This has not always been the case. In the late 1970's and early 1980's, pioneering work on adrenal and thyroid endocrinology and immune system links were postulated by Alfred Jay Plechner, DVM.

His careful research and clinical observations uncovered the relationship between the endocrine system and the immune system, and how they manifested conditions, thought before to be unrelated clinical diseases.

In his first book, *Pet Allergies*, Dr. Plechner outlined the complicated interactions of cortisol, thyroid, total estrogen, and three main antibodies as they apply to allergies and intestinal disease. Dr. Plechner's second book, *Pet's at Risk*, has further linked endocrine-immune disorders to heredity, environmental toxins, as well as autoimmunity and cancer.

Dr. Plechner dealt with these conditions every day as a practicing veterinarian, however, the fact that this information came from his research and that his findings were generated from his practice, not from a university, but in the exam room, has caused quite a lot of controversy and discussion.

Dr. Plechner has stood up to the task of defending his work, and has seen it validated in many medical circles. The last few years, he has been asked to lecture at several medical schools * here and in England. Many healthcare professionals have adopted his procedures, achieving very positive results. He has a collection of published MD journals throughout the world. A compilation of these articles appear in his 3rd book entitled, *Endocrine- Immune Mechanisms in Animals and Human Health Implications.* In addition to his clinical studies, he offers online seminars, plus two new unpublished books, as well as a medical dictionary for the pet owner.

As a practicing veterinarian, I personally collaborated with Dr. Plechner on dozens of cases over the past 15 years. These patients benefited from his work. Many of these cases had been given up on, and were at the final chapter of their lives. Using his blood tests, and carefully developed treatment protocols, many of these dogs and cats were returned to normal, healthy, happy lives.

Dr. Plechner's dedication to these pets is wonderfully evident. He is continuing to practice veterinary medicine, giving his gentle and caring touch, and vast understanding of physiology, for the benefit of those pets, that are fortunate to be under his care.

Albert Simpson, DVM.

* Author's note (Even though Al has lectured at the Broda Barnes MD Research Foundation in Conn, and was asked to lecture in England and at two major conferences here in the US, not one *medical school* has ever asked him to lecture for their students.)

****

FR: Dr. Jay Vazifdar, M.D

I was born in Poona India in 1923. My father was a Prof. of Medicine at Bombay University. At age 6 I went to England & was introduced to my future guardian family. I returned to India & at the age of 10, I went to live in England with my Guardians, the Reeves family.

I went to Berkhamsted School in 1933 and, apart from returning to India for summer vacations, I primarily lived in England.

I went up to Cambridge in 1941 for my premed. In 1945 I started Clinical studies, graduating in 1948. From 1948 till 1953 I worked in various London hospitals (Surgery, OB-GYN, pediatric & general internal medicine posts). In March 1953 I started my own family practice in the NHS. My father who had retired joined me in my growing practice!

I immigrated to the USA in 1963 as I could no longer stand the NHS & its policies!! After a year at St. John's Hospital in Lowell, Mass, I came to Meredith, NH in 1964 & have been here ever since!! I retired from professional life in 2004.

In Jan 2009 my 9 yr. old Airedale/German Sheppard mix male dog, Lucky, stopped eating, lost weight and was diagnosed with Lymphoma. A blood test panel showed an elevated calcium of 20 (normal =14 or less) & a low phosphorus.

We were told that Lucky probably had a cancer. It was recommended that he have IV's to bring down the calcium level. Not only did his level remain high but he also developed an infection at the IV site and his health continued to go downhill. The prognosis was not good.

Betsy my wife made a frantic phone call to ATRA, Airedale Terrier Rescue Association (where we had adopted him). They gave us Dr. Plechner's name & telephone number. Dr. Plechner was wonderful & very kind & he advised me to get a specific blood profile done on Lucky and to contact him with the results. When we did this, he advised us to have our Veterinarian, Dr. Guest, give Lucky a shot of Cortisone and to follow that with a course of oral thyroid.

Al called us many times to check on Lucky's progress and even told us to call him (at any time of the day) if we had questions or concerns and to keep him informed of Lucky's progress. Because of my training & medical knowledge, I was delighted to discuss his theories & experiences with cancer & immune system suppression in dogs and cats and in human patients!! I cannot tell how many times Al & I (my wife Betsy too) talked and discussed our beloved Lucky's progress.

The local Vet had by now revised the diagnosis of Lymphoma & we all agreed that Lucky had some type of cancer. Even though,

Dr. Guest concluded that Lucky's days were numbered, we followed Dr. Plechner's protocol and our Lucky gained weight and was acting his usual playful self.

Thanks to this great & wonderful Healer, Lucky had a wonderful SEVEN more months of a full, active and happy life beyond what was originally projected. Betsy and I will always cherish those extra months that Al's careful and continued assistance allowed us to share with Lucky.

I wish I was younger & still in medical practice as I sincerely believe that Dr. Plechner's work & tremendous experience should be researched & followed up in several directions. I am convinced it has a huge bearing on the cancer in humans!!

Yours,

Dr. Jay Vazifdar, M.D

****

FR: Frank J. Grasse, DVM

Back on 15 January 2003, I saw a 4 year old, black female spayed Labrador for an ear problem. Both ears were bad, with 4+ yeast in the right ear and 2+ yeast in the left ear. Topical medications were tried but the ears progressively worsened and on 14 August 2003, I added an oral antifungal. The pet was on topical and oral medications with the ears not responding and on 17 July 2003, it was started on a hypoallergenic diet. By 22 January 2004 the ears were involved in a severe otitis that I considered sending this pet for radical ear surgery – but the owner refused to have any surgery done.

I'd known about Dr. Plechner from a previous consult and called him that January. He spent a great deal of time and with his knowledge and his books: *Pet Allergies, Remedies for an Epidemic* and *Pets at Risk*, I drew a blood sample from this pet and sent it to National Veterinary Diagnostic Services that Dr.

Plechner recommended. The blood results were just as Dr. Plechner predicted. High Estrogen Levels, Low Immunoglobulins.

This pet was started on the program Dr. Plechner outlined for me over the telephone conversation. Remember this pet's ears were so severely affected that I thought surgery would be the only solution. By 24 March 2004, the ear canals were open, still infected but I could actually look down the ear canals again. By 04 June 2004 both ears looked and tested normal. Over time medications were lowered to maintenance dosages, I last saw this pet 03 September 2009, and it is healthy, happy, with normal ear canals.

The biggest problem I faced is the no laboratories other than the National Veterinary Diagnostic Services will do the testing needed to find this particular abnormality. To get samples to the National Veterinary Diagnostic Services in a timely fashion is extremely difficult in my part of the state. What is needed is for Dr. Plechner's methodology to be recognized so practitioners have an easy way to test pets with local laboratories. If this was possible, I know I would be testing more pets than I do now.

My dealings with Dr. Plechner tell me he is extremely astute and knowledgeable and his ideas should have been accepted by established veterinary medicine years ago. Dr. Plechner never talks down to me and explains these tests and theories to me giving freely of this time and experience. A pet I have described above is now 10 years old and happy and healthy thanks to Dr. Plechner.

I hope this can add to your story about a veterinarian and researcher who has made a considerable advance to veterinary medicine and to the health of many pets.

It is a true shame that the veterinary establishment has not been open to his ideas so that other pets could benefit from Dr. Plechner's treatments.

Respectfully,

Frank J. Grasse, DVM

****

FR: Nina A. Tomei, MD

Thank you for the opportunity to read your paper. It's very interesting and I look forward to learning more.

Sanibel's two week results after being on 8 mg methylprednisolone once a day and 0.8 mg soloxine twice a day (weight approx 80lb) was:

Cortisol   1.2 ug/dl (1.0-5.0)

Total T4   1.7 ug/dl (0.8-3.5)

I asked the vet to do these directly, mistakenly believing he would also order T3 and that the cost would be less, but the cost for these two tests was similar to the cost of the full panel AND overnight shipping to National Veterinary Diagnostic Services, so I will order the complete panel and send it out when her labs are to be repeated in 6 months.

My dog is doing very well--no further anal or paw itching, and she now sleeps through the night without getting up frequently (I realize now this was due to overall discomfort).   I am just concerned that she seems hungrier than before and pushier than usual about getting treats. Her weight is stable because we have kept her food quantity the same, and perhaps she just feels so much better, but I'm wondering if you have ever needed to lower the dose of cortisol in this situation?

Thank you again for all that you have done. I was thinking recently, that had you continued with a medical school education, my dog would still be suffering, and we would suffer with her.

I might have continued her Temaril P on a daily basis, never feeling comfortable with it, and never realizing I was causing her to become hypothyroid.

Thank you so much!

Nina A. Tomei, MD

The North Shore Medical Group
of the Mt. Sinai School of Medicine

****

FR: Kathy Backus, DVM

I have a Rhodesian Ridgeback who is my personal dog. She just turned 5 years old. I had attended the AHVMA conference and found out about Dr. Plechner's work when she was 1 year old.
She didn't really exhibit any clinical problems except full anal glands and urinary incontinence after her spay which I did. Interestingly I did have difficulty in removing the right ovary at the time of her surgery.

I decided to test out and explore Dr. Plechner's work on my own dog as well as my patients so I did the puppy panel on her and found her cortisol was indeed low and her estrogen slightly high. I retested a year later after seeing such great results on my patients. She was more out of balance and so I started her on the protocol. About three months ago, she developed skin masses that changed in size. RR get mast cell tumors frequently and I presumed that she had mast cell tumors.

I have successfully treated her with topical and oral neoplasene from Buck Mountain Botanicals because her immune system is so strong and responsive. I wanted to be thorough so I took her to get an ultrasound done to make sure that her spleen wasn't involved. During the ultrasound, we discovered that she was born without a right kidney and right adrenal gland!!!! We also did a digital radiograph to confirm this.

The traditional vet was amazed that she does not show any clinical signs or blood work weaknesses being a large 96 pound, active living in the desert RR. I even did a stim test on the only adrenal gland to make sure it was handling the workload well. IT is. I truly believe that getting her balanced early on saved her life as kidney failure is not reversible in dogs.

She is living a good, active life with one adrenal gland and kidney with a lot of support and nutritional supplementation and Plechner's protocol from an early age. This wasn't a sick dog, but she could've been if I hadn't practiced preventative medicine.

Kathy Backus, DVM

****

FR: Maureen - NewSage Press
Hi Al,

A wonderful vet in Corvallis, Oregon, Sharon Forster-Blouin, read your book and is very interested in your protocol. She has always prided herself in being a vet practicing "natural medicine." However, she has used your protocol a couple of times on some hard cases and has been very impressed.

She called me yesterday to get a couple more books for her staff. I gave her your email address. She has a few questions and "theories" of her own around burned out adrenals and would love to talk with you. I think you would really enjoy talking with her. She is very excited about your work. She said she was feeling burned out as a vet, and now is getting more excited about the possibilities for healing that your protocol offers.

Best,
Maureen
NewSage Press

****

FR: Sharon Forster-Blouin, PhD, DVM
Thanks so much for responding. I am a feline practitioner in Corvallis Oregon, though I certainly treat my staff's and my own dogs and end up rescuing "hopeless" cats and dogs. (I should be running a charitable organization instead of a business.)

I have just finished your book and found excitement, validation, and hope...all mixed together. I have been wondering why there is not an epidemic of adrenal disease and why only the OSU (Ohio State) folks have linked FLUTD to adrenal dysfunction. Your work validates what I have been looking for a few years though I "expect" the epidemic from a different etiology.

I have been writing "red-line gingivitis" in my records for years and can't seem to find anyone else who thinks it is its own problem. I also have been steering cats away from fish and my colleagues and the food reps ask how I can advise that without "any proof" - I just say that I find that many cats don't tolerate fish and if they are ill for any reason, get them off of it. Your work has me encouraged.

So I ran my first 3 E1 panels last week: one on a hospital cat with chronic, intractable IBD, one on my own Addisonian dog who has never tolerated Percorten and is always out of regulation, and one on a rescue pitbull with horrid food and skin allergies.

I am not sure how to proceed with my addisionian as he already receives thyroid supplements, Cortef and fludrocortisone. The rescue dog has normal cortisol but low thyroid and slightly high estrogen. And the hospital cat, a purebred train wreck Persian, already receives prednisolone but is showing some cushingoid signs (so I if I grasp your protocol, she needs thyroid supplementation since her thyroid values are low too).

Would it be possible for me to scan and email the results to you and ask for your help with the interpretation? I don't want to impose on you and I promise not to make a habit out of asking for your help with interpretations - but I could use help getting started.

If this is something that you would do, please let me know. If it is an imposition, I sure do understand the need to protect from burnout (I'm there) so no hard feelings here.

Thanks again. I look forward to your reply,

Sharon Forster-Blouin, PhD, DVM

Chapter Four

The Human Factor
Health in the New Millennium

Chain of Fools

When it all began, there was a delicate balance. The controlled chaos of survival was held in place by the great food chain...called life. Along its great links, the various flora and fauna, rose or fell depending on the nature of things. It was the potency not the strength of each species that determined its place on the chain. As the drive to survive fueled evolution, the driven moved on, the others became fodder for the fields.

We humans, having neither claws nor tearing teeth, dangled from the rungs of the food chain like salamis over a deli counter, easy pickings for prowling predators. Even still, we seemed to have a greater understanding of our own "potential". We knew that the easiest way to control the balance of nature was to make ourselves the fulcrum. We simply had to rise above nature, to control it.

Being far more timid and having less defenses we gathered together to give ourselves the illusion of strength. Gifted with a larger, more evolved brain and an immense delusion of grandeur, we knew we had to define ourselves as the alpha species. We armed ourselves with weapons and tools and we hunted and gathered and slowly climbed the chain to a much safer rung.

As our numbers grew, we stripped the surrounding wild to feed our excesses. Gorged on our destruction, we migrated on. We were driven to rise above the chaos of survival so we split and divided like malignant cell growths. With our numbers growing exponentially, our bravado fanned the flames and we spread like a brush fire across the planet. From tribe to village to town to city, we built a world where we had complete control.

As our path led us to civilization, wars, science, television and polyester, the wild continued to cycle as it's dimensions grew smaller and smaller. Our fellow fauna fell, victims to our unchecked expansion. Their numbers, once strong and plentiful, tumbled quickly down the chain from diminished to endangered to...extinct.

And now...the supposed stewards of this planet have become its conquerors. The great civilizations we built to rule this world, have left it in ruin. We once smirked in defiance at the natural world as we fingered our iPads and drank our diet sodas. Now we dangle from the top rung on the chain, our fingers slick with the blood we've spilt. We have proven ourselves to be the top predator on the food chain, even though... we had to destroy the planet to get here.

Can't See the Forest for the Trees

Here we are starting the second decade of the new millennium and we still have not been able to identify the cause of catastrophic diseases. In most cases we have been able to discover treatments for the effects of the diseases, however, we seem to still be in the dark as to the actual causes of said diseases. The reality of the situation maybe that our pets, and in many cases ourselves, may have a hormone antibody-imbalance that actually allows the body to destroy itself.

I believe that the most important hormone that regulates the immune system in the body is cortisol. One would think that the most logical hormone to treat these imbalances would be cortisone. The problem is that according to the status quo, cortisone is actually one of the most feared substances to use because its proper use has not been looked at thoroughly. Many practitioners see only a tree, but this is a forest that we are talking about.

Each and every day you and your pet both produce 30 to 35 mgs of active cortisol from the middle layer of your adrenal cortex. If you do not produce these amounts or the hormone actually produced is defective, the pituitary gland will keep asking the brain to request more active cortisol which is not possible.

Therefore, the inner layer of the adrenal cortex will respond to the brain's request by producing higher levels of estrogen and the male hormone called androgen. When your body produces more androgen, an enzyme in your fatty tissue, converts the androgen into more estrogen. And so, instead of producing the needed cortisol, the body is now creating excess adrenal estrogen.

This causes the production of a reverse T3. What does this mean? It means that thyroid hormone is bound and cannot be accepted by the receptor sites in the body. Even though your health care professional says the thyroid is normal, the hormones cannot actually be used.

What else does elevated estrogen do? It deregulates the two main families of immune cells (disease fighting cells) instructing them to not protect you from viruses, fungi and other outside invaders. Not only that, it causes them to not make antibodies to vaccines.

This is the reason that HIV progresses into AIDS. This deregulation causes these immune cells to lose recognition of the body's own tissue and they soon make anti-antibodies which begin to destroy normal tissue. This allows auto-immunity and cancer to gain a foothold inside the body.

The true thyroid test eventually will be a ratio between freeT3 and reverse T3. Many in the medical professions are not able to accept that fact yet, but you should not suffer from their reluctant realization. It is very hard to see the complete picture when your vision is limited by blinders.

While all this is occurring, the antibody production throughout the body starts to decline. This leads to a deficiency in the mucous membrane antibody. What is the importance of this? It means when this antibody level (IgA) drops below 60 mgs %, the patient, whether human or animal, cannot absorb any oral medications, rendering them useless.

This is often why a patient in the hospital does well with IV or IM medications, however when sent home with the same medication in oral dosage form, their health quickly declines due to their inability to actually absorb the oral medication. Quite often a different oral medication will be prescribed, which also proves to be completely ineffective because the patient is not able to absorb any medication orally.

Would it not be wise, to do an IgA level with every blood test, to make sure that whatever is prescribed, the patient will be able to absorb it properly? This however is not a standard procedure and is not keeping with the status quo. Most medical professionals seem not to be aware of the benefits and, more importantly, the possible consequences. After almost 50 years of research through my clinical practice. It seems very simple to me.

Are there other detrimental effects of elevated estrogen? It has been determined that elevated estrogen also causes inflammation of the cells that line all arteries in the body called endothelial cells. Could this not be a possible cause of atherosclerosis and arteriolosclerosis which frequently leads to coronary occlusion and occlusion of the carotid arteries?

Estrogen in women is usually seen as coming only from the ovaries. The laboratories have classified the various stages of ovarian estrogen, with no thought given at all to adrenal estrogen which might be an even greater source. It is very simple to identify. When a woman is menstruating, check her estrogen levels on the 7th day of her cycle when her ovarian estrogen is at its lowest and again, when the ovarian estrogen is at its highest (usually at the end of the third week). The difference in levels from the 7th day to the 27th day is due to adrenal estrogen. How hard is that!

This estrogenic inflammation can become very dangerous when the adrenal estrogen is prominent and the woman has her period which also elevates the estrogen coming from the ovaries. This exponentially raised estrogen level causes increased inflammation in the cells lining her arteries, and can lead to anything from a severe migraine headache to possibly even an epileptic seizure. Not only has this been documented in the human literature. Idiopathic epilepsy also comes from the same elevated estrogen in the adrenals in humans and both female and male dogs and cats.

There is further information on the Dr. Plechner website, https://www.Drplechner.com.

Healthfully Yours,
Dr. AL Plechner DVM & David Spangenburg

Estrogen, a Hazardous Hormone

Almost everyone has an idea what estrogen is. Most women would say "It's a hormone produced by the ovaries." Most men would say "That's a woman thing." However, that is actually not the case. Even though men don't have ovaries, their bodies still produce estrogen (sorry guys, but it is true). Estrogen is a steroidal hormone that is produced *primarily* by the ovaries but it is also secreted by the adrenal gland.

What is the adrenal gland?

Let's take a look.

The adrenal gland is an endocrine gland located above each kidney in both females *and* males. The inner part (the medulla) of each gland secretes adrenaline and the outer part (the cortex) secretes steroids such as estrogen.

Why is this important to know? Most people don't realize that too much total estrogen can lead to allergies, autoimmunity and even cancer. The fact that most people think that estrogen production only occurs in females may be the reason why these diseases are not always diagnosed and treated correctly. This wrong assumption may also be a critical reason why uncontrolled tissue growth in the male prostate and colon can occur.

Even females who are subject to the cycles of menstruation are often told that the only estrogen being produced by their system is produced by their ovaries. However, if you look at the laboratory levels of estrogen measured in a monthly cycle, everything is related to the lower level of ovarian production, at the beginning of the month (7th day) and when ovarian production is at its peak (which can be determined by the patient's physician). What causes the *total estrogen* levels in the system to increase from the 7th day to the peak? Adrenal estrogen production and, a few outside sources cause the increase.

Many post-menopausal women are thought to be estrogen deficient and are given an estrogen supplement without measuring the total estrogen. Some women, that do have an estrogen imbalance from the ovaries and the inner layer adrenal cortex, may actually need an estrogen supplement. Often that is not the case with a number of others. In those instances, the estrogen supplement may actually cause an excess of total estrogen which may expose them to the threat of a number of catastrophic diseases.

It has also been reported that many of these females are also producing an excess of the male hormone called androgen. Even if their estrogen is low or normal, the excess androgen production can create a problem.

Androgen can be converted into estrogen due to an enzyme in the fatty tissue called aromatase. Since the elevated estrogen binds (blocks) the receiver sites of thyroid. The bound thyroid reduces the activity of the liver and kidneys which further guarantees less breakdown and elimination of the estrogen and androgen. This allows the vicious cycle to continue.

If the receiver sites of thyroid are bound the metabolism of the patient usually slows which can cause the patient to gain weight. Gaining weight increases the amount of fatty tissue present which in turn produces more aromatase and obviously increases the amount of estrogen present. As you can see, increased total estrogen can create and sustain a possibly dangerous cycle. The plot continues to thicken as new information continues to be uncovered.

Just recently, it has been reported, that certain heavy metals in our environment, can actually bind estrogen receptors. They can actually increase the total estrogen levels, all the while remaining hidden. These metals (PCB, BPA and Phthalates) will function like a xenoestrogen, (environmental hormone) or "EDC" (Endocrine Disrupting Compounds). According to **Wikipedia**, *"these metalloestrogens create a chemical, mimicking estrogen which produces estrogenic effects on living organisms even though they differ chemically from the naturally occurring estrogenic substances internally produced by the endocrine system of the organism."* These stealthy compounds, created for solely monetarily motivated reasons by modern industry, are just a few of the dangerous elements that continue to threaten our fragile environment and may be a highly instrumental in the development of cancer in people and animals.

It is important to be aware of any exposure you might have to these metals, because elevated estrogen blood test results will appear normal, due to the fact that these "hidden" xenoestrogens will not be discovered in normal testing. Elevated estrogen within a human or animal body will allow any uncontrolled tissue growth (including malignant) to continue, unchecked.

Estrogenic mimicking metals include; aluminum, antimony, arsenic, barium, cadmium, chromium (C11), cobalt, lead, mercury, nickel, selenite, tin and vanadate. The main exposure to these metals for you, your family and pet's will be through your drinking water and certain food products that you all consume. Your best first step would be, to have all your drinking water sources checked for contaminants. If you are growing your own fruits and vegetables, have the soils analyzed to determine the presence of heavy metals.

Most, if not all, of these damaging metals, carry a positive ion. When they are exposed to a heavy negative ion, such as found in "living clay" compounds, like Calcium Bentonite Green Clay, they are neutralized and pass quickly through the body as excretion. These premium calcium montmorillinite supplements also contain the valuable trace mineral elements that have been stripped from our once nutritionally rich soils and are no longer found in our "factory farmed" food products. They are truly priceless to your extended family's health.

When you consider the *whole health* of both animals and people it is important to realize that there are other substances, including plants, plastic and ground water that contain varied levels of estrogen. When you take into account all of these possible sources of estrogen, one can see how just how easy it might be to be subject to an *estrogen overdose.*

Once elevated total estrogen has been identified as a problem, reducing the ingestion of estrogen will help to alleviate it. If the total estrogen is still elevated, further estrogen inhibitors (limiters) may be used but an increase in active cortisol through injection or ingestion will dramatically decrease the effects of excess estrogen production and allow you to achieve a *normal balance* between the active cortisol and total estrogen hormones.

Why is this balance important? The world is just now beginning to realize that excess estrogen may be involved in the rise in rates of allergies, Aids, Multiple Sclerosis, Muscular Dystrophy, coronary occlusion, all types of auto-immunity problems, and even cancers.

When you consider the possible medical breakthroughs that these facts might initiate. It makes you wonder why the excess of total estrogen has not been thoroughly investigated thus far by the corporate medical industry.

To answer that you might have to solve the age old riddle...

"What comes first, the Cure or the Grant?"

Healthfully Yours,
Dr. AL Plechner DVM & David Spangenburg

Aromatase and its Enzymatic
Effect on Estrogen

What is aromatase? Sounds like a **Glade** plug in, doesn't it? Aromatase is an enzyme, a catalyst that stimulates and controls chemical reactions throughout the body. It is found in the endoplasmic reticulum (the membrane network within cells involved in the fusion, alteration, and transfer of cellular materials). Aromatase is a component of many different tissues such as; blood vessels, fatty tissue, brain, ovaries, testicles, skin, bone, endometrium and the placenta and can be found in dogs, humans, most mammals and certain fish. So what does aromatase actually do?

It is responsible for changing male testosterone and female androgen into excess estrogen which augments *Plechner's Syndrome*'s deregulation of the immune system and eventually can lead to the development of allergies, autoimmunity and cancer. Factors that stimulate an increased production of this enzyme include age, increased body fat, insulin, certain gonadotrophic hormones, alcohol (not red wine), a zinc deficiency and certain diets.

Dealing with some of the above conditions, require the assistance of a medical professional but I encourage you to start as I did, for myself, my family and our pets, by adjusting all of your diets. You need to include foods that contain aromatase inhibitors, especially if you are adrenal estrogen dominant or already demonstrating signs and symptoms of *Plechner's Syndrome.*

A number of foods and supplements have been proven to reduce the effects of aromatase. The following is a list of foods and supplements that come from the family of *flavonoids* (antioxidant plant compounds) which are aromatase inhibitors and will help reduce this dangerous estrogenic effect in your pet, your family and you.

- Chrysin is a flavonoid that comes from the Passion Flower. Of the plants that inhibit aromatase, this seems to be the most potent, and most available as a manufactured supplement.

- Asperginin is a flavonoid that occurs in parsley, celery, chamomile, romaine, leafy lettuce, artichokes, blueberries, oranges and tomato sauce.
- Quercetin is a flavonoid that occurs in garlic and apples. It is also found in cabbage, broccoli and cauliflower (Important note: these vegetables, when eaten raw, can compromise thyroid hormone production),
- Reseveratrol is a flavonoid found in the seeds and skin of red grapes and quite high in the muscadine grape and its wine.
- Oleuropein is a flavonoid found in olive oil, olive leaves, cranberries, blue berries and peanuts.
- It has been also reported that extracts from both the portabella and reishi mushrooms
- Naringenin is a flavonoid found in grapefruit, sweet orange and Chinese bitter orange. These should not be eaten in large quantities because they can inhibit an enzyme responsible for breaking down estrogen which would create a result similar to elevated aromatase.

Of special interest, is the "Mediterranean" diet. It has been known to have lowered the death rate in a number of different medical ailments. What food products does the Mediterranean diet include? It consists of eating fresh fruits and vegetables and drinking red wine.

Just remember that, you are what you eat. I know that sounds clichéd but it is also very true. What you feed the family pets, your family and yourself can determine the future health of all concerned. Healthy diets can help control elevated estrogen, and the dangerous effects, caused by aromatase.

Do not allow it to undermine the immune system and it's the successful hormone antibody control that is so vital for everyone's present and future health.

Healthfully Yours,
Dr. AL Plechner DVM & David Spangenburg

How Our Hormones Influence Our Immune System

Did you know that there is a common denominator which links allergies, autoimmunity and cancer in animals and people? There is, and it is a simple hormonal imbalance which can be found in everybody; animals and people, male and female alike. It is primarily caused by the hormone we have talked about previously in this Chapter, estrogen, actually "an excess of estrogen" (that sounds like the title of a James Bond movie).

As we mentioned earlier these basic blood tests that all our doctors generally prescribe have been missing the large amount of *adrenal* estrogen. No one is measuring the total_estrogen being produced by the body and therefore, are missing the influence excessive estrogen has on our immune systems.

In a normal animal or person the amount of natural cortisol produced by the middle_layer adrenal cortex and the amount of adrenal estrogen produced by the inner_layer_adrenal cortex will determine the proper ratio which will normalize the of regulation of the immune system.

When an imbalance in this ratio occurs, the immune system becomes deregulated, not only causing the B lymphocyte to decrease its production of protective antibodies, but also restricting both the B and the T lymphocytes capacity to protect the body. Along with this decreased protection, the B and T cell lose the ability to recognize self-tissue, allowing autoimmunity and cancer an opportunity to develop. It is thought that the immune system is deficient, but the only deficiency that occurs is with the B cell production of immunoglobulin so it seems that deregulation of the immune system is probably a more accurate term.

Empirical measurements of hormone levels in people and animals are very misleading because even if the patient's hormone levels register within the normal range it still does not mean that the patient's bodies can actually use the hormone. Urine and salivary tests may indicate if a hormone is active or not, but they still can't determine whether the body can *utilize* the hormone. To

97

be able to conclude this, you must first accept the basic fact that the endocrine system's hormones actually regulate the immune system.

Specific antibody levels must be measured along with other hormones to be able to determine if a particular hormone is being used by the body or not. This is why comparative levels need to be measured as opposed to empirical levels. A prime example of this occurs when you observe both animal and human thyroid function.

The measured thyroid hormones referred to as T3 and T4 can register in the normal range and the TSH, the pituitary regulatory hormone, level may also be <u>empirically</u> normal, but the patient can still show signs of hypothyroidism. Often the patient is cold at times, overweight with a slow heart rate and seems to be predisposed to flu and other viral infections.

Why is this happening?

It's happening because of the improper ratio occurring between adrenal cortisol and adrenal estrogen. If the measured cortisol level is deficient, defective or not accepted by receptors, the negative feedback to the anterior pituitary is damaged and the ACTH (Adrenocorticotropic hormone) production from the pituitary itself negatively stimulates the inner layer adrenal cortex causing it to produce an excessive amount of estrogen which in turn binds (blocks) the receptor sites of the thyroid. This elevated estrogen can also cause the production of a Reverse T3 which will likewise bind the thyroid sites.

There is a simple test which will show if a patient's thyroid is blocked. Place a thermometer in their axilla (arm pit) before they get out of bed in the morning and if their temperature is below 97.6 degrees there is a good chance that they have a metabolic block of the thyroid.

We have looked at the dangers of excessive estrogen and we know that this increased estrogen is due, primarily, to a deficient amount of active cortisol hormone. Why is the use of cortisol so frowned on by the corporate medical establishment? It basically is due to the <u>fear </u>of using an exogenous (outside source) of cortisol, which is a steroid.

Ever since 1948, when the Rheumatology Division at the Mayo Brothers Clinic discovered the effectiveness of the "X substance" (cortisone) they also published that it was very damaging to body, very detrimental for long term use in patients. Even though this is true, the problem is that the Mayo Brothers used very high doses of cortisone. Doses, that were high enough to cause any animal or person to have severe side effects.

It is vital for us to remember, that cortisol is one of the most important regulatory hormones in the body and normally, you and your animal are producing 30 to 35 mgs of natural cortisol from your middle layer adrenal cortex every day. We already know that if that naturally produced cortisol is deficient, defective or bound, it causes an excess production of adrenal estrogen; it is this excessive estrogen that is truly dangerous.

Merely adding estrogen to normal tissue will cause that tissue to grow too rapidly (cancer?). It has also been documented that estrogen causes inflammation of the lining cells of the arteries throughout the body. These cells are referred to as endothelial cells. Medically there is a lot of interest in inflammation today and possibly the roll that inflammation may play in many other catastrophic diseases like Alzheimer's, coronary occlusion and strokes.

When menstruating woman are tested, it is obvious that the combination of their ovarian estrogen and their adrenal estrogen causes them to have excessively high estrogen prominence, This dangerous prominence can often cause inflammation of their cerebral arteries which can lead to not only, migraine headaches but many times to epileptic seizures.

My clinical studies have led me to design a simple blood test that can be included with any blood draw that is already being performed. This test has proven effective with dogs, cats, horses and humans. Most human labs can perform these tests however at this time there is only one veterinary laboratory that is qualified to do these test accurately.

The information about this laboratory and the actual animal and human treatment protocol for this simple blood test is available in the **Protocol and the Syndrome** chapter of this book and on my website under the Article button at http://www.drplechner.com

Even if your health care professional may not be familiar with my test there is no reason not to do it. If your health care professional does not want to act upon the results, you may want to find someone that will.

Healthfully Yours,
Dr. Al Plechner DVM & David Spangenburg

The Wonders and Worries of Stem Cells

No matter how you feel about stem cell research, I am sure that we all agree that there are still many serious medical problems that desperately need to be addressed. Aids, Multiple Sclerosis, Diabetes, Muscular Dystrophy, coronary occlusion, all types of auto-immunity, cancer...the list is long and in many cases lethal. When you consider all of the amazing advances we've had in medical science in just the last 50 years. The real 'medical wonder' is that there are still millions of suffering people crying out for answers.

Yes, we've had our share of 'amazing advances' but they have primarily been concerned with treatment of the effects. We have beaten some diseases into remission but we haven't scored many knock outs. Stem Cell research does offer many potential 'breakthroughs'. However, the road it travels is filled with so many religious and political potholes it seems like it can't get out of second gear.

Besides all the controversy regarding the needed research materials (adequate and efficient stem cells), researchers still face numerous problems including stem cell failure. About nine years ago, I was contacted by a physician in Belgium. He was interested in my thoughts on hormone antibody imbalances and their possible contributions to stem cell failure?

His email outlined the struggles he had been having. It seems that these patients were suffering destruction of certain glandular tissue and he hoped to remedy this with stem cell transplants. However, the results were not promising. The stem cell replacements were being rejected. All of his ministrations had led to failure.

Being driven by the precept that failure for any patient was never an option, the stem cell therapy was put on hold as he looked elsewhere for his answers. He was reexamining the diagnosed origins of the organ damage. He began to suspect that the tissue destruction might be due to a hormone-antibody imbalance.

Following our email exchanges, he began to test his perspective stem cell patients for *Plechner Syndrome* . The hormone specific blood test results indicated that these patients all suffered from the *Syndrome*. Their cortisol hormone level was low or defective, and the "total estrogen" level was elevated.

As I've mentioned in an earlier article, an elevated level of estrogen not only causes a binding of thyroid hormones, it also causes an imbalance in the immune system, which blocks the immune system's ability to determine which tissue is body tissue and which is foreign. (This may be one reason why the patient needed the stem cell transplant in the first place.) If the body's "defender cells" are attacking its own tissue, obviously it will also attack the "foreign" stem cells.

Through the use of the **E-I** hormonal specific blood test the physician was able to determine the cortisol and estrogen levels and see, first hand, the imbalance. Once the physician was aware of this imbalance, he followed the *Plechner Protocol.* After he took the necessary steps to balance the immune system, the stem cell transplant worked.

I know that there are readers out there saying, "You're a Vet! You heal animals. Why would you suggest treatments to a physician?" Although my patients (for the most part) walk on four legs rather than two and are covered by fur, feathers or scales and not denim or micro fibers they still share the wondrous bio systems that we do and are therefore subject to bodily function or dysfunction as the case maybe. What is relevant to animal health is often, also relevant to human health.

As a researcher myself, I realize that controversial scientific research, especially medical research, should not be dictated to or regulated by religious doctrine or political punditry. Science and health should rise above individual philosophies or beliefs. We can eliminate sickness and suffering in the world. It is our duty, as trained professionals, to "discover the cures".

Even so, it is sometimes the simple truths that lead to medical advancements. Many of the body's mysteries are answered by examining more closely from within than by just reaching for the latest technological advancement.

The first step in solving any medical problem is to make sure everything is working the way it was meant to in the first place.

Healthfully Yours,
Dr. AL Plechner DVM & David Spangenburg

Paying Homage to the Ancient Third Eye

The "Third Eye", better known as the pineal gland or epiphysis cerebri, was venerated by ancient peoples as having mystical powers. The celebrated French philosopher, Descartes, wrote in his **Treatise of Man,** that the pineal gland *"...is the principal seat of the soul, and the place in which all our thoughts are formed."* In humans, and dogs, this tiny pine cone shaped endocrine organ is approximately one centimeter long and is located in close proximity to the hypothalamus, which is the primary link between the nervous system and the endocrine system by way of the pituitary gland

When light or darkness passes through the retina, light-sensitive tissue on the inner surface of the eye, an impulse is transmitted to the suprachiasmatic nuclei. Located in the hypothalamus, it is the tiny region on the midline of the brain, directly above the optic chiasm that controls hormone production. It also initiates and synchronizes the circadian rhythms, which control and regulate many aspects of mammalian behavior and physiology including sleep, physical activity, alertness, hormone levels, body temperature, immune function, and digestive activity.

Nerve fibers from the hypothalamus intertwine with the spinal cord, allowing this retinal impulse to continue on its path. After penetrating the superior cervical ganglia, it makes its move to the post ganglionic neurons, which in turn finally complete the cycle by transferring this final impulse directly into the pineal gland for continuous hormone modulation and adjustment. This cycle is called the retinohypothalamic tract or the photic input pathway

The pineal gland produces a hormone called melatonin through a process called biosynthesis. Tryptophan, an essential amino acid, is synthesized into serotonin (a neurotransmitter) which, in turn, is the precursor of melatonin.. The amount of melatonin generated, is directly related to the number of foot candles of light and dark that are passing through the retina, of the eye. Any deficiencies in either one of these precursors or any inequities within this cycle will trigger the pineal gland to initiate different types of *damaging imbalances within* the endocrine system.

This cycle illustrates the true importance of the pineal gland. Descartes' remarks about the "heart" of the brain may be accurate but put into today's "tech speak" terminology it's more appropriate to liken it to the "Microprocessor" or "CPU" of the brain. It receives impulses (neurons) from the sympathetic nervous system, and in turn; interprets, translates and transmits these various neurological impulses into regulatory signals to other glands causing them to generate and secrete hormones, in the proper amounts, to attain and maintain perfect symmetry within the endocrine and immune systems.

Unlike humans and other mammals, the location of the pineal gland in birds and reptiles, is in close proximity to the skin. Therefore the light and dark "triggers", reach the pineal gland through the skin and not through the retina of the eye. This is where the "third eye" concept developed. The light impulses, that the pineal gland receives, reduce the production of melatonin. During the night, and also during the dark phase of the moon, the retro hypothalamic impulses stop, preventing the light impulses from reaching the pineal gland, allowing gland to release all of its melatonin.

It's easy to see now, how a cloudy, rainy, dark day, the dark phase of the moon and excessive tanning, whether from the sun or from a "tanning bed", might prevent the pineal gland from maintaining a proper endocrine balance which will create some serious health issues. These "light" extremes may also cause an alteration of the circadian rhythm. A normal circadian rhythm involves a pattern, based upon a 24 hour cycle of wake/sleep patterns, seasonal functions, and certain endocrine feedback mechanisms. A deregulated circadian rhythm is very common in people that are sight challenged, since there are no impulses reaching the pineal gland through the retina.

Insufficient melatonin levels in people, can lead to; low body temperature, personality disorders, a suppressed immune system, insomnia and an elevated progesterone- estrogen ratio. Many women, with breast cancer, exhibit low levels of melatonin and decreased production of melatonin has been implicated in a number of disorders including sexual dysfunction, hypertension, epilepsy, and Paget's disease, which causes excessive bone destruction and disorganized bone repair, in middle aged to elderly people.

People, that have an excess amount of melatonin production, often suffer from Seasonal Affective Disorder. SAD is thought to be caused by insufficient light input into the pineal gland, and displays symptoms including, fatigue, excessive sleep, abnormal food cravings, anxiety, depression and definite changes in sex hormones, like estrogen and progesterone. It makes you wonder if increased suicide rates, in certain areas of our country, might be caused by a lack of daylight, due to excessive clouds and rain for extended periods of time. It has been documented, that many people who feel anxiety and depression during periods of insufficient sunlight, recover their contentment and feel much more psychologically positive on bright sunny days.

Excessive melatonin production may cause depressed adrenal and thyroid function and lowered estrogen-progesterone ratio, which often leads to lower blood pressure. Altered melatonin production is also known to provide a triggering action for epileptic seizures, in both humans and animals. Melatonin imbalance in animals can lead to infertility, specific regional hair loss, sleeping disorders, and eating and behavioral problems. Melatonin also plays a major roll, in reproduction. The modulation of the pineal gland by light and dark impulses alters and controls the production of melatonin, thereby regulating and determining when, and if, a breeding season will occur in many different types of animals.

Researchers have found that the breeding season for sheep, can be manipulated with artificial light and that the testicular sperm count was markedly reduced during the non-breeding season. Melatonin appears to stop the secretion of both luteinizing and follicular stimulating hormones, from the anterior pituitary gland. This causes the hypothalamus, to reduce its production of gonadotropin-releasing hormone, which is necessary for the anterior pituitary to continue its function. It also inhibits ovulation and reduces the production of testosterone

Another interesting observation was made, when they exposed tadpoles to pineal gland extracts. They found that the tadpoles lost their pigment and their skin became completely devoid of pigment, totally transparent. The researchers have not proven this happens in birds and mammals, but it does make you wonder, might not melatonin levels, also affect pigment loss in people and other animals.

It's important for you know that certain foods can possibly cause or prevent a melatonin imbalance, which might adversely affect the health of you, your family and your pets. Melatonin is present in tart cherries, oats, bananas, rice and corn. Tryptophan (a precursor to melatonin), is present in red meat, chicken, turkey, almonds, peanuts, seeds, bananas, soy and soy products, tuna and shell fish.

You may want to consider a blood test to find out what your actual melatonin levels are, to see if any modification is indicated. A beginning pineal blood sample should include serotonin, melatonin, tryptophan, zinc, ACTH, and total estrogen. You should have the blood drawn during daylight hours. If the melatonin is normal and you still do not feel well, the blood should be drawn during the evening or before sunrise. Salivary tests are also available. This is a far more convenient way to check melatonin levels in a 24 hour period.

I am currently working with a brilliant Melungeon woman who suffers from many of the disorders that seem to plague her people and other early Americans. We have found that during certain moon phases she undergoes a Lunar Estrogen Surge even though she has no ovaries. In looking at neurotransmitters, we've discovered that her serotonin, is very elevated, and her melatonin is deficient, which may be causing the hormone disruption of her Hypothalamic, Pituitary Adrenal axis. This might help explain in part why she suffers from the moon induced Lunar Estrogen Surge and makes one wonder if there is a transference enzyme that is not present or not working that may be leading to her high serotonin and her low melatonin. Low melatonin prevents the neutralization of aromatase in the tissue, which in turn will cause DHEA, DHEAS, androgen and testosterone to be turned into total estrogen and may well be part of this Lunar Estrogen Surge. Obviously more research needs to be done, but so far the facts are quite interesting and hopefully they will soon lead to discoveries, that will help her feel better.

Researchers also believe the pineal gland contains electromagnetic receptors that monitor magnetic fields, and help the body to align itself in space. Many species from whales to man and many other animals, including birds and bees, contain a highly magnetic mineral called magnetite. Dr. Joseph Kirschvink's studies at the California Institute of Technology, have found that these magnetite crystals enable animals, from bees to whales, to navigate by using these crystals within their brains to detect the earth's magnetic field. Even though, magnetite is synthesized by the human brain and occurs throughout brain tissue, Dr Kirschvink doubts that they support any sensory capability in humans. They might, however, account for the possible influence that strong electromagnetic fields have on human health.

Dr. Kirschvink and his wife cycled honey bees through a maze, following a north or south compass, and when they affected the crystals in the bees, by introducing a very strong magnetic field, the bees flew in the opposite direction. There is even a family of bacteria called magnetotactic that contain magnetosome chains with magnetite crystals. Exposure to the earth's electromagnetic field causes them to travel up and down in the mud they live in. If the Earth's magnetic fields were suddenly reversed, the birds, bees etc., would become quite disoriented as to navigation and their alignment in space. This might possibly explain the deaths of thousands of birds, fish and bees that occurred throughout January, 2011 in the United States and across the planet.

Where do we fit into this electromagnetic world and how can we determine how much exposure to these electromagnetic fields may actually be hazardous to our health? It is important to know that these fields exist around; electric outlets, microwaves, refrigerators, alarm clocks and probably your cell phone. This may be a good reason to purchase an inexpensive electromagnetic meter, to assist you in making sure that you, your family and your pets are not exposed to too many harmful electromagnetic fields. These fields can suppress the pineal gland's ability to produce melanin and can cause damage to the circadian rhythm.

Dr. Susanne Bennett, DC, CCSP is a holistic chiropractic physician who practices in Santa Monica California and has experience with several patients suffering from melatonin imbalances and also magnetic disturbances that are affecting their pineal glands. She has determined that the pineal gland contains naturally high levels of calcium apatite, which is why fluoride has a high affinity for the pineal gland. Apparently, fluoride is attracted to bone and tissues containing high levels of calcium. Dr. Bennett has found that many of her patients, with abnormal sleep patterns, return to normal sleep patterns after she helps these patients with fluoride detoxification.

I have seen first-hand, the influence the pineal gland has on human and animal health. I agree that it is the "CPU Chip" of the brain and that it does play an important role in many endocrine disorders, either due to its production of melatonin or the effects that electromagnetic fields have on the magnetite elements within it. I hope that you now understand the influence the pineal gland has on you, your family and your pets.

Healthfully Yours,
Dr. Al Plechner DVM & David Spangenburg

Sowing the Seeds of Disaster?

Modern factory farming is creating a wonderland, a veritable vista of problem free vegetables. Problem free, however, also seems to be problematic. Through the wonders of gene engineering, they are creating genetically modified seeds for many standard agricultural products which they hope will be resistant to certain insects and pesticides. What we, the consumers, should be concerned about is that no one can predict the long term effects these altered seeds will have on our planet, the animals and us. Should we rush head on into uncontrolled genetic tampering? Look what we came up with when we split the atom.

Genetically modified soy, corn, and cotton seeds were released for planting in 1996, with canola following a year later. You're probably saying, Canola is not a plant and you're right, sort of. Canola is a genetically engineered plant (cultivar) created in Canada from the Rapeseed Plant, which is a member of the mustard plant family. I could go into the ongoing Internet based controversy about canola but that is fodder for another chapter. Just Google canola and check it out.

The USDA has received hundreds of applications for genetically engineered food atuffs and I am not aware of any environmental impact reports that have been completed, let alone filed. It would seem logical that this concept needs to be better defined, better controlled and, most importantly, not rushed. You need to be absolutely sure that people, animals and our environment are safe <u>before</u> *any* application for a genetically modified seed is even approved.

Natural mutation has led to many viral epidemics that began in one continent in horses, mutated so the virus would cause an epidemic in pigs and finally mutated again to cause catastrophic diseases in people on our continent. This all happened without genetic engineering. It was a natural biological mutation that happened spontaneously in nature. Natural mutations can be harmful enough without man's actual genetic meddling.

In my veterinary profession, this is why most of the vaccines that are used, are killed viral vaccines, so that there is no chance for a natural live virus mutation, which could turn into a catastrophic epidemic which could wipe out the entire human population. With that in mind, please consider the actual possibility of creating a genetically modified seed, which will be resistant to all of man's efforts of stopping the growth and spread of that mutated plant.

Once these seeds were planted in agricultural fields, the winds, wildlife and insects spread the pollen from these altered crops to other naturally seeded fields. It has already been shown that a normal field of an unmodified crop can be completely over taken by the genetically modified crop and these results can spread exponentially. Sounds like science fiction, nope, it's science fact. Is there an end in sight, or is this just the beginning of the end? This uncontrolled spread can start growing in non-agricultural areas also. A prime example of this is in North Dakota, where the spread of genetically modified, canola (you remember canola) is already out of control.

As a veterinarian that has fostered and continues to live on a wildlife preserve, I have enhanced the habitant for all of our wild species of animals by planting different types of clover and vetch which not only provide leafy food for the cloven animal, but seed for the various wild bird populations. This cultivation also stores nitrogen in the soil for better growth of the surrounding habitant including the forest. My concern is that many of the seeds used for planting other wildlife food plots, might contain Brassica napus (rape plant) which is a super source of food for wildlife, but if those seeds have been genetically modified, their spread could prove to be highly damaging to other plants and eventually overwhelm our environment. We should be concerned for the new generations of animals that subside on those food plots and the changing and mutating environment they live in.

You need to be aware of the problems that can occur when wildlife is feeding on genetically modified plant products. Often with the first generation of animals and people the results may or may not be significant. It's within the second and third generations, you begin to see problems. Even though we may not experience negative effects, what time bombs are lurking within us for our children and our grandchildren to inherit? What if the generations to come continue to ingest plant products that come from genetically altered seeds?

Let's take a look at a Russian study involving three generation of the same family of hamsters. All generations were fed genetically altered soy.

- The 1st generation, overall, they saw their general health start to decline.
- The 2nd generation saw an increase in infant mortality, 5 times higher than normal.
- The 3rd generation was all sterile.

Obvious this was a study in hamsters but do really think it's wise to even consider eating these potentially hazardous, genetically altered, "plant products". Should we even allow the "modern factory farming industry" to blindly pursue their bottom line, PROFIT, all the while showing no concern about the potential health risks to our future families? Not to mention, the entire population of the flora and fauna of our planet.

Studies have linked genetically modified plant products to...

- Cancer
- Severe viral Infection
- Damage to the immune system
- Allergies, including food sensitivities

The Institute for Responsible Technology has prepared a list of altered foods and food products that should be avoided...

- Soy
- Corn
- Sugar from beets
- Canola oil
- Cottonseed oil

- Hawaiian papaya
- Certain types of zucchini
- Crookneck squash

I am sure the list will grow. Apparently, 800 genetically engineered food applications that have been submitted to the USDA for approval. Remember a plant product can be grown and sold as "organic", ah, but does it come from a genetically modified seed?

Always read the labels! Even though some European products say that they are not derived from a genetically modified seed, some of these labels have been proven to be false. Recently, the European Commission gave permission for the production of a genetically modified potato. This altered potato contains a gene that causes the production of an enzyme which can provide a resistance to several antibiotics. We can only hope that this genetically modified mutant potato will never find its way into the United States but considering that we are just a part of a global marketplace we're going to need more than hope.

Be proactive, aware, ask questions at your produce market and grocery and keep yourselves up to date. Get in touch with your congressman. It's up to all of us to stay alert to potentially dangerous food products. Consumers still control the marketplace. Refuse to buy genetically modified food products. Everyone please remember, before you ingest, chew and swallow, the life you save may be that of your child.

Healthfully Yours,
Dr. AL Plechner DVM & David Spangenburg

Mother Earth's Remedies
for the Atomic Age

Through the years there have been many articles and scientific papers singing the praises of certain types of clay referred to as "living clays". Since the dawn of life on this planet, these clays have offered a multitude of health benefits to human, animals and plants alike. Especially important benefits, in these days of the "Atomic Age", these clays have the ability to neutralize and detoxify surfaces that have been exposed to radiation. It has been clearly documented that during the Chernobyl disaster in the Ukraine applying these "living clays" externally through clay baths and lotions did cleanse and decontaminate skin that had been exposed directly to radiation.

Internal and external use of these clays is recommended during times of extreme radiation exposure, similar to what has happened in Japan following the recent earthquake and tsunami. External applications of these clays in conjunction with internal ingestion of the clays and iodine tablets are proving to be the fastest and most efficient way to remove radiation from the body. The Chernobyl disaster in the 80's taught us a few important lessons that we are Drawing from today.

On April 26, 1986, the Chernobyl Nuclear Power Plant in the Ukraine suffered a great explosion. That and the ensuing fire released huge quantities of radioactive contamination into the atmosphere over Western Russia and Europe.

According to Wikipedia (in a nutshell)...

"Reactor four suffered a catastrophic power increase, leading to explosions in its core. This dispersed large quantities of radioactive fuel and core materials into the atmosphere and ignited the combustible graphite moderator. The burning graphite moderator increased the emission of radioactive particles, carried by the smoke, as the reactor had not been encased by any kind of hard containment vessel. ...The battle to contain the contamination and avert a greater catastrophe

ultimately involved over 500,000 workers and cost an estimated 18 billion rubles, crippling the Soviet economy (effectively putting and end to communism in Eastern Europe?)"

A Russian publication, *Chernobyl*, concludes that,

"985,000 excess deaths occurred between 1986 and 2004 as a result of radioactive contamination."

How did the Russians use calcium bentonite clay to fight this invisible killer? Russian scientists and technical workers, first coated their bodies with "living clay" even before they put on their radiation protective suits because it absorbs radiation so well. The next step was to quickly bury the damaged nuclear reactor with calcium bentonite clay, and cement to reduce the amount of uncontrolled radiation seeping out of the damaged nuclear reactor.All the people exposed to this lethal radiation were asked to include the "living clay" in their established decontamination routine when they showered or bathed.

The "living clay" was even included as an ingredient in the commercial chocolate bars available for the residents living in the areas affected by this toxic catastrophe and also added to all the animal feeds for the animals being raised for human consumption. calcium bentonite clay was used to contain and clean up the radiation at Chernobyl. How is this possible, that a natural deposit of organic materials can protect living beings against the insidious dangers of nuclear radiation?

Like the trace element packed, Calcium Montmorillonite Clay, Calcium Bentonite Clay has a uniquely strong negative ionic charge. When it is activated with water it works like a strong magnet, affecting anything with a positive ionic charge (i.e., toxins, pesticides, radiation). The clay has the unique ability to **adsorb** (causing substances to stick to the outside surface of a clay molecule similar to the way a strip of Velcro works) and **absorb** (Drawing substances into the clay's internal molecular structure like a sponge absorbing water). This "living clay" captures these toxic and dangerous substances removing them as the clay is eliminated or washed off.

The tragedy of Chernobyl, back in the eighties, has, at the very least, enabled the nuclear cleanup squads in Japan, here in 2011, to diminish the hazardous health effects threatening all those within the affected zone. Just distributing iodine tablets to those workers and others who were exposed to the extreme radiation leaks will not save their lives. "Living clays" must also be used (both internally and externally) to help them detoxify and shed the radiation from their bodies and the bodies of their animals before permanent radiation damage is allowed to occur. These work well with most nuclear materials except strontium and plutonium

It is recognized that iodine alone does not protect against radiation exposure from uranium, cesium or plutonium. The added use of "living clays" not only detoxifies these radioactive elements but also eliminates the residues of most heavy metals and other toxins that we are all exposed to on a daily basis. It has been well documented, that radiation and electromagnetic fields definitely affect your hormones and alter the body's immune response by means of the *pineal gland*, (a small endocrine gland in the vertebrate brain) thereby causing major disruptive changes within the body.

These edible calcium montmorillonite clay supplements, like NUTRAMIN and TERRAMIN contain geothermally charged particles, ION-MIN, which set up an electromagnetic polarity in the body that causes not only radiation but also heavy metals and other toxic molecules, within our environments, to bind to the negative ions which are then neutralized, denatured and excreted from our bodies through the urine and feces. There is even a product, TERRAPOND, which has been found highly effective in cleaning up oil spills and purifying pond and lake water.

According to the World Nuclear Association, as of February 2011,

"There are now over 440 commercial nuclear power reactors operating in 30 countries, with 377,000 MWe of total capacity. They provide about 14% of the world's electricity as continuous,

reliable base-load power, and their efficiency is increasing. 56 countries operate a total of about 250 research reactors and a further 180 nuclear reactors power some 140 ships and submarines."

Now, just consider how much nuclear waste is actually being created currently, across our planet. Spent nuclear fuel is a relatively stable form of uranium called uranium 238. It has a half-life of over four billion years, Uranium 235 (U-235) (half live of 700 million years) and plutonium fuel (half live of 24 thousand years) decay a "bit" quicker and can actually be reprocessed into new fuel. Still, how can we contain the radioactive waste that will be around long (!) after our great, great, great, great...(you get the idea) grandchildren exist, especially when we will be producing more and more every day.

Melt downs and other nuclear accidents have happened and will continue to occur, that alone should prompt us to be more proactive. If we are going to continue to use nuclear facilities to create energy, we need to design and build far sturdier and more secure containment structures.

The recent earthquake and tsunami in Japan, March 11, 2011, is a tragic example of how a remote natural disaster, can have global consequences. Three of the plant's reactors, suffered numerous major fuel rod meltdowns and dangerous radioactive strontium, at 240 times over the safe limit, has been detected in seawater surrounding the Fukushima-1 plant. The emergency vents, much celebrated by American officials as the safety devices which will prevent American nuclear plants from catastrophic hydrogen explosions, failed miserably in Japan.

Knowing that the negative ions, found in the special calcium montmorillinite clay deposits, are effective in containing radiation, I believe that the living clay should be combined into the concrete building materials mix that is used for housing or storing anything nuclear. I also think it is wise for all families (pets included) to add special calcium montmorillinite clay supplements to their daily diet to proactively protect against these dangers that lurk in our everyday life.

I get mine online at **California Earth Minerals**. Check out, http://www.californiaearthminerals.com or Google calcium montmorillinite clay for more information.

Healthfully Yours,
Dr. Al Plechner DVM & David Spangenburg

CHAPTER FIVE

His People Speak

True Stories of Life and Death, Courage and Commitment

Biscotti and the Fight of Her Life

When I first sought out Dr. Al, he was on sabbatical in the Idaho wilderness Even though he was "retired" he answered my call for help because I had a dog in trouble. I already knew Dr. Al was brilliant. But I was I was astounded to find out how much he really cared. It is clear that he truly loves the animals he treats and for whom he consults.

Dr. Al helped me with a bulldog named "Biscotti," who was adopted from a rescue that guaranteed her to be healthy. (which is another story for another day....) I soon discovered that Biscotti came with a lot of "physical" baggage. Her litany of issues included megaesophagus, aspirate pneumonia, glomerulonephritis, myasthenia gravis, h. pylori, and irritable bowel syndrome. The poor baby was literally wasting away.

I ran Dr. Al's EI-1 test - ENDOCRINE-IMMUNE BLOOD PANEL TEST - when I first adopted her, and it had all the indicators of the Plechner Syndrome. I was directed by the rescue to a prestigious and well-appointed veterinary clinic which had all the diagnostic and surgical "bells and whistles."

It was supposed to be the premier practice for bulldogs. The rescue, beginning to realize that Biscotti was not quite as "healthy" as they had originally billed, promised to pay her medical bills there. (It didn't, but that is also another story....) Despite thousands of dollars in diagnostics and treatments, Biscotti's condition continued to deteriorate.

The clinic refused my pleas to consider Dr. Al's protocol, even though Biscotti was obviously declining along with the EI-1's that I

119

continued to have run. I was advised that if I wanted Dr. Al's protocol, I could take Biscotti to California where Dr. Al was just returning to practice. I was finally "fired" -- they knew I was already unhappy, and undoubtedly also knew this was not going to improve when they were not going to be able to help Biscotti.

By this time, Biscotti was critically ill. Her protein/albumin levels were so low she had to be transfused. I was finally able to convince a veterinarian in a small local clinic to give Dr. Al's protocol a try. I believe she consented because she knew euthanasia was going to be the only other option. Dr. Al walked us through the protocol, and listened patiently to my many fears along the way.

I continued to monitor Biscotti with monthly EI-1s and conventional labs (i.e., CBC, chem panel, complete urinalysis, and UPC ratios). Anyone doubting the validity of Dr. Al's protocol would find it difficult to argue with the conventional lab results that documented Biscotti's healing. Only some megaesophagus -- requiring elevated feeding -- remained,

What else can I say? I've seen both the insidious effects of the Plechner Syndrome and the healing success of the Plechner Protocol. Dr. Al is amazing -- his energy, his open-mindedness, his sense of inquiry, his determination.... Unlike so many others who hold the degree, he has not forgotten why he became a DVM.

Pegg Bauer

Malachi, a Very Special Doberman

This is a story about a Doberman, not just 'a' Doberman, my very special Doberman, Malachi, and the very special veterinarian that is in our lives, Dr. Al Plechner.

Malachi isn't a dog I purchased to be my pet, he isn't special just because I love him, he is the once-in-a-lifetime special dog, for me. How do I know? I've had Dobies in my life for over 45 years, so that's how I know Malachi is special!

I have owned and loved Dobermans since 1962, and then started breeding the majestic breed 10 years later. I wanted to do it right, so did x-rays of hips, as well as their necks, thyroid tests, and vWD testing when it came along. When the DNA test for vWD became available, that was used rather than the blood test which isn't as accurate.

I had been breeding Dobermans for about 10 years when, through a friend, I had the opportunity to meet Dr. Plechner, and that was 30 years ago! Since that time, I have used his E.I panel to test every dog I planned to use in my breeding program. If they were too far out of balance, they were spayed or neutered and placed as pets. If the E.I. panels were just slightly off, we selected pairs with E.I. results that complemented one another.

Malachi's 'Mom' is the result of this 30-year testing program, and I bred her to a top winning Champion. While he had not had an E.I. test done (I don't know of a Doberman breeder that does the test, which is a shame) he did have lots of other testing, Cardio, vWD, thyroid, etc. Five puppies were born C-section, and because the female rejected the litter, I bottle-raised the puppies, which I thoroughly enjoyed! I knew quickly the black male was the one I wanted to keep for myself. He had a self-confident attitude from the get go, he had substance and good conformation, and what a look in his eye...it's called 'the look of eagles'.

My husband had to spend six months in Brazil on business while Malachi was growing up. This boy stepped up to the plate, he became my companion and protector by the age of 6 months. He was a big guy, looked like an adult, and acted the part. He wasn't vicious, but he wouldn't back down, he was serious 'stay away from my Mom'! I should have named him Shadow because to this day, he has to be on my lap or a head on my shoulder when I'm at the computer, at the very least his head's on my foot.

His eyes look into mine with adoration. He is strong, but wants to please and has been easy to train. Most will say 'it is the Doberman temperament'...yes, it is, but, his is magnified. As I mentioned above, since 1962, I have had a Doberman I've loved very much in the house, they have all been wonderful...this one is special and I can't describe further how or why.

It was a good thing I decided to keep him rather than sell him. By the age of a year or so I knew he probably had a hormonal imbalance. He had an unusual coat; it was thick, oily but not shiny, it was rough, with lots of flaking on just the center of his lower back, and he shook his head from Dry rough skin inside his ears, but they weren't infected. He had a good appetite, but had a very sensitive stomach, anything new had to be given in extremely small amounts or he'd get diarrhea, he did not have an upset stomach, but always very soft stools. He definitely was not my normal Doberman; they had cast iron stomachs and could eat about anything!

A problem! By this time Dr. Plechner had retired and left the Los Angeles area! I began the search for a veterinarian that would do the E.I. Panel, as well as Dr. Plechner's protocol, if required. I had no luck, even when I described the success I'd heard about from people that had used the protocol. I faxed pages from his latest book at the time, 'Pet Allergies, Remedies for an Epidemic' to veterinarians. Nope, they were not interested, he was 'out of the mainstream', and they didn't believe in using Medrol long term. I just couldn't believe it, even with the success stories? Although Dr. Plechner is very willing to assist in evaluation of test results and medication dosing, I often got the feeling there was envy, one veterinarian tossed the book back at me, saying NO!

Well, we learned to live with the issues; they weren't all that serious and were easily managed. However, at age 6 he began having chronic Prostatitis. Our veterinarian put him on medication, Malachi would get better, and in a few weeks it would return, medication and he would get better, a vicious circle. I had always had a bad feeling about having him neutered, but I knew he needed to be neutered, and took him in. Again, a bad feeling in my gut, but had no choice, it had to be done.

Malachi was already on a medication prior to the surgery because he leaked heavily on his dog bed while sleeping at night. After the surgery, there was a major problem! He dripped urine when he walked around the house, and when he barked, look out! The veterinarian did urine tests to be sure he didn't have an infection; he didn't, but the vet put him on antibiotics to be sure. They didn't help. My precious Malachi, my companion, had to be either in the garage or outside, the Drip was just too constant and heavy to have him inside on the carpet. Malachi was so sad outside, separated from me, he didn't understand what he'd done wrong. I was miserable too!

Then, I got the news Dr. Plechner was coming out of retirement and back to the Los Angeles area! As soon as I heard he was back, I made an appointment for an E.I. Panel on Malachi. After all the years, all the testing, and all the successes I'd seen and heard about, I was positive Al Plechner could help him.

As soon as Al saw him, he knew he had a hormonal imbalance. He did the E. I. panel, and when the results came in, Malachi was put on the appropriate dose of medications. BUT, there was no change!

I was devastated, Malachi was not absorbing the medication, I thought it was hopeless that he would never be inside with me again! Al Plechner is an extremely sympathetic understanding man, and I'm sure he realized what I was thinking. I believe it is because he himself truly loves animals. He told me not to worry, he would use a series of injections, and was sure they would work; and then we would try the pills again.

The injections did the job! Hallelujah, he no longer leaked, I could have Malachi back in the house with me; he could travel in the van with me! Also, all the previously mentioned problems, with his ears, coat, bowel and stomach were eliminated also. I cannot explain the joy I felt, the relief too. Now, the pills are working, and as usual, Dr. Plechner was right!

There are not words to explain how grateful I am to Dr. Plechner. Years ago I told him he was the best...and I'll tell you today, he is STILL the best!

Roz Wheelock and Malachi

The Protocol VS Feline Leukemia

Dr. Plechner has been treating my animals for over fifteen years. He is a dedicated and caring veterinarian and I cannot begin to express my gratitude for all that he has done for the animals in my family. There are countless stories I have of how he has corrected the imbalances that have manifested in many of the cats that my husband and I have owned over the years. Luckily we live in Southern California where he practiced veterinary medicine for years.

When he retired I was beside myself, because I never found anyone who was as caring and who really understood that animals were like "canaries in a coal mine". They were affected by years of inbreeding (whether pure bred or mutt) as well as exposure to increasingly hostile environmental elements.

He understood that a simple blood test called an EI1 test, could explain whether the body's endocrine immune system was functioning correctly or not. If that system was out of sync, then an animal's body would start to break down and all sorts of things could happen. Once Dr. Plechner corrected the syndrome with his very simple protocol of administering a physiological dose of a steroid, miracles would happen.

The good news is Dr. Plechner came out of retirement, because people simply missed him. I was lucky enough to find that out when I was in Texas where I have another home. I had started to foster a Texas cat named Dot who tested feline leukemia positive in March of 2011. I contacted Dr. Plechner who told me he would be happy to work with any vet in Texas. I have a very open minded vet in Texas and told him about Dr. Plechner's protocol and he agreed to do the blood work on Dot and we began his protocol in October 2011.

She has had four EI1 blood work tests and based on those results Dr. Plechner and Dr. Pohler adjusted her medication. I was back in Texas for a visit this past week and brought Dot in for her fourth EI1 test and asked Dr. Pohler to retest her for feline leukemia. On March 6, 2012, the feline leukemia test came back negative. Just one example of the remarkable Plechner protocol at work!

I could go on and on. This is just one example. Dr. Plechner is, of course, helping and advising medical doctors now as well. He is not only a remarkable vet. He is a remarkable human being. I feel so blessed to know him.

Hallie Foote

Hausy's Story

A few years back we had a severe emergency with our German Shepherd, Hausy. He is jokingly referred to, by the surrounding neighbors in our area, as the "big lug". He makes his rounds each day as the patriarch of the surrounding 1 mile radius going from house to house for his "treats". In other words, everybody loves the Haus.

Well, late one evening we just can't seem to find him in his usual spot...we call and call, but no Haus. We finally assume he's out on a date and we turn in for the night. The next morning...still no Haus. We begin to panic a little and search all areas of the property and surrounding houses. Finally, we come to find him lying hidden in a ditch and bleeding from all extremities. Absolutely horrified, we gently wrap him in a blanket and rush him to the emergency center.

Once there we sit and wait...and wait...and wait. When we finally get to check on the Haus...he has so many tubes in him...IVs and 4 machines. Two vets working on him round the clock, blood transfusions every 4 hours. Needless to say, we were scared to death. After three full days of this, there is still NO IMPROVEMENT,

Now, know this, this facility is the best in our area but 72 hrs. and 4,000 dollars later they notify us that there is nothing more they can do and as soon as they pull the plug he will probably be gone. This was a moment beyond comprehension...to lose a family member, it seemed impossible that this was happening.

Through tears, sobs and a prayer a friend tells us about this special vet whose mission is to take on the tough cases. Considering we had nothing to lose but our best friend, we wrapped him in his blanket, put him in the back of our car and raced as fast as we could to Dr. Plechner's office. As we turned him over with a plea for help, Dr. Plechner stated that he knew what needed to be done and that he felt he could do it. Wow, are you sure?! We go home to wait and walk and hope.

Finally, we receive a call. Hausy is improving...the bleeding has stopped...he's going to be OK?! What? How could this be? He said it was a "completely different protocol". We added, "By the best in the business". Who is this man and what is his gift?

Five days later, Hausy's on his way home with a program to follow. All of us were hugging and kissing Dr. Plechner (including Hausy) and thanking him for saving his life.

After this incident, Hausy lived to a ripe old age of 17 and we became lifelong advocates of the Dr. Plechner Method referring people in need of help his whenever we encountered them. We tell them, they don't have to have their animals put down; they only have to follow the protocol of this magical wizard of the Wookie's kingdom........

Karen Judkin

The Struggles of Sophia

Soon after our marriage, in the spring of 2001, my husband Robert and I decided we needed an addition to our family. Her name was Sophia, she was just eighteen months old, and she came from an Italian Greyhound Rescue. Even though her skin was raw and itched terribly we feel in love with her the moment our eyes locked. It was clear from her medical records that her immune system was weak. Ever since she was a puppy Sophia had been treated for allergies, and had a history of skin, ear and urinary tract infections.

Our first step, obviously, was to change her diet. We tried a novel protein diet, hopefully one made up of animal protein she hadn't already been exposed to. As weeks passed without improvement, we tried various other protein diets. When these also failed, we began to wonder if she simply could not tolerate animal protein at all so we reluctantly tried a vegetarian diet. However, when she still showed no signs of improvement we realized that it was going to take more than diet change to help Sophia.

Sophia had such a steady course of testing and treatments it seemed like we were living at the Vet's office. She was tested for demodex mite overgrowth and treated even though the scrapings came back clear. Midway through our vet suspended treatment, as Sophia failed to show any improvement. She was also tested for various allergens in her environment, but nothing really stood out so we were back on square one.

In an attempt to relieve the incessant itching, our vet suggested various antihistamines, both prescription and over-the-counter. Sadly, she did not respond and showed no improvement. We bathed her with medicated shampoos and applied leave-in conditioners to ease her discomfort. Yet it often seemed that the mere act of bathing her set her skin afire and she would scratch terribly after a bath, even one with just clear water. Trying to reduce infections, we always washed her feet and her nails immediately after a walk.

Sophia had been on several rounds of antibiotics as well. It seemed as soon as one infection resolved, another took its place. She'd even been on oral Prednisone but, oddly, it was hit or miss, responding favorably to one course, with no response to another. She also had frequent defecation, at least several times a day. Food seemed to go right through her. Later we would learn that she had malabsorption, her GI tract couldn't absorb food or oral medications easily.

Nighttime was a particular challenge for us. Sophia sleeps in our bed, and the noise and shaking of the bed as she scratched for hours prevented us from getting much sleep at all. Most mornings, between 6 and 10, Sophia would finally sleep a few hours in the early morning probably due to shear exhaustion. We even went to a dermatologist. However, after reading through the notes of all of Sophia's prior treatment she told us that our regular veterinarian was doing a very thorough job, and that she felt she could not assist us any further.

Fortunately, I came across Dr. Plechner's first book "Pet Allergies, Remedy to an Epidemic". After reading it thoroughly, I felt as if someone had flicked a switch and the lights came on. I truly believed that I had identified Sophia's underlying problem. I phoned Dr. Plechner directly and explained our situation. He was very interested and graciously gave us his time. He asked me to have my veterinarian phone him. After all his efforts, my veterinarian was more than willing.

The two doctors devised a plan to test Sophia's blood for a hormonal imbalance that Dr. Plechner had discovered. It directly affects the immune system. He had also devised a successful method to replace the diminished hormones, after which the immune system does the rest on its own. It made sense. All of Sophia's conditions appeared to be immune-mediated and we had yet to test her hormonal levels. This was a very exciting step and we held our breaths hoping for some helpful information from the blood test results.

When Sophia's first Endocrine-Immune panel came back in September of 2001, every single value on it was either "high" or "low". There wasn't a single "normal" one. Her adrenal hormones, thyroid hormones, and immune globulins (part of the body's defense against allergens, viruses, bacteria, fungus) were all registering at abnormal levels! Despite this seemingly devastating news, everyone was excited. We had finally uncovered some very valuable and seemingly helpful information Sophia's underlying problem, the great enigma, might soon be solved!

Dr. Plechner worked closely with my vet to correct Sophia's hormone deficits. Initially, she received injections of adrenal hormone to correct her cortisol hormone deficit. Because her adrenal glands were secreting too much estrogen and not enough cortisol, her hormones were not at normal levels. When most people hear the word estrogen they think of ovarian estrogen. However, Sophia is spayed and does not have ovaries. Therefore, this was adrenal estrogen that was flooding her body.

In all mammals, both male and female, the adrenal glands manufacture estrogen for our systems. Sophia's adrenals were essentially in overdrive. While desperately needing to produce cortisol they were producing too much estrogen instead. She had an abundance of estrogen but a shortage of cortisol. The solution was to increase her levels of this hormone through physiological (low dosage) injections of cortisone.

Next up was addressing Sophia's thyroid hormone shortage. According to the panel her T4 ("storage" thyroid hormone) and T3 ("active" thyroid hormone) were in the low range, meaning she was hypothyroid. As mammals, our bodies take T4, and convert it in our bodies to T3, which our bodies can properly utilize. For this to take place we also need normal healthy cortisol hormone to aid in this "transference". The upshot is that we needed to give Sophia's body what it could not produce and then wait for her body to do the rest. And it did.

The evidence was readily apparent that Sophia's body had begun to utilize the injectable adrenal hormone, and was converting the T4 oral thyroid medication to T3! Her intricate endocrine system was once again beginning to run the way it was intended. Her immune globulins, those important little foot soldiers of the immune system, began to rise to normal levels as well! They had been severely low when we started, down to one third of what a healthy dog should have. It was no wonder she had so many infections.

Within ten days we saw very obvious improvement. Her infections began to resolve and her skin healed. Within sixty days, Sophia seemed like a different dog! The scratching had ceased. Her skin, which months ago had begun to resemble raw hamburger, was now clear and healthy. What an amazing difference! In the months that followed, our veterinarian regularly tested Sophia's hormonal levels and immune globulin levels.

She was now able to switch to daily adrenal oral medication, in the form of hydrocortisone, as well as the thyroid medication. Incidentally, years later, we switched to Medrol for her adrenal medication and it has worked out very well, a bit better even than the hydrocortisone.

Sophia's thyroid and adrenal levels normalized first, as evidenced by her good health and her blood test results. Then each month we saw improvement in her immune globulin levels as well. Those levels did take a full year to normalize, but it was worth the wait. They have remained stable for the past 8 ½ years, which is something rarely seen in veterinary or human medicine.

Sophia is due for a tenth birthday soon and she has Dr. Plechner and our veterinarian to thank for that. I'm really not sure how Sophia could have survived in the state she was in as a young dog. Along the way, whenever I needed help or our veterinarian needed advice on Sophia's treatment, Dr. Plechner has always been there for us.

Later, my husband and I adopted a second Italian Greyhound from Italian Greyhound Rescue. Herbert is three years younger than Sophia and the best friends play together and live life to the fullest. Sophia maintains her daily medications and continues to have her blood tested regularly. She enjoys a home-prepared diet, and continues to do well! We've had a few glitches and the occasional setback over the years, but we've always been able to get back on track. Dr. Plechner has always been there to guide us.

Sophia's good health is not only a testament to Dr. Plechner's Protocol, but to his dedication and personal commitment to helping animals afflicted with this often misdiagnosed affliction. We thank him from the bottoms of our hearts.

Michele

The Clunker Boy and the ADTEIT

I can't exactly remember when our story starts but I'd say 2001. I don't have the early test results any longer which would tell me exactly when I first contacted Al and in turn, Jason, at his lab where Al had all the serum sent for testing. Originally, I had heard about Al through the Airedale Terrier network and an email group **(ADTEIT · Airedale Endocrine Immune Testing)** on Yahoo to which I belonged.

Al's story and his work first came to light because of Kirk Nims but basically came to the forefront for me because of a woman in Australia, Sue Forrester, and her Airedale Terrier whose name was Aemon. I do hope she has contacted you or contributed their story because it was a shining example of Al's determination, generosity, and commitment.

In any event, I was living with a couple of Standard Schnauzers as well as one Airedale Terrier at the time. One of the Standard Schnauzers - Jordan by name - developed visible symptoms which led to a visit to my long time local vet to get his thyroid checked. The levels weren't right and the normal treatment had no effect. I remembered immediately what I knew of Al and his work so I called him. (I live in Eastern Washington - Wenatchee -; Al was at his practice in Los Angeles).

He was kind, interested and patient from the very start. He was also determined to solve Jordan's problem. Serum was drawn, shipped to NVDL and the results were sent to Al. To make a long story short, Al's name for Jordan became the Clunker Dog because it took us 18 long months of trial and error in adjusting food and meds before we managed to get Jordan's levels in balance. Since his coat stopped growing while his system was so out of balance he was nearly hairless for almost all that time. When I first saw the new growth I was beyond words.

I'd had a long standing and great relationship with my local vet so luckily for me when I walked in the first time and said here's what we're going to do and told him about Al, he didn't fight me on the idea. I gave him Al's book to read but they didn't actually talk for a while. I was the liaison. About 6 months into the trial and

134

error (the try and try again) phase, I made a trip down to LA to talk to Al in person about Jordan. I never lost faith.

Even though my vet remained skeptical for quite a while he knew better than to try to deter me once I'd decided that Al held the key. Interestingly, my vet, Dr. Ed Womak at Cascade Veterinary Clinic here in Wenatchee, is now one of the vets listed on Al's web site as being a vet who practices the Plechner protocols. All that came about because of Jordan and me. Ed now has multiple patients on the protocols.

Sadly, Jordan died in January of this year. However, he was 12 ½ yrs old. I firmly believe that without Al's help and determination in those early days, Jordan would have had a much shorter life. He had some tough times but basically he did well and I am certain that we had a lot longer and more enjoyable time together than we would have, had it not been for Al.

I am grateful beyond words to Al Plechner. He never took a dime from me for all the phone calls and all the consultations - he helped because he could and because he was that committed to helping an animal in need. , In my estimation, he was and still is a truly remarkable man. In memory of Am/Can Ch. Uhlan out of the Blue, aka, Jordan,aka, the Clunker Boy.

Joey Warren

Bridget; a Little Dog with Big Problems

Bridget is a sixteen and a half year old Lakeland Terrier and has had many health problems throughout her years. We have taken very good care of her as well as her sister who passed away at age 13 due to improper medications that led to kidney failure. Her sister had inflammatory bowel disease which would have been an easy fix for you.

Bridget has always been a strong willed dog and her small size did not stop her from being very alpha towards her older and larger sister. She's suffered from allergies and always seems very congested and has difficulty breathing. Because of her allergies, Vets continue to want to put her on special injections. Although I did purchase them (for a large amount of money) thank God I never used them on her.

At age 12 she had 10 teeth extracted due to gum disease, and at that time we took blood tests for allergies. We found out that she had allergies to many foods and veggies as well. We started to home cook her meals of things she could eat. But as time passed by she also became allergic to them as well. We must constantly switch her foods around.

At age 14 she started to have tremors; her head would shake as well as her entire body. I thought it might be ear or tooth infections so I took her to several top Vets. When we went to a neurologist; she was shaking and learning to the left. She had problems with her balance and kept falling down. He didn't even look into her ears. He just gave her meds and said she could not hear and perhaps the meds would help. They never did,

While at another Vets they found fungus in her ears. At last, someone listened to my cry for help. However, though she recovered it was only to relapse again. The vet gave her acepromazine 10mg- (a tranquilizer) TO CALM HER DOWN and she HAD A SEISURE and I almost lost her right in my arms. She again started falling and flipping over and they thought she had a brain tumor. Again I went to specialists and the doctor said he did not think it was a brain tumor and again gave her more meds. She began to have a chronic cough that would not stop, I took her to the animal hospital where she saw a pulmonary specialist who informed us that she had chronic bronchitis and needed to be put on an inhaler for the rest of her life, though she would never be cured.

This poor dog was trying to hang on and I knew that there was something very little wrong with her but no one could pin point it, UNTIL I FOUND YOU. After a blood test that you suggested and a treatment plan that I followed, she began to slowly show signs of recovery, and is almost back to normal or as good as normal could be for a 16 1/2 year old dog.

We thought she would never see her 16th birthday and now she will definitely see many more. Now you have her on thyroid meds and .1 ml of steroids for the rest of her life. I will continue with the blood tests every 6 months because she is almost back to normal and her immune system is back on track just as you said it would be.

I have given your book to many of my friends, and whenever I see a dog or cat in need I pass on the information to their humans and the lucky ones have gotten their Vets to follow your protocol as well. Every day that Bridget lies down beside me, kisses me and sleeps in my arms I thank you from the bottom of my heart. Whatever time she has is quality time and she sure is enjoying every minute of it and it's all because of you.

I thank you for caring for all our companions and I only wish that you could reach everyone in need and show them how simple a cure is when you care as much as you do. Thank you for all that you have done for my little "Bridget". You are a man of great compassion and conviction, and we are truly blessed to have found you. Attached is a photo of Bridget and myself on her 16th Birthday, everyone in town thinks she's a puppy!!!! I expect you will do the same for me, only kidding.

Dimitra and Bridget Barton

Merlin's Three Lives

Every day, I thank God for Dr. Plechner. He saved my beloved wolf hybrid, Merlin, twice. The first time was when Merlin was a puppy; his system was so out of balance, they weren't even sure he'd make it. For the next three years, Merlin's health improved and flourished under Dr. Plechner's care.

When Dr. Plechner retired, - I now know it was out of frustration, because his fellow veterinarians, appeared not interested in finding a better way - I found what I thought was a well-respected animal hospital with a broad minded owner, and assumed that all would be well. Well, you know what happens when you assume. The Vet at this new facility decided that the medication that Dr. Plechner had prescribed, (based on accurate blood test results) should be discontinued and I was told Merlin's replacement therapy had been changed.

The first reactions I noticed were gradual changes in his health, behavior and personality. I hoped he was simply maturing. However, after the "first time" groomer, at the animal hospital, bathed Merlin, he had a very severe allergic reaction. I knew that something was wrong and I was now on alert.

His thick and previously luxurious coat became sparse on one side of his body. Soon it began to fall out in clumps, leaving large, round, weeping sores. Even worse, he began to lose his sight, due to a lack of proper hormone regulation of his imbalanced immune system. All this just because this new vet "assumed" that Dr. Plechner's medications were not applicable. I guess he was never taught you don't try to fix something that's not broken.

When I found Dr. Plechner's website, I knew my prayers had been answered. He was back in practice in Southern California, not only because of the public outcry to come back, but because he really missed taking care of all his animal patients. Very soon, after our visit with Dr. Plechner, and the return to the correct replacement medications, Merlin began to show improvement. His coat is growing in again, his energy is returning to normal and his eyesight is much better.

I, of course, think Dr. Plechner is a genius and that every school of Veterinary Medicine, should include in its curriculum, courses on Dr. Plechner's discoveries in the field of endocrinology and immunology. Every day I spend with Merlin I still thank God we found Dr. Plechner... two times.

Marilynn Margulies

The Treatment of Champions

I believe it was about 1980, when I first met Dr. Al Plechner! I liked him immediately! The veterinarians I have used over the years have all been competent; treating what were thought to be 'typical' conditions; skin and/or coat problems, ear or eye infections and the occasional intestinal sensitivity. Through the years I've wondered about the causes of these conditions. Is it genetic, nutritional or just a weakness in various breeds? Are these issues just here in the US, or are they global? After about 10 years of dealing with these 'typical' conditions, I was soon to learn that these aggravations don't need to be 'typical' problems.

Dr. Plechner smiled as he came through the treatment room door, then actually put his hands on my Dobermans and greeted them first! Can you imagine? I'd never, in all my Dobies' vet visits, experienced that! Watching his 'hands on' approach, it was obvious from the first, that he truly loved and cared about animals. I was use to a more reserved office technique. I even had one vet ask me to place my Dobies rear towards him in order to give the Rabies vaccine!

As we chatted, I explained that I was a 'small time' Doberman breeder, and while I wanted to produce quality dogs, I was mainly interested in developing a line with a good disposition and good health. Oh boy, that was his opening! He began sharing about how his research into hormonal imbalances made him aware of what he called the 'Plechner Syndrome', and the treatment protocol he had developed to deal with it.

He didn't do all the talking as some do in order to 'brag on themselves'. He gave me numerous opportunities to ask questions. When I did, and that was often, he took extra time to describe, in terms I could understand, the tests he'd created, the Plechner protocol he was using based on the test results, and what response he had seen in patients. He was so enthusiastic about it, that I caught the enthusiasm too. He was encouraging and confident that we could accomplish what I wanted for my line. I had to give this dedicated man a shot to see what we could do.

Even though it's been years since, I still remember his face when he saw the first litter of 10 robust puppies that I had brought in for their first test. They were from two matched 'Plechner Syndrome' tested parents, who were out of parents that had also been matched by using his Syndrome Panel testing. Dr. Plechner's eyes lit up when he saw these big, solid pups running all over his office. He smiled in his 'quiet' way, but his voice was excited when he said something like "Roz! These are incredible pups!" I knew it too but I was amazed (and pleased) at how sincerely excited Dr. Plechner was about them. They might as well have been his! He couldn't get over the difference from other people's pups he had seen.

I also recall the day I phoned him to say we had finished our first totally tested, and healthy Champion, out of totally tested and healthy parents.

He said, "That's awesome, congratulations!"

More than just his words, it was obvious in his voice that he was as excited as I had been when I took that final win. I was confident now that I had an opportunity to reach my goal and this would all complement Al's goals as well.

I encouraged owners to call me with any questions or concerns throughout the lifetime of their dog and many did, but mostly they were simple 'puppy' questions. I wanted perfection and when a few of the adults developed allergies, I'd get discouraged and call Al. He was never too busy to take my calls and then (with his patient understanding) remind me that nothing in medicine is 100%. He'd tell me that I was doing the best I could by using all available testing.

There have been a few occasions when owners called because their vets were either stumped or said they couldn't do anything more and that they were going to lose their dogs. One female was suspected to have been stung by a Scorpion another had eaten a pound of chocolate candy and two had been poisoned! I have so much faith in Dr. Plechner I've always suggested that the owners immediately call him and, no matter how far the drive, they should take their dogs to him for evaluation before giving up. He always took the calls, and the time, to talk with the owner, or consult with their vet. He was incredibly generous with his time, even when he knew they were too far away to make the drive. That is the kind of man he is. With Al, it's not about the money, it's about the animal!

Thankfully, most were able to take their dog in, and all were saved. However there was one exception. That 'one' was doing great but after a short period of time, the regular vet took him off the 'Plechner Protocol'. The dog deteriorated quickly, and died. Apparently there are vets out there that can't tolerate being wrong, and the animal loses because their owner listened to them.

It seems to me, that some vets are only interested in running up a big bill. They see an owner in tears because they love their precious pet, and know most will spend all they can in order to save their animal. A big tab isn't what drives Al Plechner, he wants to help the animals live longer, healthier, and better quality lives. I always kid him about losing office fees and medication income from my now healthy dogs and puppies. He just laughs and says that's the point of our doing his Plechner Syndrome panel on my potential breeding dogs!

Because of the initial testing, I've never had to use Dr. Plechner's protocol on even one of my dogs but a few years ago, I thought I was going to have to put my dear 6-year old house female down. She had somehow been injured by running and playing and was losing the ability to get up or walk with any stability. She'd fall just when walking. My local vet x-rayed her neck and found it was jammed like an accordion! An animal chiropractor did all she could and even though new x-rays showed her neck now had normal spacing and was in alignment, the dog still had no stability.

Because he had always liked sweet 'Faith' (but more likely because I just needed sympathy) I called Dr. Plechner not even dreaming he could do anything. He immediately said her body wasn't healing itself and that we should do a panel. We did her panel, and put her on the 'Plechner Protocol. In two weeks, she seemed better, but was she? I was worried that I was just wishing her better. The end of the third week proved she was! Faith was actually able to get up and to run the property like her old self! When I called Dr. Plechner and told him, he was thrilled, but I honestly don't think he was surprised. I'm guessing that he knew all along I'd be calling with that news.

What I found hard to believe, is that, after all these years working on the testing and breeding program with Dr. Plechner, why I didn't contact him immediately? Why did I wait until I was out of options? Dr. Plechner gives his total commitment to each individual animal and its owner, no matter how 'unique' our personalities are. For the majority of his career he's been very dedicated to his research of the 'Plechner Syndrome' he's found in sick animals that came into his office. He immersed himself in developing the testing to uncover the syndrome and then in creating a treatment protocol to adjust and maintain the newly balanced system. An important reminder; he did it all on his own time and money.

Although, throughout the years I've known him, there have been times he appeared fed up, tired of the stubborn attitudes of other veterinarians, and such. Thankfully, he has been extremely driven and dedicated, so he stuck with it.

How discouraging it must be that even though they have been told about the results, so few other veterinarians are willing to investigate or even just inquire about this successful, treatment protocol, a treatment that repeatedly brings supposedly doomed animals back from the "end of the line".

I know about discouragement because I too have been unable to convince other veterinarians to even try a (what they call) "out of the mainstream" testing and treatment protocol. I have tried to locate veterinarians out of my area, even out of state, that would do a 'Plechner Syndrome' Panel, and the Plechner Protocol if required, for several people to whom I have sold Dobermans.

When Dr. Plechner left the Los Angeles area for a few years, I could not convince even my own local veterinarian of 20 years to do the test for me. Even though, Dr. Plechner was willing to evaluate and assist with medications and even after I related three actual incidents where dogs were saved by the Plechner protocol. Friends couldn't get their veterinarians to do the test, even when requested. It is extremely difficult for me to understand, why trained doctors of medicine refuse to even try an "outside the box" approach when 'mainstream' treatment is <u>not</u> (!!) working. Especially when death is the only other and such a final answer!

I thank Dr. Plechner for all he has done, and still continues to be doing. Without his encouragement, without his patience with me (and with my puppy owners' too) through all the phone calls, I never would have been able to develop the Dobermans that are recognized by other Dobie owners in dog parks, and even Driving down the street in other cities. As I have told Al, over and over, "I just wish I'd found you sooner!"

Roz Wheelock

Rocky

I count myself extremely fortunate to have found my way to Dr. Al Plechner. His expert diagnosis and treatment of a hormone condition (Plechner's Syndrome) affecting my German shepherd, Rocky, has made all the difference in the length and quality of Rocky's life.

The diagnosis of this condition had eluded other vets in spite of extensive, and ultimately unnecessary, testing and speculation. Dr. Plechner's years of innovative and informed observation of the many patients he has successfully treated are surely factors that set him apart.

His example of compassionate care, rigorous research and willingness to consider progressive alternatives to conventional treatment is far too rare.

Thank you Dr. Plechner!

Andrea Morgan

Dr. Plechner, Healer and Life Saver

I have Dr. Al Plechner to thank for saving not only 11 of my cats' lives, but my own as well. Just short of 4 years ago, I received an e-newsletter from an Animal Communicator I know, who was featuring Dr. Plechner on an upcoming teleseminar. You see, I am a Certified Natural Health Consultant. I am also certified in Iridology and have completed a Graduate course in Classical Homeopathy.

Having been in practice for 24 years, I have done plenty of additional research and taken numerous seminars on animal nutrition and homeopathy as well. I thought to myself, do I really need one more seminar – what could I possibly have to learn that I don't already know. (Note to self: don't EVER think you know it all.) I ignored several more emails, then the night before the class, they said they had two spots left, and the signup fee was only $25, so I thought, oh, what the heck, I'll go ahead and sign up, this must be a sign that I keep getting these emails and there are still 2 spots left.

I signed on to the teleseminar the next night and began listening half-heartedly because I just didn't know what this was going to be about. After all I had spent about half my life continually studying Natural Health and taking care of up to 18 cats of my own with Homeopathy, herbs and giving them human quality food. Dr. Plechner was discussing his "Endocrine-Immune" protocol. I knew a lot about both systems, but wasn't really quite sure what this particular name and these two body systems had to do with each other.

After about 10 minutes, he had my full attention. I was certainly recognizing the symptoms he was describing in my own animals as well as many others I'd cared for in years of doing animal rescue work. Then after more discussion, I realized that what he was describing was what was wrong with me. The teleseminar was scheduled to be an hour long and the moderator asked for questions from the attendees at the end of the hour. There were certainly many questions, including from me. The moderator tried to end the seminar at an hour and a half and Dr.

Plechner said, please let them ask their questions and I guess we finally wrapped it up at the 2 hour mark. That sums up Dr. Plechner -- willing to give of his time and all of it that he has to help animals and educate the people who care for them.

I immediately ordered Dr. Plechner's book, "Pets at Risk" and read it in a couple days of getting it. The book is now completely dog eared, red lined and highlighted all the way through. I've read it countless times since then. I've given away at least 7 copies. I also ordered his other book on the human condition of this syndrome so that I could understand it as it applied to my own health. Despite being involved in Natural health for many years, having a husband for a chiropractor and spending thousands of dollars seeing the best Natural Health care practitioners from all over the world, I was still suffering with my own health. I suffered from violent headaches every single week for 20 years which completely debilitated me and nothing we did in the Natural Health world made a difference. As time wore on, I literally got weaker and weaker and spent more and more time in bed. I could not even stand up to fix a meal (more about that later).

Based on what I read in the book, we began having our cats tested, the sickest ones first, as all of our cat household had become ill due to a newly adopted kitten who had come into the house apparently carrying Panleukopenia and given it to all of our cats. We had made the decision many years back not to ever give our cats vaccinations due to the disease they cause. Unfortunately, this decision in this case only was deadly for us. There is no test for Panleukopenia and typically, by the time the symptoms show up, it is frequently too late for the kitten or cat.

This kitten had been properly quarantined at a foster home for 6 weeks and tested and checked out at our veterinarian for Feline Leukemia and Feline HIV. We only found out several years later that the foster home had previously cared for a kitten with Panleukopenia who did live, but had neurological problems as a result of the disease. Meanwhile, I was dealing with a house full of sick cats with a disease I knew nothing about and barely heard of.

Panleukopenia is a disease that attacks and inflames the intestinal tract and the sick cats will hang over their water bowl wanting to drink, but can't because their mouths and entire gut is inflamed. They certainly cannot eat. Their body can quickly shut down and they simply die. Kittens go the quickest since their immune systems are not fully developed yet. This is why most of our cats did survive because they were older, but one of our cats died immediately, her sister a few days later. Four cats were in and out of the Veterinarian Emergency Room for days and weeks on end along with days spent at our regular vet for nursing care on fluids. The others all spent time at the vet as well.

We went into debt for probably close to $14,000 to care for them all. We did Chinese herbs for them, Homeopathy and everything else we could think of. Thankfully, the rest pulled through. We had 11 cats at the time. And fortunately, our local Veterinarian was into Natural medicine and did acupuncture, so he was a tremendous help and should be credited with saving the rest of our kitties along with the talented ER Vets.

Each of the first 4 cats we tested had "Plechner's Endocrine Immune Imbalance". Missy, a tiny 16 year old tabby was already having kidney failure, stopped grooming herself and was eating next to nothing. I had seen cats go from kidney failure many times and knew that she did not have much time. She got her first two shots of the steroid injections the first month and within two weeks; this kitty was a different cat. She began eating well again, her coat became shiny again and she gained a new energy she hadn't had in a while. As I sit writing this, our little Missy will be 19 years old in 4 months and she still runs around the house, flying up the cat trees and carrying her ball around the rooms, howling and having a grand time.

If you're reading this and wonder, does my pet have this syndrome?, wonder no more because they probably do. Every single one of our cats wound up on what I call "cortisol replacement" with Prednisone on a daily basis. Common ailments for pets who suffer from this include any or all of these: itchy skin problems, aggression, seizures, spraying, chronic cystitis or urinary blockage in males. Well, you're reading the book; you'll see all of what this can cover.

Frosty, a Lynx point Siamese who was a rescue kitten had problems from the beginning with itching skin. At some point, he began to scratch himself bloody in the muzzle in his whiskers. He wore an e-collar off and on for a year and was back and forth to the vet with steroid shots constantly. We finally realized that he had these violent scratching episodes shortly New Year's and the 4th of July. That was because our neighbors happen to have a lot of money to blow on some very high end fireworks and shoot them off for hours on those holidays. This terrified the poor cat. His cortisol would bottom out and he got the violent itchy attacks. Once tested and on the proper dose of Prednisone, Frosty went 3 years with no itchy problems whatsoever. Remember, the Adrenal glands are the "fear" glands. They give you the "fight or flight". But in our daily stressful lives, our cortisol is depleted and there are other causes for this as well. Chronic genetic inheritance sets the scene for it too.

The little kitten that we adopted, Baron, had aggression problems. If you tried to love on him, he would turn around and shred you for no reason, hissing and spitting and slashing. Evidently, it was scary to him if you even tried to hug him. He began spraying as well even though he was neutered. We finally started him on 10 mgs of Prednisone per day and his aggression stopped. He became a much sweeter kitty. He's still a bit of a handful, but he makes us laugh and that's just his personality. We love him to bits.

Here comes the sad part of the story.

Frosty developed Diabetes as part of the aging process and because our wonderful, favorite Vet was a 45 minute Drive and very stressful for the cats, we had to check Frosty's blood sugar and took him to a local just to make it easier on him. This vet, of course, vigorously objected to the high steroid use, saying it caused his Diabetes and demanded we Drop his Prednisone from 20 mgs to 2.5 in a day. Well, you don't take any animal or human off steroids that fast. You have to drop it down slowly. Any first year intern would know this. Unfortunately, I went into freak-out mode and even though I knew better, particularly because of my own health situation, I began dropping the dosages on several of our cats.

I got Frosty all the way down to 7.5 before I realized he was having a lot more problems and contacted Dr. Plechner again and he tried to help us save this kitty with long distance advice. There was too much going on the despite Herculean efforts and more vet bills, Frosty got weaker and weaker and we finally put him to sleep just two weeks prior to my writing this. Dr. Plechner's first book warned several times and he told us also, that if you take the pet off the cortisol replacement, all of their symptoms come back like a raging fire. So, dear readers, if you decide to put your pet on Dr. Plechner's protocol, know that it will be for life, or your pet will die a miserable, slow death.

As for me, not long after we saw this working with our kitties, I realized that I needed to do something about my own health. I knew that I had cortisol deficiency from Dr. Plechner, of course, but also from reading Dr. William Jeffries book, "Safe Uses of Cortisol". I went on a mission to find a Holistic Alternative Medical Doctor to help me fix my own health. Went through two idiot doctors before I found one who knew what he was doing. I found a discussion group on the internet and when I could hold my head up, I spent thousands of hours of research and reading to learn literally everything I could about this imbalance.

For people, it always involves adrenal and thyroid hormone replacement. I was one of the lucky ones because I found a local doctor who knew how to help me. And by this time, I had developed debilitating, painful Fibromyalgia. So now, I not only had years of weekly violent headaches, I was in constant pain all the time, all over my body. There's a lot to my story, but just 3 months shy of 4 years from meeting Dr. Plechner on a teleseminar, I am healthy, well and free from pain. My own book will be coming out very shortly.

Oh, and those 7 copies of books of Dr. Plechner's that I GAVE away to people – no one did anything with the information to help their pets. So I challenge YOU to help your own pet. This information saves lives and IT WORKS. Read the book, and then find yourself a Vet locally who will work with you and Dr.

Plechner's lab and his consulting. It's YOUR pet, the Vet works for you. I'll tell you though, it's not easy. They're going to have to be open-minded and willing to do whatever it takes to get the pet well. That's what it's about, helping the animals, not keeping the doctor's ego going. I've heard it said that, "The mind is like a parachute, it only works when it's open."

Lisa A. Parker, CNHP, HMC

Shyanne Star

In September 2007, I picked out my Shyanne Star from an animal rescue based out of Central Indiana. She was about 10 weeks old she was scratching her head, neck and ears more than "normal". I had switched her to Raw Food when I got her so I figured it wasn't the food. I assumed she had Dry skin so I decided to try Emu Oil spray to moisturize her skin and to help with the scratching. I used it almost every day throughout the winter and it appeared to work fine.

Everything seemed to settle down for the most part until July 2008, and Shyanne went back to scratching. Now she was "chewing" at her legs and wherever she could reach on her back and it just kept getting worse. She got to the point where it seemed that she could not leave herself alone. She would go days and nights without sleeping — she was too busy chewing and scratching. Neither one of us was sleeping. Shyanne's constant itching kept waking me up, throughout the night

In August 2008, I went to the vet and was given "Revolution" to treat for scabies (if there was any) and Hydroxyzine for her to relax and not scratch. This supposed "remedy" did not work at all and I was extremely worried about her. The vet, not knowing what to do, sent us to a dermatologist to look at Shyanne's case. The dermatologist wanted her put on a food trial, bathed daily with a soothing shampoo and a spray conditioner to moisturize her skin.

The food trial was absolutely horrible. I had to give Shyanne a meat that she had never had, so we were stuck with elk or Ostrich. I found Ostrich meat. I was told to cook the ostrich and add baked potatoes, calcium powder, safflower oil and vitamins. Shyanne kept right on scratching and got a real bad case of diarrhea. They gave me a pill to stop the diarrhea and I was told to stop the meat and only give cooked rice. That was terrible—how can you only give your dog cooked rice. Dogs are not supposed to eat rice, they are carnivores.

Luckily one day, I was speaking with Claudeen McAuliff, a dog nutritionist and the woman who created ESSFACID, and she told me about Dr. Plechner. She suggested that I look at his website,

Drplechner.com and to read up on his research. She said me that Dr. Plechner was able to help her with her dog. I checked him out. Dr. Plechner has been researching unrecognized Endocrine-Immune defects since 1969.

So...on September 10, 2008, I sent Dr. Plechner an e-mail outlining everything that Shyanne and I had been through. He called me personally from California the following day. After talking with Dr. Plechner, I went to my vet and gave her the address of his website to read and told her I wanted to do the tests. For the tests, we had to refrigerate the blood work and send it to a special lab in California that was familiar with the tests that Dr. Plechner wanted.

The blood test is called: Endocrine Immune (EI-1). The EI-1 checks for total estrogen (this includes estradiol, estrone, and estroil) as well as cortisol, thyroid hormones T3 and T4, and IgA, IgG, and IgM. Our findings were unbelievable. Shyanne's estrogen level was high which binds her thyroid and her immune level was 42. Dr. Plechner also believed that Shyanne has an allergy to meat that has wings or feathers. This would explain the episode with the Ostrich. He decided to have her stay on Beef until January, and then we could gradually add different proteins back to her diet—but would still have to watch her carefully.

The HEALING PROCESS BEGINS: Shyanne has had two series of shots of Depo-Medrol and Vetalog once a week for two weeks. After the first shot, Shyanne slept through the night without waking up! I woke to check on her as she has never slept through the night. Two weeks after her last shot, she was placed on Thyroid pills and a low dose of steroid which will be her maintenance. At the end of October Shyanne's IgA (immune level) reading went from 42 to 82. The doctors are very happy with Shyanne's progress and so was I.

In the month of January, Shyanne starting scratching again and I became concerned. I decided to REALLY read the labels of the brand of food I was feeding Shyanne. Even though it is beef, there are chicken and pheasant eggs in the mix. That explains the scratching.

It is very important that you know what your dog has an allergy to and read the labels. I had never thought about eggs in the raw meat mixture.

After reading ingredient labels on the internet, I know what brands Shyanne can eat and what she cannot. Shyanne is doing much better, but it will take time to get the chicken out of her system I know she will be scratch free soon. February 12, 2009, Shyanne's IgA (immune level) reading went from 82 to 96. She is now "under control" and is a happy and HEALTHY girl.

Dr. Plechner, thank you so much, for personally calling me from California. Thank you for taking the time to listen to my story and all that you did, to help me find out, how to help my sweet Shyanne Star.

Sincerely,
Renae Vollman

Jazzy's Story

(Jazzy's Story, as told by Ken - her biggest fan and who is humbly honored by her presence in his life.)

I feel extremely fortunate to have found out about Dr. Plechner early in 2004. I heard him on a radio show, was spellbound by what he had to say and instantly ordered his book. When the book arrived I read most of it, and - armed with a tiny, tiny understanding of Dr. Plechner's premise of the Endocrine-Immune imbalance, I began calling local veterinarians. My hope was to find at least one who would be willing to read Dr. Plechner's book and then work with Dr. Plechner, me and Jazzy to improve her health.

At the time, Jazzy had what everyone thought was Irritable Bowel Disorder (IBD). She would be fine for several days or a couple weeks at a time. Then she would have days when she would vomit right after eating - IF she ate.

As a person who has been interested in alternative medicine for decades, I had previously sought alternatives for treating Jazzy. For example, we had taken her to a holistic veterinarian and for a few months we tried different homeopathic remedies. Unfortunately none of the remedies actually remedied the problem.

When I heard Dr. Plechner, I was encouraged we might actually make some positive strides in Jazzy's health. Not too long into my search, I found a veterinarian who suggested coming in for a consultation. On the appointed day, Jazz, I and Dr. Plechner's book arrived at the office. I explained about the apparent IBD and the treatment we had so far sought. I told the local veterinarian about hearing Dr. Plechner on the radio and that what I had learned so far of the Endocrine-Immune problem made complete sense...to me. I remember to this day what the local veterinarian said: "I'm normally pretty conservative in my approach. I am open to taking a look. I'm going on vacation next week. I'll take the book with me. If I think there is something to it,

I'll call you when I get back." I was thrilled the man was open minded enough to do this.

Lo and behold, a week or so later he called. He said to bring Jazz in for an exam and some blood work. So, off we went. While we waited for the results, I set up a consultation with Dr. Plechner. I don't have those first results right in front of me, but I remember Jazzy's estrogen was too high, her cortisol was too low and her IgA was too low: a classic I-E imbalance, the way I understand it.

Shortly thereafter, our local veterinarian and I got on the phone with Dr. Plechner. I found Dr. Plechner friendly and easy to speak with from the outset. Also, just as I had heard him on the radio, he certainly came across as anything but ego-Driven. Based upon Jazzy's test results, he recommended a combined shot of Vetalog and Depo-Medrol. He explained this would give Jazz's system a jump start (and a longer-lasting infusion) of the cortisol her body needed. Dr. Plechner said this would stop the excess estrogen from being produced and then the IgA would come up. Once that had happened, then Jazz would ultimately be able to absorb tablet prednisone.

Our local veterinarian again was open minded enough to follow Dr. Plechner's advice and administered the shot. Once again, I don't remember the specifics, but I recall that we eventually followed with tablet Prednisone and sometime later retested Jazz's blood. I do remember it wasn't very long before we saw all her numbers move into the recommended ranges. Jazz also appeared to generally feel better, and she was no longer having those days of nausea and vomiting.

I'm not a chemistry professor, a scientist, an MD or a veterinarian, but there sure seemed to be a noticeable correlation between her E-I numbers, the administration of the combined shot, followed by the tablet prednisone and her overall state of wellbeing. It appeared self-evident, at least to me. From mid-2004 to January of 2009, Jazzy generally seemed to feel quite good and we only had blood work done every six months or so.

In January of 2009, the time came once again for some tests to be run. Jazzy's IgA came in at 73, just above the bottom of the range. However, nearly by accident, I found out the blood sample had taken a week to get to the lab. When I mentioned this to Dr. Plechner he said that the result could not be relied upon. He expressed some concern that the number may actually be lower, because in this battery of tests Jazz's glucose came in at 280. Our local veterinarian was somewhat concerned about the high glucose and said that she might be diabetic. I think he also said something about the prednisone might be the cause of her high glucose.

Anyway, a couple weeks later we ran a new glucose test, a total estrogen test and an IgA. This time I sent the samples overnight to NVDS. The results showed estrogen a little high, glucose at 312 and IgA at 69 - a little low. [I should back up and say that a couple weeks prior to this, Dr. Plechner and I had begun talking about possibly increasing the steroid, as Jazz was getting older and perhaps she wasn't absorbing enough. He thought this may be causing the higher glucose, as well. When these latest results came in, Dr. Plechner suggested we change to prednisolone and lower the dose by 5mg. He explained to me that prednisolone is usually more bioavailable (especially for cats), and we could therefore lower the dosage. We made the change to prednisolone, waited a couple weeks and retested the glucose. As Dr. Plechner had suspected it might, it had in fact, come down. Once again, to me, there appeared to be a correlation.

Unfortunately, I don't know what happened - if Jazz could taste the prednisolone or if she was just plain tired of the cottage cheese/rice/turkey mixture she'd been eating for a couple years, but she began having some challenges eating breakfast; this is the meal when she receives the steroid. Sometimes she wouldn't eat all of it, and this meant she was not getting the entire dosage she required every day.

About this time, Dr. Plechner and I began discussing the possibility she might need another injection to jump-start her system since her numbers were out of range; and now she probably wasn't getting enough steroid every day, so the situation was exacerbated. Meanwhile, I was quite busy making arrangements to go away for a week. Because of this distraction, I was clearly not paying enough attention to Jazzy's needs. I was committed to go, and so I did.

Nearly every day while I was gone, I checked in with Linda to get reports on Jazz and find out if she was eating or not. Linda told me that breakfast was becoming even more challenging and that, for the most part, Jazz was not eating all of it. Now I see, in retrospect, this meant the passage of time without her receiving the necessary steroid was mounting.

The week progressed and the story stayed about the same: Jazzy not eating all her breakfast. Linda said Jazz even began to show less interest in dinner. This was a real red flag for me. Now I was anxious to get back to see for myself.

Finally, a week after I had left, I arrived back home. As soon as I saw Jazzy it was very evident she had lost weight. That evening at about 9:30 - way past her normal eating hour, I served her dinner. She had no interest in itâ€¦none. She wasn't talking either, and now I was really concerned, as she's normally quite vocal.

The next morning, Wednesday, I called our local veterinarian and took her in for an exam. He Drew some blood and I asked for extra so I could send to NVDS for an IgA. Our vet examined her and gave her some fluids, since she was a little dehydrated. Jazz and I went home to wait for the results. I spent the rest of that day attempting to tempt her with four different cans of food (Limited Ingredient) in the hopes she would eat. She barely did, having only 2 and½ozs for the day. Normally she would have an entire can, which is 5.5ozs. The next morning, the call came. The results:

- Glucose 222 (had come down a little - apparently with the increase of the steroid)
- ALT (Serum Glutamic-Pyruvic Transaminase - I had to look it up) = 2236 - incredibly high: 100 is the upper range
- ALP (Alkaline Phosphatase - I looked it up also) = 423 - very high: 62 being the upper end.
- AST (Aspartate Aminotransferase - again, I looked it up) = 3122 - incredibly high: 55 is the upper end.
- SPEC fPL ((feline pancreas-specific lipase) = 22 - very high: 3.5 being the upper end.

Our vet said with numbers like these an ultrasound was the next logical step, as there may be a tumor. My jaw fell on the desk and I'm sure my neighbors could hear my heart thumping in my chest. How could this be? Just a couple of weeks ago she was fine.

I made some calls and got us an appointment for an ultrasound later that same day. I gathered Jazzy and my courage, and we drove the 10 miles to the animal hospital. After waiting a while, a young man came out to get her. He explained everything they were going to do (except the part about shaving her tummy). He said they would have the result within an hour.

For the next 45 minutes, I paced back and forth in the parking lot. I kept trying to think positive thoughts: "She is fine." "She will be fine." It was a challenge, to be sure. My mind kept trying to run away with the negative. (On another note: why is that? Why do we - for the most part - knee-jerk to the negative?) I was frightened and very upset about what was happening and what was next.

Finally they came and got me and took me to an exam room. Waiting, I paced some more. Then a very serious looking veterinarian came into the room. Barely a smile on his lips when he said, "Tell me about your girl." I gave him the Reader's Digest version of Jazzy's health history. Of course he looked askance at me when I mentioned Dr. Plechner and the fact that Jazz is on a regular regimen of prednisone.

As I began the telling of the tale (or is it tail?), tears were welling in my eyes: this was a nightmare I never wished to have. After my recounting of Jazz's story, he finally said, "There is no evidence of a tumor." Thank God, I thought to myself and I cried for joy. One hurdle crossed. Then he said the evidence pointed to pancreatitis and hepatic lipodosis. Both serious by themselves, let alone at the same time, he said. I said I didn't know what hepatic lipodosis is and he said it basically means a fatty liver condition. He also said it could be secondarily caused by the pancreatitis. He explained, "Pancreatitis usually causes nausea and the lack of eating would cause her body to begin digesting stored fat, which would cause too much fat in the liver." Okay, makes sense to me.

We discussed further treatment. He wanted to aspirate her liver in order to make sure there wasn't a tumor. "No," was my quick response. I just kept thinking that she's really is okay, that this is some kind of accident or some anomaly. They gave her some fluids and we headed back home. When we got home, I called Dr. Plechner to tell him what had taken place. He agreed there was no need for further investigation of her liver. He said probably the best thing to do while we waited for the IgA result, was to get her to eat. But, and here's the part that scared the hell out of me: Dr. Plechner said that sometimes, especially in cats, the pancreas can become inflamed and damage might occur to the ducts leading out the pancreas and create autolysis (self-digestion) and cause the pancreas enzymes to digest itself.

Someone wake me, please.

I am so very thankful that this scenario did not occur!

The next day, Friday, Jazz seemed somewhat improved. She ate more than Â½ of a can. The following day, Saturday, she appeared to be about the same, but she only ate about 2.5ozs for the day. Sunday morning, April 5thâ€¦she was not so good. Jazz had a very restless night; didn't sleep but about 5 or 10 minutes at a time. I know because I slept (or tried to) on the floor next to her and every time she changed her position, I woke up. By morning I think we were both exhausted.

When we both gave up and got up, I put a couple different flavors of the Limited Ingredient food in front of her. She only ate one small bite. She walked away and went to her little fleece pad in the dining room. Not good, I thought. A short time later, I found her on the bed, facing toward the wall - not looking out into the hall as she would usually do. This was also not a very positive sign. By late morning, I had reached my anxiety limit. I was too upset to contemplate navigating a car, so I called a neighbor and asked if he would Drive Jazz and me down to the animal hospital where I had taken her for the ultrasound. Yes, he said, and he came right over.

I held tears all the way to the hospital as we talked about our past animal companions. When we arrived, I carried Jazz inside. I was crying on and off while waiting for someone to come get us. They took us to an exam room and I talked with a different veterinarian about what they could do for her. She told me they would put her on IV's and probably give her an antibiotic and maybe something to quell the nausea. It seemed like the best that could be done for her right then. I said "goodbye" to her and I cried on the way to the front desk. I hated leaving her there, and I knew it was the best thing for her.

Befitting the average daily cost, the hospital was quite extensive and impressive: they even have visiting rooms. Every time I went to see Jazz, they would escort me into a small, comfortable room, complete with sofa. There I'd wait a couple minutes and one of the nurses would enter from another door, with my beautiful girl in their arms. Every day she had a different colored 'sock' on her right leg. I called it a sock, but really it was the wrapping for the IV needles. What was unmistakable each time I saw her was the Light (Inner Light) in her eyes; it was bright and seeking and life-affirming. Her life force was clearly visible. She has always had a life force much larger than her physical size. I enjoyed our visits immensely and looked forward to the next one, which was just a few hours later.

For the next three days, I went to visit Jazzy three times each day. I wanted her to know that she was not going to be left there, as she had been much earlier in her life. Sunday was a long day. I visited her two more times. I was exhausted by that night.

Finally, after an interminably long several hours, Monday morning arrived and with it, the IgA test result. No big surprise: it was 57. The low end of the scale is 70. In a strange way, I was actually thrilled to see this result. Now I felt we very likely had the reason for all these effects. In a previous conversation, Dr. Plechner had explained the mechanism of this scenario to me: not enough steroid = too much estrogen = low IgA (therefore lack of antibody in the gut, therefore the pancreas is not protected); estrogen too high = inflammation running rampant, and so on.

That same morning, I met with the attending vet, the same who had originally talked to me on Thursday after the ultrasound. He discussed what they were doing for her. Before I even had a chance to bring it up, he said: "I'm not going to give her a shot of Depo-Medrol. It could kill her. With her liver in the condition it's in, when it hits her liver it could just take her out." Not that I expected them to do it. Still, my heart sank when I heard those words. Time was passing, and with it I felt, were her chances of surviving all of this.

I came home from the hospital and called Dr. Plechner. He was wonderful. He gently and caringly counseled me, like a true friend, a better-informed brother. His care and concern came through loud and clear. No one else had given me anywhere near the time that he had given already. No one else had any suggestions. It seemed they were okay with standing by and watching whatever was going to happen. And this was completely and totally not acceptable to me.

When Dr. Plechner and I talked, he suggested that it was time for the shot - right now; no time to lose. I asked if he would be willing to talk to our vet and see if he (Dr. Plechner) could persuade him to administer it. Dr. Plechner said absolutely he would talk to him. I called our vet's office, gave them Dr. Plechner's number and begged for our veterinarian to make the call.

I waited. I paced. I was frightened: what will I do, if he says "No"? I really began to think about that possibility. What will I do if he says no? I wondered about my options and started thinking about putting Jazzy in the car and Driving the several hundred miles to go to Dr. Plechner. Would my elderly car make it? How would the trip be on Jazz? Do I even have the money for gas? There were too many questions to consider and right now, no answers. I was prepared to do anything for her, ¦anything!

I sought alternatives: what can I do, if the local veterinarian won't give her the shot? I began making calls to friends. I called everyone I could think of and asked for their thoughts and ideas, and prayers. I followed every idea, every lead; no matter how seemingly insignificant. Unfortunately, it seemed to be one dead-end after another; one frustration after another.

I had what felt like one final idea. Step by step I followed that idea, and it actually started to appear that it just might work. A contingency plan was beginning to take shape; a plan based on Dr. Plechner's work and what we had done for Jazz several years prior.

That night dragged on.

Morning arrived, even though to me it felt like afternoon. Our vet called; my heart thumped. He said he just couldn't bring himself to give her the shot; that it goes against everything he's ever been taught. In wanting to appeal to his common sense I gently reminded him that two months earlier we watched her glucose come down, after we'd increased the prednisone. He replied, "Yes, I remember." Then, with tears in my eyes and sobs in my voice, I told him I would sign any and every piece of paper he wanted from me, stating I would hold him harmless from whatever the outcome was, until the end of time. He said, "I just can't do it."

I called Dr. Plechner and told him of our vet's response. I could hear the disappointment in his voice. I told him I had a contingency plan. I told him what it was and he was very happy to hear the news.

*** Before going any farther, I need to make it clear that throughout the preceding week, Dr. Plechner was steadfast in his assistance to me. I realized that this man, who is hundreds of miles away, is not my cat's hands-on veterinarian, and he's giving me much more time and showing more concern than anyone else. Prior to April 2, I thought I had a pretty good idea of the veterinarian named Dr. Al Plechner and the depth of his caring for animals. Now I was also getting a look inside the man named Al Plechner and what I could see was humbling. The extent of his passion and humanity for helping animals appeared depthless. ***

That day, Tuesday, I went to visit Jazz three times, as usual. She did appear to be vastly improved from Sunday, and she was eating much better. The plan remained to bring her home the next day.

Wednesday morning I had a meeting with the hospital veterinarian. They had rerun her blood work and he brought me up to date on her condition. Her ALP was up a little. But, the ALT was down by 50%! He really didn't have much to say about that, merely, "Hm. She's improving." Curiously to me, he did not appear to be curious. I wondered if these positive changes in her blood work might have been because she was getting 5mg of IV prednisone each day. Business having been concluded, I left the hospital happily carrying my best pal in the world. I was elated! She's going home.

The rest of that day she did okay. She ate some, but didn't seem to have much energy. This was to be expected, I imagined, as she had been through a lot and also was probably stressed from being away from home and surrounded by other animals. I was beyond happy to have her home; the place just wasn't the same without her. I feel pretty certain the house had missed her, too.

The next morning, Jazz was slow to rise. She had, however, slept through the night on the bed next to me - which she hadn't done since this all began. She ate a little and then lay down on her fleece pad on the floor of the dining room. She didn't move much the rest of the morning. I was beginning to be concerned all over again. Clearly, she was back sliding already. I did not have a good feeling about where she was headed if this was allowed to continue. It only took a couple hours of observing her for it to become crystal clear that something needed to be done. I put my plan-in-the-wings, into motion.

By the time the plan came to fruition, my heart was on the floor - with Jazz, who had not moved much since early morning. I could see she was sinking and I was praying - hoping that there was still time; that it wasn't too late for her to recover. The plan came into being at 11:30AM on Thursday. Now, we wait, and pray.I stayed close to her for the rest of the day. Gradually, slowly at first, she began to move around. Then, she got up from her bed and ventured into the kitchen. This was a very good sign! I was crying for happy at the sight of her in the kitchen. I fed her as often as she was interested in eating. She slept well that night.

The next morning, as soon as she got up, she was ready to eat! Within 25 hours, she was clearly - without a doubt - taking a turn FOR THE BETTER. If I had not been there to witness it, I'm not sure I would believe it. Literally, as each hour passed, she appeared to be feeling better and better. This is NOT an exaggeration! I thought this kind of miraculous occurrence only happened in films or in Fairy Tales. I was witness to an absolute real miracle! Jazzy's appetite really began returning in earnest. Except for those long-gone when the IBD would flare up - which were BEFORE we met Dr. Plechner, she's always loved to eat. Now, my beautiful Angel-in-Kitty-Clothes (as I like to refer to her) was eating like she used to, even better.

I can't describe how this turn-around felt to me. My world was righting itself, from having been completely upside down and twisted in knots. This exquisitely precious being called Jazzy was returning to health, minute by minute.

The following Tuesday, only 5 days after implementing the plan, I took her to see our veterinarian. He had called that morning and asked how she was doing. As it happened, she did seem a little "off" that day, so I decided to take her in for a quick once-over and some blood work. Our vet repeated the SPEC fPL and the liver enzyme tests and a couple others.

Note: All of this may need to be under the heading of "Opinion." However, this is me talking to you right now: one to one. It's my "opinion" that what follows really belongs under the heading "Fact." What I observed over those first days (and now weeks) is nothing short of - if not actually - a miracle. To me, it's a fact that she has not only improved to her pre-illness condition, she has improved beyond that point. I say this because of what's to follow. Our vet called me the next day with the test results. Here they are (and these are "facts"):

- ALP - now 276, down from a high of 423 = a 30% reduction in a few days
- ALT - now 252, down from a high of 2,236 = an 88% reduction in a few days
- SPEC-fPL - now 5.3, down from a high of 22 = a 75% reduction in a few days
- Glucose - now 254, down from a high of at least 300

It is now April 30, only 21 days since the plan was implemented. I have not had any blood tests redone since the 14th. I will repeat these and an IgA soon.

Dr. Plechner called me a couple days ago and asked after Jazz. I was touched by his call. Obviously, this is an unusual man - not only a wonderfully uncommon veterinarian; he possesses a huge heart. I happily reported to him that she is doing better than even I had hoped. I told him she appears to be drinking from the Fountain of Youth. She's acting more energetic and she is more 'vocal' than I have seen and heard in a couple years. He was genuinely thrilled to hear the news, as I was to relate it to him.

From the bottom of our hearts, we thank Dr. Plechner for his knowledge, his humanity, his empathy, his caring and his heart. During this journey from Jazzy's dire illness, to her restoration to health, I feel we experienced an infinitesimal portion of the ridicule and doubt and incredulity Dr. Plechner most surely has faced for the last 44 years. We, therefore, especially wish to thank him for his indefatigable courage; his courage to go against the grain, to swim upstream, to buck the system, to stand his ground and have the courage of his convictions - the courage that comes from the KNOWING that his work, works, and saves lives.

Dr. Plechner, Jazzy, Linda and I humbly thank you for all that you have done and continue to do. We thank you for helping give Jazz her health and her life back. I pray Jazzy and I have many more years together, for I can't imagine life without her. It is with great love, respect and appreciation that we dedicate this Story with a Happy Ending to Dr. Plechner, a true humanitarian, and in our opinions, a Nobel Prize winning man.

Jazzy, Linda and Ken

Larry's Last Chance

This e-mail is purely to thank you from the bottom of my heart for your heroism to take a new approach to save pets through your love of animals. I came across your Pets at Risk book in January of this year at a time where I was taking my cat Larry to vets to figure out why he was not eating and, losing weight. If I had not come to my stage of observing him instead of being devastated and, accepting the diagnosis (Lymph Cancer) of the last two vets he would have been put down already.

I wouldn't give up on him when I noticed him stretching and, cleaning himself. I couldn't believe that a cat sick with cancer would be capable of these two healthy behaviors. I was well into acknowledging that holistic approaches can and, do help animals and people.

By the grace of God your book arrived at my local bookstore right during that time. Your book had symptoms of my cat Larry all over it. I contacted both vets in New Jersey on your website. They both were at least an hour away but, with a car all things are possible. When the one vet couldn't take him right away it turned out the other could. Dr. Mark Newkirk in Margate, New Jersey diagnosed Larry within ten minutes of having inflammatory bowel syndrome.

Six and a half months later Larry is reversing back to health. He had, as Dr. Newkirk put it pain all over. Everything from his lymph system, stomach, liver ...everything was messed up not excluding that he was blind in one eye from glaucoma that lead to buphthalmos and, blind from phthisis in his other eye.

Dr. Newkirk put in 110% of his energy for Larry. There was a time when he and, I weren't sure Larry would make it. He ended up being in the hospital for two separate two week visits because he was losing a lot of weight to dehydration to intense diarrhea the Dr. couldn't control. After Dr. Newkirk's last resort the diarrhea got under control. Larry got all the way down to almost four pounds.

We are talking about an eleven year old large framed marked tabby who once weighed thirteen pounds. He started gaining weight two months ago and, is around six pounds now. His next vet appointment is tomorrow. His last appointment was the sign of his first real progress. His steroids were reduced to one instead of two and, he gained 7 ounces.

I'm sorry to make this story so long Dr. Plechner but, I wanted you to get the real picture. It is no small miracle that Larry is alive today. It took all of us to keep Larry alive today. Your book played the most important role in his recovery and, it seems that a thank you isn't enough. His first many years it seems the vets weren't so good. I believe things are making up now. No more conventional food and, I keep him to the prescribed diet the doctor ordered.

Again, thank you thank you so very much Dr. Plechner. For what it's worth we may never get to meet each other but, through your information that saved Larry you will always be remembered by me. And, will always be remembered for the primary loving man who saved my family. May loved ones always follow you. God Bless always.

Mary E. Pollara & Larry

Sierra's Story

Dr. Plechner, I would like to THANK YOU for taking such good care of Sierra. Right after her exploratory surgery to find the leak in her lungs, it was discovered that she had cancer. After a couple of weeks, she stopped eating. I had spoken to the surgeon earlier and she stated that we had done all we could and it was out of our hands.

As I took her to you to be euthanized, it didn't feel right as she seemed to be very alert. Sure enough, you said that her color looked good and after reviewing her files from the surgeon that her type of cancer most likely originated in the spleen. You then concluded that she probably had a hormone imbalance.

After giving her a shot of a cortisol and some thyroid medication, I took her home and (after two days of not eating) she ate like a champ! The instant change in her demeanor was incredible! The next day she was chasing her tail again- something I hadn't seen in over a month. It was like I had a new dog.

Unfortunately we caught the cancer too late and she did eventually succumb to it. You gave me another wonderful month and a half with her though, and for that gift I am full of gratitude. I am convinced that if we had found it sooner, your treatments would have given her a much longer life. If I had known about your studies years ago, I would've taken preventative measures and Sierra may never have even developed cancer.

I feel so blessed to have met you. To find a vet that really cares about animals and is continuously looking for solutions is a rarity these days. I've been a dog owner for 16 years and I have never been so touched by a Doctor's kindness and generosity. You're compassion is unparalleled. Words cannot express the depth of my gratitude.

Lydia Castro

Reo's Vision

Well, 3 independent veterinarians this week all confirmed that they think Reo has some functional vision! Reo saw her veterinary acupuncturist, her original vet for a CBC blood Draw, and our "new" vet, with whom we work on the endocrine issues and injections. They were all informal "tests" done in the office, but she could track cotton, navigate the exam rooms (complete with furniture and chair legs), and her PLRs were quickly responsive. Everyone was floored.

I am over the moon with happiness, and hope that she continues to make progress. I'm surprised how she can navigate new places - including going up a few stairs. She surprises me every day. If she does continue to improve, we will go back to our ophthalmologist who gave us "no hope" for Reo, to get his assessment. I'd also like to do an ERG, as Reo was flat line at her SARDS diagnosis. I would just LOVE to see if there is some activity - my curiosity is too much.

I know I've said this before, but THANK YOU so much for all that you do, and your support. I honestly could not have gotten through this time without the support of *you and Caroline Levin.* But, I truly believe in the biochemistry/endocrinology/physiology of it all, so we stayed the course, and seem to be reaping the rewards! I told all of the veterinarians that I just want to create awareness for this type of treatment, so hopefully we could help other SARDS dogs in the future.

Honestly, our original vet is still having trouble wrapping her head around all of this. They were expecting Reo to lose muscle mass from all of the hormones (particularly the injections, which it seems they are still against, for whatever reason!). They think she looks great - she's healthy, bright, alert, and sassy! :)

Her CBC revealed this week slightly higher liver enzymes, but no one is worried about that, as they are only slightly elevated. Also, slightly elevated phosphorous (I think maybe due to the pumpkin that I give her - I've read that is high in phosphorous). We'll probably test her 3-4 times/year, just to make sure all is good, but for now, I am so happy. The vet ordered a T4 test with the CBC, and it came back NORMAL, so I suspect the EI-1 will show the same.

I will let you know when we get the EI-1 results back, in case we need to alter the dosage of any hormones (maybe Drop the L-thyro back down to 0.1 mg).

Thanks again! :)

Lynn

Shadows Lymphoma

I have just read your article about cortisol imbalances and their role in the development of cancer. I want to thank you so very much for your dedication to and love for animals which I know are the things that drive you to do the research that you have.

My 16 year old cat, Shadow, just received the devastating diagnosis of gastric lymphoma. I know that you have seen firsthand the sadness, helplessness, and confusion this disease presents to a Mommy like me, and the desperation I feel for information. My vet determined that surgery would be too risky, and that cortisone therapy would be the best place to start.

I have read so many conflicting and frightening articles on this issue, but yours has given me peace about this course of treatment and an arsenal of information that has brought me to a place of better understanding. I am so very grateful for doctors like you, and I must admit that your insight has made me feel the most relaxed I've been in the last two weeks! If only human doctors were as dedicated as you...

You should be proud of what you have accomplished and all of the wonderful and beautiful care that you bring to your patients and their families alike - and even to me, a perfect stranger!

God Bless You and I pray that you continue to make amazing strides in approaching and striking out this senseless killer.

Sincerely,
Heather Vinarski

Saving Missey

Dr. Plechner started treating my Missey in late January, 2011. Missey had been diagnosed having a thyroid problem and was being over dosed with Soloxine as her T4 levels were staying extremely low. Missey kept losing weight, she was down to almost 35.8 pounds, even though she was eating at least four times a day and not little meals either.

Her weight should have been at least 60 pounds. Missey is a Lab/Pit Bull mix, medium size dog and was diagnosed with Myofactorial Muscle Disease. Thanks to Dr. Plechner, she is now 68.3 pounds. I didn't find out until a couple months later that Missey was most likely a week to a week and a half away from death. She was slowly, starving to death as her intestines were compromised and she was not getting any nutrition.

In late January I noticed Missey staggering around, looking very weak and acting like she was extremely hungry all the time. She slept most of the time, this is not normal for Missey. Dr. Plechner started her immediately with injectable Vetalog and Depomedrol intramuscular injections, and then we did her immune testing, which took a week. All her levels were extremely low.

Missey went for injections every ten days and was retested every three months. The vet that is working with Dr. Plechner, is Dr. Angela Erickson of Animal Health Practice in Bantam, Ct. She told me that she has been in practice for 15 years and has seen dogs with this same problem, Missey is the only dog, that has survived. Missey and I have had a very hard year (2011).

Missey is now stable and doing extremely well, thanks to Dr. Plechner and his research of over 40 years. I now have medical problems and will also be having Dr. Plechner's EI test soon. I have a pre-cancerous condition and can live a long life if I also do his protocol. Thank you again, Missey owes her life to you.

Carol Skowronek

Volume Two
Healthfully Yours Handbook
for
Whole Animal Health

The following is a collection of articles, opinions, blogs etc., some of which have appeared on numerous websites including Dr. Plechner.com, The Opinion Sector and the Healthy Pet Network.

Diet and Nutrition

From Tragedy to Nutrition

In March of 2007, a tragic outbreak brought tears of grief and cries of outrage and soon became a major turning point in my life. The careless acts of others made me realize a major responsibility I had accepted but then took for granted and it was just dumb luck that spared me the loss felt by so many.

It began with numerous reports of renal failure in pets in North America, South Africa and Europe and led to a major recall in the US, involving several major pet food companies and totaling 5300 different pet food products.

Most of the recalls came from Canadian Pet Food manufacturer, **Menu Foods** which is the manufacturer of such "quality diverse" product lines including the high priced "Gourmet" -"Natural" - "Holistic" Brands such as; Nutro Ultra, Natural Life, IAMS, Eukanuba, to the low priced "generic" - "discounted" - "store brand" Brands like Walmart's Old Roy's, Winn Dixie, and Springfield Prize.

The pet foods recalled contained wheat or corn gluten, and/or rice protein made in China which were contaminated with melamine. The Chinese company's used melamine, to falsely increase protein levels (during mandatory tests) of the wheat and corn gluten, and rice protein they sold to the recall related pet food manufacturers. The combination of melamine and cyanuric acid found in the "protein elevators" is known to cause renal failure.

Even though the FDA received reports of several thousand cats and dogs who had died after eating contaminated food, it could only confirm 14 cases due to the fact that there is no centralized government database of animal sickness or death in the US. Conveniently, for the guilty parties, the actual number of affected pets will never be known. The actual death toll could potentially reach into the thousands.

I'm sure that you will remember it was a very frightening and angry time and it proved to be the catalyst for many pet lovers. We began to research just what our animal's food actually did contain. The results were so frightening and disgusting it caused some of us to start taking a more proactive role in overseeing our pet's diets.

Pay No Attention to the Printing On the Label

You remember the scene in The Wizard of Oz, when Toto pulls the curtain back and reveals the "wizard" to actually be a hoax. The wizard, desperate to maintain the deception, cries out, "Pay no attention to the man behind the curtain...". That scene is a good example of the ingredient listing on pet food labels...mostly smoke and mirrors, and a lot of deception.

Now, we're not saying that commercial pet food manufacturers are liars. Let's just say that the ingredient listings on their pet food labels contain a lot more bull-waste, than a cattle car. If they actually believed in the "quality" of their product there would be a lot more facts and a lot less deception on their labels.

It is good to realize the important fact that, good foods for us and our pets are simple. That's right, good nutrition is simple. Therefore a good adage to follow is, "The longer the ingredient listing, the worse the food actually is." You don't need a lot of fillers just a few naturally nutritious ingredients. Let's take a look and we'll "break down" the facts from the fiction.

Ingredients are listed on the label by weight. The ingredient weighing the most in the product is listed first; the ingredient weighing the second most is listed second, and so on, until all ingredients are listed. The most important fact is; when you look at the label you need to realize that 90% of the actual diet inside is covered in the first <u>three</u> ingredients. Are those three ingredients protein, carbohydrates or both? Consider those three ingredients carefully and remember they are your pet's primary diet.

A food with no corn, wheat or soy is recommended. Meat should be your two top nutrition sources. The best commercial foods contain MINIMAL grain (preferably rice), no 'by-products' or 'animal digest', no artificial preservatives like BHA or BHT, ethoxyquin, no fillers such as beet pulp, rice flour or brewer's rice.

If beef, chicken or whatever meat protein, is the 4th or 5th ingredient, basically means that the bull or the chicken or whatever meat is listed came by the barn and waved. Most commercially produced animal foods are filled with <u>filler</u> then artificially enhanced with the vitamins, minerals, protein, carbohydrates etc. needed to meet the FDA's daily <u>minimum</u> requirements.

Did we hear a sigh of relief, out there? "It has the FDA's stamp of approval!" but who actually determines dog food standards? The Association of American Feed Control Officials (AFFCO) determines how the nutritional adequacy statement on the label or bag of dog food is worded. Basically all the statement says is that the pet food manufacturer formulated the food inside to meet the minimum daily requirements of your dog "to keep it alive". It says nothing at all about the quality of the ingredients used.

How about labels that proclaim that their dog food is complete and balanced and safe for <u>all</u> dogs? All you need to do is, just follow the "feed by weight" directions and your pet is good to go. That may be true as far as their poop is concerned; however, **The Animal Advocate** sums up the possible dangers behind this illogical statement...

"'Complete & Balanced' food. Think logically: A 40 pound Keeshond sheds; a 40 pound Kerry blue terrier does not shed; would these two need the same coat producing nutrients? A 45 pound Bulldog has thick bones, a 45 pound Pharaoh Hound has thin bones; would these two need the same amount of bone building minerals? A 50 pound Basset Hound and a 50 pound Standard Poodle have different energy levels; would they need the same caloric intake? A 60 pound Labrador Retriever is one of six dog breeds that produce skin oil; a sixty pound Collie does not produce skin oil; would these two have the same need for dietary fatty acids?"

The Animal Advocate at http://www.wdcusick.com/01.html

How did it all begin? What led us from sharing scraps by the camp fire to stumbling down aisles; lined with endless shelves, filled by countless brands and varieties of pet foods?

Even though commercially mass produced, dry and canned pet foods didn't become the popular thing until after World War II, the first processed dog food was actually introduced to the public way back in 1860. Ohioan, James Spratt started selling biscuits made of wheat, beet root, vegetables and beef blood called "Spratt's Patent Meat Fibrine Dog Cakes". Other companies soon got into the act and the dogs really started barking.

When the 1930's ushered in the depression, people started tightening their belts and had to find cheaper dog food. Raw meat scraps were better served at the family's dinner table. That's when pet owners started packing in the carbohydrates and began feeding their pets more cereal and grains.

The pet food industry began during the 1940's with canned "meat" pet foods leading the way. Dehydrated dog food followed closely in 1943 and following World War Two, pet food manufacturing shifted into high gear.

It's important to note the fact that, during this time period, cereal companies needed to do something to do with their tainted grains which were "unfit for human consumption" because they were rancid, moldy or just plain contaminated. Some bright businessmen saw that the meat industry had the same problems so they mixed it all together and called it "pet food". Voila', the commercial pet food industry was born.

The "industry" wasn't really concerned with nutrients. In its quest to strengthen their bottom line, they became more concerned with shelf life and economy. They felt it was their job to "fill your pets up", not to keep them happy or healthy. Simple, basic pet food formulas became more complex as the "industry" started adding byproducts, additives and enhancers to the mix...

******

What Does The "*By*" In Byproducts Actually Mean?

Back in 2007, when the melamine tainted pet food was killing dogs and cats around the world; many of us shook off our laziness and complacency and took a real good look at what they put into pet foods. Those who did were so shocked by what they found they vowed their pets would never eat commercial food again and started home cooking their food.

We still do, however, emergencies came up and we had to go up and down the pet food aisle reading labels till we found some safe options. We found some natural and holistic pet foods that had nothing to hide so they said it all on their labels. Yes, there are some safe, commercial pet foods available. Even so, there are still pet foods out there that, like icebergs, have more below the surface than they want you to know about. That's why someone coined the phrase *by-product*. We feel that the term by-product is beyond misleading it is what we consider a subversive term; however, "good meat" by-products are often organ meats from mammals, fowl and fish that "north American" humans do not eat for whatever reason. I know the term organ meats, does sound weird but they usually are a good source of protein.

There are many definitions for the term *by-product*. I personally like the one from Princeton; *"a secondary and sometimes unexpected consequence."* **Wikipedia,** states that the commercial enterprise which attempts to regulate the quality and safety of fodder and pet food in the United States the **Association of American Feed Control Officials (AAFCO)** defines "Meat by-products" as *"clean parts of slaughtered animals, not including meat; lungs, spleen, kidneys, brain, liver, blood, bone, and stomach and intestines."*

You still need to be cautious as you try to decipher just what the labels are actually saying. Eileen Layne from the **California Veterinary Medical Association** points out,

"When you read pet-food labels and it says meat meal or bone meal, that's what it is - cooked and converted animals, including dogs and cats." You read right *"millions of dead American dogs and cats are processed each year at plants across North America"*.

Canine and Feline, cannibalism? That was the straw that broke *my* camel's back, that and the 4 D's. The 4 D's; Diseased, Disabled,

Dead and Dying, that's where all the "meat" comes from. Difficult as it may be to believe, according to **Spear-Bar Kennels**...

"Road kill, slaughter house rejects, animals that die on their way to meat packing plants - all are acceptable ingredients for pet food under the "4D" rule: ! Steroids, growth hormones and chemicals used to treat cattle for infestations - including insecticide patches - end up mixed into the final product. Meat from grocery stores past its final due date is also added to the mix, as are the Styrofoam trays and plastic wrap they were packed in."

If that's not bad enough, **Spear-Bar Kennel**'s website added that these "meat" products were also marinated with "Chemical Cocktails"...

"The addition of euthanized pets goes beyond morally repugnant - it also introduces a host of chemicals not listed on pet food labels. At the rendering plant, time cannot be spared to remove even the green plastic bags the pets came wrapped in, let alone the insecticide laden flea and tick collars they were wearing. Even the very chemicals used to put these pets to death also find their way into the final product."

http://spear-barkennels.com/Feeding.php

Many years ago I helped Senator David Roberti pass a bill in the State of California which made it illegal to use any dead or euthanized dog and cat parts in dog and cat foods. We were successful but that was just California. The **Pet Food Institute**, the trade association of pet food manufacturers, acknowledges the use of by-products in pet foods as additional income for processors and farmers:

"The growth of the pet food industry not only provided pet owners with better foods for their pets, but also created profitable additional markets for American farm products and

for the byproducts of the meat packing, poultry, and other food industries which prepare food for human consumption."

I know this was supposed to be about by-products but I just have to discuss the smell. I know for a fact if you ever fed commercial dry pet foods to your animals you'll have to acknowledge *the smell.* You know what I'm talking about, a *just short of overpowering, definitely rancid odor* that hits you when you first open the bag. What could that "pungent" odor be? The **Animal Protection Institute** says...

"It is most often rendered animal fat, restaurant grease, or other oils too rancid or deemed inedible for humans."

So do they throw it away? No Way! Not in America. They give it to our beloved dogs and cats...they can't read the labels and they don't vote. The **Animal Protection Institute** continues...

"Restaurant grease has become a major component of feed grade animal fat over the last fifteen years. This grease, often held in fifty-gallon Drums, may be kept outside for weeks, exposed to extreme temperatures with no regard for its future use. "Fat blenders" or rendering companies then pick up this used grease and mix the different types of fat together, stabilize them with powerful antioxidants to retard further spoilage, and then sell the blended products to pet food companies and other end users."

"These fats are sprayed directly onto extruded kibbles and pellets to make an otherwise bland or distasteful product palatable. The fat also acts as a binding agent to which manufacturers add other flavor enhancers such as digests. Pet food scientists have discovered that animals love the taste of these sprayed fats. Manufacturers are masters at getting a dog or a cat to eat something she would normally turn up her nose at."

******

The Culprits

Recall! That's one word we all dread. Whether it's an automobile, toy or pet food it means, bring it back because we screwed up. If it's pet food, it could mean a visit to your Vet or even worse. We've had quite a few recalls but what really scare us, are the ones we <u>don't</u> hear about. The following is a partial list, from the **Born Free USA** website,

__http://www.bornfreeusa.org/facts.php?more=1&p=359__
•

"When things go really wrong and serious problems are discovered in pet food, the company usually works with the FDA to coordinate a recall of the affected products. While many recalls have been widely publicized, quite a few have not.

- *In 1995, Nature's Recipe recalled almost a million pounds of dry dog and cat food after consumers complained that their pets were vomiting and losing their appetite. The problem was a fungus that produced vomitoxin contaminating the wheat.*
- *In 1999, Doane Pet Care recalled more than a million bags of corn-based dry dog food contaminated with aflatoxin. Products included Ol' Roy (Wal-Mart's brand) and 53 other brands. This time, the toxin killed 25 dogs.*
- *In 2000, Iams recalled 248,000 pounds of dry dog food distributed in 7 states due to excess DL-Methionine Amino Acid, a urinary acidifier.*
- *In 2003, a recall was made by Petcurean "Go! Natural" pet food due to circumstantial association with some dogs suffering from liver disease; no cause was ever found.*
- *In late 2005, a similar recall by Diamond Foods was announced; this time the moldy corn contained a particularly nasty fungal product called aflatoxin; 100 dogs died.*

- *Also in 2005, 123,000 pounds of cat and dog treats were recalled due to Salmonella contamination.*

- *In 2006, more than 5 million cans of Ol' Roy, American Fare, and other dog foods distributed in the southeast were recalled by the manufacturer, Simmons Pet Food, because the cans' enamel lining was flaking off into the food.*

- *Also in 2006, Merrick Pet Care recalled almost 200,000 cans of "Wingalings" dog food when metal tags were found in some samples.*

- *In the most deadly recall of 2006, 4 prescription canned dog and cat foods were recalled by Royal Canin (owned by Mars). The culprit was a serious overdose of Vitamin D that caused calcium deficiency and kidney disease.*

- *In February 2007, the FDA issued a warning to consumers not to buy "Wild Kitty," a frozen food containing raw meat. Routine testing by FDA had revealed Salmonella in the food. FDA specifically warned about the potential for illness in humans, not pets. There were no reports of illness or death of any pets, and the food was not recalled.*

- *In March 2007, the most lethal pet food in history was the subject of the largest recall ever. Menu Foods recalled more than 100 brands including Iams, Eukanuba, Hill's Science Diet, Purina Mighty Dog, and many store brands including Wal-Mart's. Thousands of pets were sickened (the FDA received more than 17,000 reports) and an estimated 20% died from acute renal failure caused by the food. Cats were more frequently and more severely affected than dogs. The toxin was initially believed to be a pesticide, the rat poison "aminopterin" in one of the ingredients. In April, scientists discovered high levels of melamine, a chemical used in plastics and fertilizers, in wheat gluten and rice protein concentrate imported from China. The melamine had been purposefully added to the ingredients to falsely boost their protein content.*

Subsequent tests revealed that the melamine-tainted ingredients had also been used in feed for cows, pigs, and chickens and thousands of animals were quarantined and destroyed. In early May, scientists identified the cause of the rapid onset kidney disease that had appeared in dogs and cats as a reaction caused by the combination of melamine and cyanuric acid, both unauthorized chemicals. The fallout from this recall is ongoing as of May 2007 so please be sure to check the FDA website for the most recent updates."

So far, in this 'look behind the pet food label' we have learned some really disgusting facts. The main one being, don't believe a word that they say. I think it's time to take a look at just who "they" are. "They" are a multinational pet food industry that makes $16.1 billion per year in the U.S. alone.

According to the article, "What's really in Pet Food" on the **Born Free USA** website,

http://www.bornfreeusa.org/facts.php?more=1&p=359

They are merely extensions of even larger multinational corporations who owe allegiance to no country and worship only their bottom line...profit.

"What most consumers don't know is that the pet food industry is an extension of the human food and agriculture industries. Pet food provides a convenient way for slaughterhouse offal, grains considered "unfit for human consumption," and similar waste products to be turned into profit. This waste includes intestines, udders, heads, hooves, and possibly diseased and cancerous animal parts.

The pet food market has been dominated in the last few years by the acquisition of big companies by even bigger companies. With $15 billion a year at stake in the U.S. and rapidly expanding foreign markets, it's no wonder that some are greedy for a larger piece of the pie.

- *Nestlé's bought Purina to form Nestlé Purina Petcare Company (Fancy Feast, Alpo, Friskies, Mighty Dog, Dog Chow, Cat Chow, Puppy Chow, Kitten Chow, Beneful, One, ProPlan, DeliCat, HiPro, Kit'n'Kaboodle, Tender Vittles, Purina Veterinary Diets).*

- *Del Monte gobbled up Heinz (MeowMix, Gravy Train, Kibbles 'n Bits, Wagwells, 9Lives, Cycle, Skippy, Nature's Recipe, and pet treats Milk Bone, Pup-Peroni, Snausages, Pounce).*

- *MasterFoods owns Mars, Inc., which consumed Royal Canin (Pedigree, Waltham's, Cesar, Sheba, Temptations, Goodlife Recipe, Sensible Choice, Excel).*

- *Other major pet food makers are not best known for pet care, although many of their household and personal care products do use ingredients derived from animal by-products:*

- *Procter and Gamble (P&G) purchased The Iams Company (Iams, Eukanuba) in 1999. P&G shortly thereafter introduced Iams into grocery stores, where it did very well.*

- *Colgate-Palmolive bought Hill's Science Diet (founded in 1939) in 1976 (Hill's Science Diet, Prescription Diets, Nature's Best).*

Private labelers (who make food for "house" brands like Kroger and Wal-Mart) and co-packers (who produce food for other pet food makers) are also major players. Three major companies are Doane Pet Care, Diamond, and Menu Foods; they produce food for dozens of private label and brand names. Interestingly, all 3 of these companies have been involved in pet food recalls that sickened or killed many pets.

Many major pet food companies in the United States are subsidiaries of gigantic multinational corporations. From a business standpoint, pet food fits very well with companies making human products. The multinationals have increased bulk-purchasing power; those that make human food products have a captive market in which to capitalize on their waste products; and pet food divisions have a more reliable capital base and, in many cases, a convenient source of ingredients.

Waste products, are ingredients? We hate to leave you with that pleasant thought but just remember to be aware, at all times, of just what your pets are eating. When you find a food that looks fit for your pet, do some more research.

Google the manufacturers, look for reviews and possible recall history. Make sure it's safe before you even buy it. Your pets are counting on you to do the right thing. First and foremost, always make sure you read the label.

Healthfully Yours,
Dr. Al Plechner DVM & David Spangenburg

Just Because It's Supposed to be Healthy, Doesn't Mean It Can't Kill You

How's that for an alarmist title. Or is it? People are constantly trying to lose weight and to feed or eat healthy so they keep eating their way through all the fads and crazes hoping to discover the miracle diet. One that keeps them sleek, healthy and happy and still allows them some of their dietary guilty pleasures. This, while not being impossible, usually is, for the most part, highly improbable.

There is (sad to say) no gain without pain and sometimes these healthy_foods may not be all that healthy and occasionally may actually be hazardous to you or your pet's health.

Soy is fast becoming a popular substitute for dairy and meat products. To many it seems like it is a healthy alternative, however, like an iceberg it has some hidden dangers lurking beneath the surface. Soybean ingredients and soy milk can cause definite health issues, possible negative health effects include:

- It may stop iodine from properly combining with an intermediate amino acid causing a reduced production of thyroid hormones (hypothyroidism) which will affect the metabolism.
- It may stop the absorption of calcium. This is particularly significant with pets with kidney disease and osteoporosis.
- It may stop the absorption of iron. Any person or pet with an anemia beware.
- In females it can lead to abnormalities in the reproductive tract and can give rise to infertility.
- Possible dangers for children include learning disorders, attention deficit disorder, dyslexia, etc. It can also cause pancreatic and growth related problems.
- Soy milk estrogen is harmful for babies or puppies.
- Manganese presence in soy milk is sometimes large enough to cause damage to the cortex.
- It can contribute to skin problems like sudden and severe eczema, acne, blisters, canker sores, swelling and hives.
- Isoflavones present in soy milk can cause diseases like leukemia and breast cancer.
- The level of phytoestrogen is high in soy milk, which decreases the testosterone present in males and can affect the production

189

of sperm. Phytoestrogen can also lead to early puberty and early adolescent development.

- It can block the action of trypsin and enzymes which are required for proper protein digestion.

Studies continue on the effects of soy on human and animal health and results are being posted on both sides of the argument. I do have to say, however, there are enough negative findings to give one pause. Obviously the amount of soy one consumes is a determining factor in these findings but when you consider its presence in an increasing number of both human and pet food labels the possibility of it being an actual health hazard are very plain to see.

I guess when you are trying to pick the 'lesser of the two evils', the decision always falls back on you and me, the consumers. You just need to do your research and determine just how much you are consuming.

Healthfully Yours,
Dr. Al Plechner DVM & David Spangenburg

The Hazards of Some Raw Diets

Raw diets are becoming very popular amongst pet owners. Some people have a tendency to think that animals should eat their food raw and natural. That dogs, should dine as their wolf ancestors did so long ago. The pet food industry has heard these calls and is producing numerous raw diets for the market place.

Commercially Prepared

Be very careful of Commercially Prepared Raw Diets that contain meat. All of these pet foods manufactures claim that their organic meats are completely safe but think for a moment about all of the human_food products, meat and vegetables alike, that have been recalled due to E. coli, Salmonella and camphrobacter.

You will see a number of veterinarian endorsements for commercial raw food diets but an equally important fact for you to consider is; just as MD's are influenced by large_prosperous pharmaceutical companies, vets are influenced by academic departments and professional associations that rely upon funding from large prosperous pet food companies. Hill's Pet Nutrition, makers of Science Diet and a range of prescription only food is a major sponsor_of the American Veterinary Medical Association.

Can you say, "conflict of interest"?

The BARF raw diet is among the many commercially produced raw diets available and is and is probably the most recognized. Its proponents are scattered throughout the internet, wildly singing its praises. There are, however, many raw diet detractors who warn of the possible dangers involved, primarily involving the possible contamination by bacteria and deadly parasites.

Craig E. Greene DVM MS DACVIM, writes in his highly regarded textbook, *"**Infectious Diseases of the Dog and Cat**"*...

"...animals, immunocompromised or healthy that eat raw meat are susceptible to bacterial infections. E coli and Salmonella are among the more serious infections that are transmitted through meat that is not properly cooked."

Most manufacturers claim that freezing raw diet recipes "reduces the potential of parasites" but you'll notice they didn't say it <u>eliminates</u> the potential. Many studies done on commercial raw diets have detected salmonella in up to 20% and Escherichia coli in 64% of the diets tested. Racing Greyhounds, which are usually fed raw meat that has been graded "not for human consumption", have been infected by E. coli H157:O7 which causes severe vasculitis, cutaneous necrosis, renal failure and death.

According to Ann Martin, in her **BNet** Article *How safe is a raw diet?*

"The US Centers for Disease Control and Prevention (CDC) has found that a high percentage of meat and poultry contains at least one strain of bacteria. Hence, the agency advises that you thoroughly cook meat and poultry. Toxoplasma, a parasite found in warm-blooded animals, can also be transmitted from raw or undercooked meat. David T. Roen, DVM, writes, "A veterinary neurologist told me the other day that they have seen au increase in seizure disorders in dogs and cats caused by toxoplasmosis, especially in areas where raw meat diets are trendy."

Her article, which can be found here...

http://findarticles.com/p/articles/mi_moFKA/is_6_67/ai_n1 3788104/?tag=content;col1

...also points out that...

"It's clear that puppies can suffer nutritional inadequacies on a raw food diet. Josepha DeLay, DVM, and Jenny Laing, DVM, from the Ontario Veterinary College at the University of Guelph, in a 2002 paper titled "Nutritional Osteodystrophy in

Puppies Fed a BARF Diet," describe two litters of 6-week-old dogs who showed hind limb collapse, weakness and failure to thrive. One litter was fed a BARF diet beginning at 2 1/2 to 3 weeks of age. The second litter began the diet at 5 weeks. "The dames had been fed the same diet during gestation." All pups were weak, in pain and were either unable to stand or had abnormal gaits. DeLay and Laing concluded that lesions in the pups' bones resulted from the diet's abnormal calcium-to-phosphorus ratio and a likely absolute calcium deficiency."

Studies have proven that even though the majority of dogs may not exhibit symptoms of E. coli contamination, they can none-the-less pass the contamination to other animals or people. Considering the outbreaks in recent years we all know that these disease outbreaks can kill or debilitate children, the elderly, and individuals with compromised immune systems. So, it seems that although raw diets can seem natural and be nutritious they can also play host to dangerous and sometimes lethal micro-organisms. Like so many food products in both the human and animal world they are subject to manufacturing safety standards that are, more often than not, substandard.

Though their advertising campaigns suggest that all the products they use are the finest quality available, the reality is that the corporate pet Food Company's first concern is their bottom line, the almighty (?) dollar. Still there are those who feel that, dogs should dine natural and raw as their wolf ancestors did so long ago. Others feel quite the opposite; Ann Martin tells us that...

Geoff Stein, DVM, wrote: "The problem with these 'natural' diets is the misguided assumption that 'natural' is better. It's 'natural' for wolves to die of salmonella once in a while." He added that wolves would probably be healthier if they ate cooked meat.

Home Prepared

While we are looking at potentially healthy but possibly deadly diets, we obviously need to look at homemade pet diets. Since the tainted dog food atrocities of 2007, commercially prepared pet foods have come under fire again and again. Just take a look at a 2010 update on the recall...

http://www.petfoodsettlement.com/

And the list of offending companies, it is 17 pages long.

The '07 pet food scare and the information that followed were major turning points for pet owners the world over. Many of us started home cooking our pet's food and we haven't looked back since. Even so, you need to be careful what you include in your pet's diet, especially if you are feeding a raw diet.

We like most of the vegetables and fruits in homemade raw diets but still worry about the uncooked meat. I deal with so many compromised immune patients that if exposed to one of these bacteria they would probably perish. Be aware that raw fish, especially salmon, may harbor parasites that are dangerous for dogs and liver fed in large amounts can possibly lead to Vitamin A toxicity.

Cooked bones may splinter and puncture or obstruct the digestive tract. Even raw bones can cause problems. Weight-bearing bones from cows and pigs are very dense and can easily injure a dog's teeth by causing slab fractures of the teeth. If you are thinking of switching to a raw diet make the change gradual. Give your animal an opportunity to adjust to the change. Any abrupt change in diet can cause diarrhea and other stomach upsets.

Eating and feeding certain raw vegetables can also damage the thyroid gland causing enlargement (goiter) leading to the reduction of thyroid hormones and iron deficiency.

Possibly offensive Vegetables include:

- Bok choy, broccoli, brussel sprouts, cabbage, cauliflower, garden kress, kale, kohlrabi, mustard, mustard greens, radishes, rutabagas, soy, soy milk, soybean oil, soy lecithin, soy anything, tempe, tofu, turnips.

Minor offenders include:

- Bamboo shoots, millet, peaches, peanuts, pears, pine nuts, radishes, spinach, strawberries, and sweet potatoes.

These all are referred to as Goitrogenic and if served uncooked can possibly be harmful. If you are feeding a Raw Diet and want to include any of these food items make sure they are cooked first before serving. Again, beware of soy products, raw or cooked.

Table scraps have been a staple in many pets' diets ever since dogs and cats first took their place as human companions. Most people don't like to waste 'left-overs' and sharing your food with your friends is a common practice, however, you need to realize that what may be good for you can possibly cause health problems for your animals.

Table scraps that are greasy and have a lot of fat can cause the production of excessive digestive enzymes which can inflame the pancreas leading to Pancreatitis. Signs include; bloody vomit and/or diarrhea which could cause dehydration and even death. Table scraps can also contain certain seasonings that can be lethal. Nutmeg has been known to cause tremors, seizures, and death in dogs. The thiosulphate present in cooked or raw onions can upset the digestive tract, cause hemolytic anemia, and even death. Garlic also contains Thiosulphate but in lesser amounts than onions.

Some folks think that raw eggs can add good nutrition; however, the avidin in raw egg whites can cause vitamin B deficiency, skin problems and can even skeletal deformities. There is also the possibility that e. coli or salmonella may be present in raw eggs.

Be careful of using certain carbohydrates because they can cause food allergies. Many human and animals should not eat wheat because they can have a wheat allergy called a gluten enteropathy. The same can be said about corn, corn meal products and flours.

195

We don't want to scare you away from "healthy diets" but you do need to know about the possible dangers involved. If you feed your pets home prepared diets, make sure you research your possible ingredient choices thoroughly.

You also need to know all that is involved in serving those ingredients both raw and cooked. Our modern day pets need all the help they can get to survive their human induced genetics. A complete diet, properly prepared is one way to help.

Healthfully Yours,
Dr. Al Plechner DVM & David Spangenburg

Soybean Products, Their Nutritive Value and Possible Health Implications

Soybean ingestion has been shown to definitely cause health hazards in people especially in human infants which is where the use of soybean milk started here in the United States. Soy milk was first used for infants in 1909, by Dr. Ruhrah, a pediatrician. It was a used as a substitute for breast milk or cow milk that caused the infants severe gastrointestinal problems (upset stomach and intestines.)

From the 1940's to the 1960's, clinical studies have reported vitamin A, K and B12, and zinc, iron and calcium deficiencies in Soy milk. It's easy to realize how these deficiencies might cause anemia, osteoporosis and metabolic problems with the continued use of soybean milk, or soybeans in general.

Hardly any of this research has been done in animals, so I think you can begin to see why I worry about its effects on our pets. In 1939 it was found that soybeans included in poultry foods, interfered directly with thyroid function. It caused an enlargement of the thyroid gland called a goiter.

Can you imagine the possible ramifications, health wise, in a human or other animal that already has a thyroid disease? This might cause a "double whammy" of further complications for the patient.

Initially it was thought that normal growth patterns occurred with infants who consumed soy milk instead of breast or cow's milk. They actually discovered this was not the case due to the fact that soy was deficient in methionine. Methionine is an amino acid necessary for normal growth. How do you think this might affect the growth of your puppy or kitten?

Another growth inhibiting factor is that soy also contains a protein enzyme inhibitor which retards growth and metabolic function. Can you imagine the disastrous effect this might have on animals in general but especially with those animals that already have a digestive enzyme deficiency.

How can you determine if your dog has this kind of deficiency? Check the wrists of your dog and if they are bowed, your dog has this deficiency. It shows that the dog was unable to absorb calcium correctly as a puppy and now has lengthened ligaments. Any soybean product ingested could exacerbate the problem by allowing that dog to have not only anterior cruciate tears and ruptures but also the possibility of more malnutrition problems.

In the 1980's they discovered that soy contain phytates which actually bind calcium, zinc, iron and copper. Even though these elements are allowed to enter the blood stream, are not recognized by the body's receptors, and are excreted in the urine.

Taking only calcium into consideration, you need to realize that normally the body tries to keep a 1 to 1 or a 1 to 2 ratio of calcium to phosphorous. What does this mean to you and your pet?

If you or your pet has kidney problems, often there is phosphorous retention. If the soy is binding (stopping) the absorption of calcium and the phosphorous is high, in keeping with the proper ratio, the body will take the calcium directly from the bone, and if you continue the ingestion of the soy product, osteoporosis can occur in both you and your pet.

Soy contains high (possibly toxic) levels of manganese. In children, high levels of manganese are associated with learning disabilities, attention deficit disorders and behavioral problems. Do you think this might also affect your puppy or kitten when it comes to house breaking and many other behavior related problems? These facts about soy and its possible effects on infants, has been taken from a wonderful book written by Kaala T. Daniel, PHD, CCN, entitled, **The Whole Soy Story**. For more information, on the problems of eating soy, this is a must read book.

I created the first commercial hypoallergenic foods probably in the world more than 3 decades ago. I did use soy for the protein because at the time it was considered to be hypoallergenic also. It seemed to work for a while, but soon I realized that most of my patients, that had a need to change to a diet they had not been exposed to, had *Plechner Syndrome* and eventually developed allergies to the soy also. At that time I was not aware of all of the other possible problems that soy created.

Soybean problems have been well proven in people and, even though there have been limited studies, it obviously affects animals as well. Why take a chance. Until more is known about soy, I think it is best to be guided by whatever has been proven so far. If you and your pet are better able to sustain yourselves by eating soy, seemingly without all the inherent problems, then do so, however, please be warned that the liabilities appear to far outweigh the assets.

Healthfully Yours,
Dr. Al Plechner DVM & David Spangenburg

Weighing in on a Problem

In this age of runaway obesity, diabetes at epidemic proportions and heart disease leading the pack of the Top 15 Causes of Death in the US, weight loss is obviously a frequent topic at the water cooler. Uncontrolled weight gain in our pets and, sad to say, ourselves is thought to occur because there's just too much eating and not enough exercising. Why can't we lose the weight? We have Jenny Craig and other Weight Loss programs yammering from our TV's, pet food companies pushing their reduced calorie kibble and raw diets even Mickey D's is slipping apples into their Kid's Meals. For some of us *critters*, nothing seems to work.

The fact is that there are some animals and people that have tried to do everything right and still have failed to lose even an ounce. It seems like no matter what they do, (or have done for them) they just can't shed the fat. People write in all the time asking, "What can *we* do, when we've done everything else?" Sometimes, in cases of continued obesity, you need to have your health care professional (animal or human) check the patient's thyroid hormone level.

If the T4 level is checked and found to be normal they shouldn't stop there. Why not also check the T3 level which is the actual "active" hormone level? This is a must, due to the fact that if the T4 (stored Thyroid) level is high and the T3 (active thyroid) levels is normal or low, your pet and/or yourself may have a cortisol imbalance that prevents the T4 storage from transferring the storage into the active T3. This will cause obesity, no matter how little you or your pet eats or however hard you exercise. And no, a lap band will *not* be the answer for either of you.

Often, both T3 and T4 are normal. How can this be? My dog and I have uncontrolled weight gain, our heart rate is often slow; we both are lethargic and chill easily. Oh, oh, sounds to me like the time has come to measure estrogen levels from the inner layer adrenal cortex.

First of all, the inner layer adrenal cortex secretes estrogen in *both females and males*. If the estrogen is in excess, it creates a reverse T3 hormone that binds (blocks) the receptor sites so your body does not recognize the thyroid hormones. Therefore, you and your pet become hypothyroid (low thyroid production) even with normal thyroid hormone levels because the elevated estrogen levels have made them unavailable for the body to use.

You need to have an endocrine/immune system, blood serum panel done to be able to correct the weight gain, otherwise all the restricted diets, all the exercise, all the weight loss gimmicks in the world that you or your pet may try will not help you lose weight. Besides being frustrating, it is extremely unhealthy and in a number of cases, downright deadly.

You need to have your health care professional perform the simple endocrine/ immune blood serum panel, so the imbalance can be corrected so that it is possible to achieve a normal weight while following a proper diet and exercise program. If you really are normal but overweight due to eating incorrectly, then weigh your food and the food you give to your pet. Both of you need to eat more vegetables and fruits. Definitely do not eat or feed carbohydrates at night because it will definitely become "table muscle" (a huge belly) while you are both sleeping.

It is a good thing to know that dry pet food has "three times" the calories of wet food! If you're feeding "dry" add fresh vegetables and/or fruit to a lesser volume of dry food. Short of time? Cook up a great stew on *your* weekend and keep in the fridge to be added as needed. Eating is a very enjoyable and necessary function for us all, animal and human alike. Reducing obesity in both your pet and yourselves will help both of you to live a happier, healthier and longer life.

Healthfully Yours,
Dr. Al Plechner DVM & David Spangenburg

Antioxidants, What They are and How They Bum Out Free Radicals

Antioxidant, we have all heard the term being used but what are they and what do they really do? An antioxidant is a substance that protects normal body cells from the damage done by free radicals (a highly reactive atom or group of atoms with an unpaired electron).

How do free radicals occur? When the body's metabolism is converting food to energy, oxygen can be added to an element or compound causing it lose electrons (oxidation) which creates the Free radicals. Free radicals have been implicated in the changing of the structure of normal cells causing catastrophic disorders, like heart diseases, auto-immunity, cancer and many other severe disorders.

Each of the antioxidants has a function and they work together to protect each other forming an antioxidant network. When any one of these antioxidants finds a free radical, the antioxidant combines with the free radicals, engulfs it and incorporates it within itself.

Each of these antioxidant networks has their own job to do. They are fat soluble, like vitamin A, vitamin D, and vitamin E and seem to only effect the surface of many cells that are fat soluble and made of a fat called lipid.

The inside of the cells are water based so that usually, only water based antioxidants, can get into the cell itself, like Vitamin C. However it has been discovered that the antioxidant, lipoic acid, can do its job not only within the cell and also on its surface as well.

Although I may not be qualified to extol on all the good benefits of antioxidants, I do know they can make a difference with estrogen inhibitors. I have researched the adverse effects of elevated estrogen, which can be very damaging to the body's systems. Many of these antioxidants appear to reduce the elevated adrenal estrogen with their estrogen inhibitors.

There are apparently hundreds of naturally occurring antioxidants that are manufactured in the body and also occur in foods and supplements. The antioxidants that occur in the body come from vitamin A, vitamin E, vitamin C, Coenzyme Q, and many others. Many of the following fruits and vegetables contain antioxidants plus estrogen inhibitors...

- Berries, broccoli, cabbage, citrus fruits, figs, grapes, green beans, melons, millet, onions, onions, pineapple , squashes, tapioca, and wheat flower...all contain estrogen inhibitors and antioxidants......

However...

- Apples, cherries, dates and pomegranates

...do not

You or your pet may have an allergy to some of these, if so, their value to you or your pet may be greatly reduced. Always remember, no matter how healthy the food or supplement may be, even if it is totally natural, it can also be harmful to you or your pet. Look for signs on your pet's body and/or listen to your own. In this negatively altered environment, being aware will help you to be forewarned.

Healthfully Yours,
Dr. Al Plechner DVM & David Spangenburg

Trace Minerals, it's the Little Things That Count

Micronutrients also known as trace minerals; have existed throughout the earth for more than 13 million years. They are natural products, created by the actions of the earth that offer profound benefits for our pets and us. Unlike carbon, hydrogen, nitrogen, and oxygen, elements common in organic molecules, these alimental elements are inorganic nutritive substances that must be consumed and absorbed by animals or plants to nourish their whole health and wellness and to support and maintain their biochemical processes.

These essential micronutrients, which include; sodium, zinc, iodine, magnesium, calcium, and potassium, were once plentiful in deposits buried deep within the earth's soil and rocks. Safely stored in protected layers across the globe, they steadily released their essence into the food chain via vegetal conduits sustaining the flora and the fauna of earth's growing garden.

This give and take functioned well throughout the centuries, however, as the alpha fauna numbers grew to unsustainable levels, uncompromising and progressively more destructive modern farming techniques Drew these nutritive rich layers to the surface to be washed away by excessive irrigation and exposed to the scouring wind. As Jeremy Rifkin points out in his book, *The Hydrogen Economy*,

"Traditional farming relied on the planting of diversified crops that attracted a range of insects, some of which are natural enemies of insect pests. Eliminating crop diversity in favor of monoculture crops left the fields without the beneficial insects, and crops became more vulnerable to insect pests, requiring a steady rise in the use of pesticides. Much of the sprayed pesticide runs off into the groundwater and becomes a major source of water pollution in every agricultural region of the world.

The pesticides also destroy the remaining soil. The soil contains millions of microscopic bacteria, fungi, algae, and protozoa, as well as worms and arthropods. These organisms

maintain the fertility and structure of the soil. Pesticides destroy these organisms and their complex habitats, hastening the process of soil depletion and erosion. American farms lose more than four billion tons of topsoil annually, much of it because of the high-tech farming practices introduced over the past half century.

By the 1970s, the U.S. had lost more than one-third of its agricultural topsoil. The depletion and erosion, in turn, have required the use of ever-increasing amounts of petrochemical fertilizers to maintain agricultural output. Marginal returns have set in. More and more energy inputs are required to produce smaller gains in net energy yield...

Moreover, high energy agriculture is now a major contributor to global warming. Reliance on petrochemical fertilizers has increased the release of nitrous oxide, a potent global warming gas."

Once bared to these and other devastating forces, these fragile deposits were leeched from their safe harbors and continuingly squandered by questionable actions. Turning the global garden into an environmentally damaged wasteland, teetering on the edge of extinction, devoid of earth's rewards and filled with examples of man's remorseless arrogance and supercilious nature, creating, what we call, a *Medical Ice Age*

.As **Wikipedia** points out, these micronutrient deficiencies are extensive and globally pervasive...

"...50% of world cereal soils are deficient in zinc and 30% of cultivated soils globally are deficient in iron. Steady growth of crop yields during recent decades (in particular through the Green Revolution) compounded the problem by progressively depleting soil micronutrient pools."

...and adds that.

"In general, farmers only apply micronutrients when crops show deficiency symptoms, while micronutrient deficiencies

decrease yields before symptoms appear. Some common farming practices (such as liming acid soils) contribute to widespread occurrence of micronutrient deficiencies in crops by decreasing the availability of the micronutrients present in the soil. Also, extensive use of glyphosate (broad-spectrum systemic herbicide*) is increasingly suspected to impair micronutrient uptake by crops, especially with regard to manganese, iron and zinc."*

In 1931, the **Ford Foundation** reported that **modern day farming techniques account for loss of many nutrients in foods that Americans eat.**

"Due to intensive farming practices, poor crop management, increasing uses of pesticides, erosion and other abusive factors, the crops that are produced from these soils, are seriously depleted of nutrients"

In 1931 (!), the **Ford Foundation** found this to be a very critical alert and now, 79 years and an *"Inconvenient Truth"* later, don't you think it is far more critically important to find out just how many of our animal's and our own ailments are due to a micronutrient deficiency. Just how *healthy* are our diets when our supposedly 'healthy' foods have been grown in "nutritionally deficient" soil?

Long before the **Ford Foundation** report, we began to see regional health outbreaks that made us aware of the growing deficiencies. During the '20's and '30's, an area in the Northwestern U.S. around the Great Lakes began to be called the "goiter belt" because of a high incidence of the Thyroid disease. In Michigan alone, glacial melting flushed the iodine from the soil and water table causing 40% of the population to suffer from the disease.

To remedy the outbreak, salt manufacturers followed an already proven Swiss practice of adding sodium iodide or potassium iodide to table salt and iodized salt began to be sold commercially in Michigan on May 1, 1924 and by the end of 1924, Morton Salt Company began distributing iodized salt all across the country.

Even though iodized salt is the most cost-effective measure available to improve the general health worldwide. Iodine deficiency still affects about two billion people globally and is the leading preventable cause of mental retardation.

So we're feeding ourselves and our pets "healthy" foods but are we really providing and receiving all those necessary micronutrients now that they are no longer occurring naturally in the soils? More and more trace mineral deficiency related health problems are finding their way into our news cycles.

Copper helps in the maintenance of artery walls. Incidences of aneurisms increase in areas where copper is deficient in the soil. Pigs raised in tight cement enclosures develop a respiratory disease called "thumps" due to an iron deficiency anemia. If raised naturally, on dirt containing iron, this would never happen.

Even though it is hard to imagine, our once fertile soils are becoming completely deficient of these small but mighty trace elements and minerals. The causes are due to being overworked, misused and/or broken down agriculturally and environmentally. The soils in general have been depleted, however, there are still a few deposits whose natural potency is so rich that their rarity almost makes them more valuable than gold.

I have used Trace Minerals for many years. Not only for treating; dogs, cats, horses and birds but I have also used it to supplement my own diet for over 30 years

Healthfully Yours,
Dr. Al Plechner DVM & David Spangenburg

Trace Minerals, Things Just Keep Getting Better

It's been nearly 25 years now, since they published my findings, about trace minerals, in the November 1985 Issue of *Pet Age Magazine*. Since that time, we have come to realize that a lack of micronutrients has played a tremendous role in the development of modern day diseases. Even worse, I have a sinking feeling that we are really just seeing, the "tip of the iceberg".

It is obvious that the roots of many of the physical diseases we are seeing today are firmly entrenched in the nutritionally deficient soils our foodstuffs are "grown" in. Sure, vegetables today grow large with thick skins, bright colors and long shelf life, however, they are lacking some simple natural ingredients, mainly, the trace minerals that our bodies desperately need to function as they were designed to.

The "farming industry's" business sense tells them, people buy vegetables like they buy their cars because of their looks. People buy large, brightly colored produce that has no blemishes and seems to stay "fresh" longer. So the "industry" has geared their factory farming techniques to produce just that type of produce. It doesn't seem to matter to them that the product they're selling has all the nutrients (and even the taste) that "wax fruit" offers...zero, zilch, nada.

It also doesn't seem to matter to them that their chemical fertilizers, insecticides, weed killers and other "scorched earth" techniques have stripped the soil of the desperately needed, natural vitamins and health sustaining trace minerals. The "bottom line" is that these ruthless methods make it easier to produce cosmetically improved food stuffs that store longer, are safer to ship and have the shelf life (and all of the nutrition) of a plaster clown at a thrift store.

As you admire the size of that melon or the color of those egg plants you need to be aware that micronutrient deficiencies are causing worldwide diseases in people and animals. These trace minerals are critical elements that direct important bodily functions. They are the very keys that allow other vitamins, nutrients and supplements, to pass through the cell membrane to enhance the production of energy and oxygen for the body to use to help fight off disease.

Since my initial exploration of the possible uses of micronutrients in the late 70's and early 80's, a remarkable amount of painstaking academic research has been completed on this natural, calcium enriched, trace mineral packed and hydrothermally ionized montmorillinite clay created through natural processes by the earth.

N.A.S.A.'s Manned Space Center funded a study by **Cal Tech** Scientist, Dr. Benjamin H. Ershoff. It seems our Astronauts were developing bone density loss and rapid onset osteoporosis due to the long periods they spent in zero gravity on extended space flights. Led by Dr. Ershoff, **N.A.S.A.**'s scientists conducted extensive studies on calcium related compounds including calcium montmorillonite. These comprehensive tests included studies of animals who were experiencing calcium reduction similar to space conditions.

Their studies proved that consuming calcium montmorillonite living clay actually increased bone density and muscle tissue; whereas those that were given typical calcium supplements showed no improvement of the bone loss! Ccalcium montmorillonite was shown to fuel the body to stimulate healthy bone mass retention and tissue strength. It has been used daily by all of NASA's Astronauts ever since.

During this time, other scientific investigations were being done by Dr. Paul A. LaChance. Administering this clay to male rats, hamsters, mice, miniature pigs, kangaroos and other mammals, over a period of time, also proved positively that normalization and re-calcification of bone density did occur, only when calcium montmorillinite was administered.

In study after study, it has been proven and documented that this simple, power packed compound is 100% effective! Why not apply this same clay, to millions of people and animals that suffer from many types of bone density loss or an inability to absorb other forms of calcium? This clay has high levels of calcium in a form that is "chelated" which allows the body to absorb only the trace minerals and amounts that it actually needs.

In my profession the use of a calcium supplements in a large breed puppy is often thought to be dangerous. Some Animal Health Professionals believe that excess calcium may actually create excess bone growth with a bone malady being the end result. This will not happen with this product as the chelated calcium will only be absorbed and used, if the puppy's bone growth dictates it.

Bone loss is very common with chronic kidney disease in people and animals. The kidney disease often causes the retention of phosphorus and as the body tries to maintain a 1 to1 or 1 to 2 ratios between calcium and phosphorus, the body automatically removes the calcium from the bones and ligaments. The high level of calcium contained in this living clay will help stop this. Research facilities in Asia; have scientifically proven that this clay also causes elevated blood urea to be concentrated out of the blood and into the intestines which allows it to be excreted much quicker.

Dr. Howard E. Lind has done a large number of successful studies showing the anti-bacterial effects of calcium montmorillinite and its ability to neutralize toxins. These results are very important in people and animals that are sensitive to certain antibiotics. At the same time, this remarkable product will help neutralize toxins that may occur in our foods or the foods that we feed our animals. This is an important fact considering the large number of pet food and human food stuff recalls that seem to be increasing yearly.

Other health benefits that this ionically charged compound offers include; relief from Acid Reflux and/or Irritable Bowel Syndrome, due to the high level of chelated calcium and the external use of this clay, as a paste, has a wonderful healing effect while adding micronutrients back into the outer layer of skin referred to as keratin. Many world famous healers have use this product internally and externally for thousands of years.

I have been in practice as a veterinarian and animal health researcher for over 50 years of my life and I am totally sincere in my recommendation for this amazing trace mineral clay. I have seen it in action first hand and have even used it personally.

We really do not know the extent of diseases that are caused by micronutrient deficiencies. My suggestion is that you try edible calcium montmorillonite living clay for your animal and for yourself and your family and feel the difference for yourself.

Healthfully Yours,
Dr. Al Plechner DVM & David Spangenburg

Changing your Pets Diet,
Could Hurt More Than Their Appetite

You've done a lot of research, spent a lot of money but you finally found something that is healthy for them to eat. And, they even like it! Just when you think it's safe to go into the dog food aisle, you hear that there's a new diet available and it's supposed to be even healthier and nutritious than their present food. Ah, but you know those Pet food manufacturers are always looking for new avenues to attract pet owners. Adding new ingredients that appeal to the owner's human appetites, which may not be so healthy for your pet's body.

Most of you know, you never switch new foods immediately. It is best to add a small amount of the new food to the old food gradually over 7 days before totally switching over to the new food. This will allow your pet's digestive system to adjust to the new diet with little to no adverse reactions. Your pet's response to the new food depends upon the enzyme production by your pet's pancreas.

The pancreas is a significant organ that determines the amount of digestive enzyme produced to deal with the various foods your pet ingests. The exocrine pancreatic enzyme production is designed for the breakdown and digestion of proteins, carbohydrates and fats. Each time a new food is introduced to your pet's system, changes in the enzyme production from their pancreas also occurs. There may be a delay before the pancreas adapts and adjusts its enzyme production to the new diet. During this time, diarrhea is likely to occur.

If your pet seems to react poorly to different proteins and carbohydrates, it could be because the food is badly formulated and/or the ingredients are inferior. If the quality of ingredients or the formula is not in question, it is possible (actually quite likely) that your pet has food sensitivity. If this is the case, your pet is suffering from a hormone antibody imbalance, which is causing this reaction to the food.

212

If this is the case, changing foods, trying to find one food that agrees with your pet is fruitless and is slowly but surely pushing your pet to a point where nothing on earth can be eaten by them without causing horrible side effects. Yes, you might find a new food that your pet will tolerate for a while, but within 3 to 4 months, your pet's deregulated immune system will be creating antibodies to this food which will start causing adverse reactions all over again. If you don't identify and control this hormone antibody imbalance, the day will come, when your affected pet will not be able to consume any food on earth.

Feline reaction to foods not only causes inflammation of the pancreas thereby damaging the exocrine function (external secretion) of the gland. Adverse reactions can include damage the endocrine function (internal secretion) of the pancreas, which effects the production of insulin. This may cause the cat to develop high blood sugar. This condition is referred to as Diabetes Mellitus. This can be a transient or permanent change in the cat, depending on the amount of cell damage.

To determine if your cat has this type of diabetes, the pancreatic enzymes need to be checked along with the blood glucose and the white blood cells called eosinophil. Eosinophils respond to an allergic reaction by inducing a histamine release. Their percentage should not exceed 3 % in a normal cat or dog. If this level is over 3 %, the cat or dog may be allergic to the diet, and a hypoallergenic diet should be considered. Be sure to make certain that your pet is free of internal parasites, because they also can cause an elevation of eosinophils.

Once this has been done, and the eosinophil and pancreatic enzymes count returns to the normal range and the inflammatory damage to the pancreas was only temporary, often the production of insulin will return to normal, and the cat may no longer be diabetic.

Often a bladder inflammation may occur due to food allergy causing cystitis, with blood. Skin inflammation is also another sign of a food allergy. Most of the inflammation occurs in the flaps of the ears, the feet and the skin of the ventral (lower) abdomen. Areas around the eyes and face may also be included.

I should note that mast cells contain histamine and are concentrated in these regions. If the inflammatory reaction is more severe in one ear or the other, this is probably due to a greater concentration of mast cells in one ear as opposed to the other. If a urinalysis is done, and the urine is normal, the dog or cat has a hormone antibody imbalance causing the reaction which is ignited by the food.

The pet food industry continues to cash in on the need for "hypoallergenic" diets. Their cost effective method is to use "hydrolyzed protein", which is protein that has been broken down so its particles are, supposedly, too tiny to arouse the immune system defenses. This type of protein is basically a flavor enhancer which contains MSG. MSG in this form does not have to be listed on the label but if you see "hydrolyzed soy" or any other "hydrolyzed" products listed; you're feeding your pets (and yourself) MSG.

Many of these "hypoallergenic" diets are also free of grains and contain sweet potatoes and other food stuffs which are high in estrogen. Excess estrogen can lead to estrogen dominance which can cause; behavioral problems, urinary incontinence, hormonal skin disorders and other miseries for your pet, including catastrophic diseases.

The food industry is also pandering to the "organic" food market. You need to realize that although "organic" is on the label, "organic" primarily means, cleanly grown without pesticides and petrochemicals. There is a new concern for all of us, in this age of our "corporately controlled food industry". The danger is not just what is sprayed on the plants it is also, what kind of seeds are they using to grow the plants. More and more of organically (and non-organic) grown products are coming from genetically_modified seeds. These "modified" grains and vegetables are also being fed to our meat producing animals. This may not seem important to you now, but I guarantee it will be significant for your offspring.

For a more in-depth look at genetically modified seed products check out our article, *Sowing the Seeds of Disaster,* in the **The Human Factor, Health in the New Millennium** chapter.

Make it a challenge to be aware and try to avoid all of these genetically modified food products. Who knows what effects they will have on the genetics of our planet and all living things on it, in the years to come.

Healthfully Yours,
Dr. Al Plechner & David Spangenburg

Breeding

Good Breeding, Gone Bad

The crowd cheers as she crosses the stage, her body lean after months of exercise and measured amounts of just the right foods to attain and maintain the correct muscle mass and structure. Her silken hair radiant under the stage lights, is styled and teased to perfection. As she advances to the podium it's like a symphony of movement; muscles flexing and contracting, skin tightening and relaxing, each step rehearsed and practiced hundreds of times over and over again.

She performs like an automaton driven by the spirit of a nymph, sleek and sure with just a wisp of urgency. Her face set in a designed smile that shines from her eyes like a ray of sunlight just escaping a mountain's peak. She works the audience like an elegant actress, shining even brighter in their growing adulation. Trained, poised, pampered and elegant, a more regal bitch you've never seen.

She's a champion, as were her mother and father, grandmother, grandfather and so on, and so on down her long, long line. She is definitely blooded, a dog of good breeding, precisely pedigreed and completely without function. A dog designed to be perfection, nothing more and certainly nothing less. She carries the delicately balanced genes of physical faultlessness, straining mightily to maintain their equilibrium, just one step away from a possible mutant malignancy.

216

Designer Animals, Have Become the Rage

Rage, is a sign of our times. Frustration, desperation...traffic, there are many things that can push a human over the edge but what leads animals into acts of rage? The RAGE syndrome in animals is simply; extreme, unprovoked and unpredictable behavior that often leads from a "dominance stare" to full-blown attack on people (including their beloved owner) forgoing the intermediate stages of standard "dominance aggression".

When you think of rage in dogs most people would nod their heads and say, "Pit Bulls and Dobermans, yep, those dogs can rage!" Well they'd be surprised to know that Springer Spaniels are the most likely breed for the 'sudden bite'. They are actually known for the *"Springer Rage Syndrome"*. Some say it's "breed dominance aggression" others say there's a genetic factor influencing the syndrome. We tend to lean towards the center, they are both contributing factors.

We are experiencing more and more of this type of aggression as the 'genetic ice age' continues to grow. As the gene pool continues to creep closer and closer, a hormone antibody imbalance comes along for a "free ride" causing the RAGE syndrome to occur.

For healthy survival of the domesticated species (both canine and feline), the genes that are being passed on to the next generation, need to come from different gene pools. Breeding practices that are based on human needs and human desires are pushing the genetic envelope to a breaking point.

Working or hunting dogs are two breeds that are still bred for purpose. So many others are designer animals where breeding has very little to do with the function and health of that animal. They are bred to fit specifications that are more quirky than quality. It almost seems like they are being bred to a name.

We have Bagel Hounds, Boxerdoodles, Whoodles, Schnoodles, Puggles, Chugs and Brats. They sound more like snacks than dog breeds. Ah, but isn't that the human way. Who else would take the complexity of breeding and turn it into whimsy. Taking genes and putting them in a blender? It's like mixing strange cocktails. Who knows what you'll end up with, a *Doodleman* Pinscher with anger issues?

This kind of tampering with structure genetics is bound to create difficulties. RAGE comes from a endocrine/immune hormone antibody imbalance that allows the adrenal estrogen and androgen to be very high which, in turn, may cause a Jeckle/Hyde effect. The high estrogen binds (blocks) the thyroid hormone and reduces the mucous membrane antibody (IgA).

This imbalance can cause the pet to become food sensitive which, in turn, can trigger it to be horribly aggressive with its family, if the wrong food or food snack is given. If this RAGE presents itself in your pet, be very careful with foods and have your health care professional do an EI blood test. Not only to identify the imbalance but also to control it so that no human gets hurt and the pet does not have to be euthanized.

What happens if an 'imbalanced' RAGE pet is fed a certain type of food that triggers a reaction? Many years ago a friend of Al, who was not only a fine dog trainer but also an animal behaviorist, asked him to assist with a client's dog. As Al remembers it, the trainer was working with a 4 year old Labrador retriever that was aggressively biting the husband, wife...and the child.

After several weeks of training, it seems that the aggression still prevailed. This is typical with a dog suffering from the imbalance. Training will be expensive and always prove to be of little help. Once the imbalance has been identified and controlled, the owners will be able to train their own dog.

Knowing that changing the food, might help stop the aggression, Al suggested a change of diet, until actual testing could be done. This was in the 80's and he had just created the first Lamb and Rice diet for the original owners of the *Nature's Recipe* brand. Al suggested changing over to this diet. Almost immediately, the aggression stopped because the imbalanced immune system had not yet become reactant to the lamb and rice.

The frightening displays of RAGE abated for over two weeks, but reoccurred suddenly when a left over piece of steak was accidentally given to the dog by the child. One half hour later the dog bit the owner so badly, she had to go to the emergency room.

Cats suffer from the same imbalance but seem not to react as badly as dogs. Still, the imbalance can be serious enough that a cat will stalk and bite their owner. Signs of the condition can appear less serious in cats and present itself only as 'annoyance', like when you try to pet your cat on the back and they hiss and/or turn around and try to bite you.

70% of the cats with this imbalance, will display a slim red line on their gums were the gum meets the enamel. Al refers to this as a gingival flare. In dogs, this sign is only present in 30% of the cases. It is important to realize that even though gingival flare is not always present in the RAGE syndrome in your dog or cat, the endocrine/immune imbalance almost always is!

Occasionally you might see a "Charlie Manson" canine. It is a rare occurrence but it can happen that a dog is born in a mentally challenged state, dangerously teetering on the edge of RAGE. The slightest emotional fluctuation can set them off. Their EI panel is normal but they still present a serious threat to humans and other animals. In this instance, the owners will have a very difficult decision to make.

There are also times when an animal can be pushed into an accidental but still severe bite. Al had a client with a sweet little Dachshund. A neighbor child was playfully chasing it and fell on the dog.

The small dog was hurt and reacted quite normally by biting the child. Incensed that her child was badly bitten, the neighbor wanted the dog to be put down. Thankfully calmer minds prevailed and the animal was not euthanized for merely defending itself.

Healthfully Yours,
Dr. Al Plechner & David Spangenburg

The Dangers of Gene Bending

There was a time, many years ago, when dog breeders had a mission. Pure and healthy breeding to promote their breeds natural function. Today's breeds are a product of designer breeding, mixing traits and structure to insure size, coat colors and other surface appearances. Producing litters like lines of fashion with no thought about the possible genetic consequences.

These proliferating practices have continued exponentially for many decades. The results are, ersatz breeds which are, in realty, genetic cripples, predestined by Mother Nature not to prosper. These unfortunate animals are condemned to poor health and shortened life spans. "Holes" have been "dug" for many breeds, Inescapable destinies most may not be able to avoid. However, there is still hope for these unfortunate cash and crash casualties.

Often when a breed becomes popular, a number of irresponsible breeders jump on board because they think that they will make lots of money by being fur peddlers. The sad truth is that they can. A good example of this inhuman practice is the beautiful but medically troubled, cavalier King Charles spaniels. I love the breed, but they are plagued by health problems.

By the age of only 5 years, over one half of all King Charles spaniels' hearts are afflicted by mitral valve disease (MVD). This terminal illness afflicts almost all Cavaliers by 10 years of age. If that wasn't bad enough, Syringomyelia (a disorder of the brain and spinal cord, is persistently pervasive in the breed. The disorder attacks the spinal cord and the brain and can possibly lead to paralysis. Either of these genetic defects are a deadly price to pay just for "points" in a dog show.

You cannot breed perfection! "Gene bending" comes at too high a price. Is perfection worth possible allergies, autoimmunity and even cancer? The struggles of a low sperm count, early abortion and absorption of the fetuses can all possibly be controlled and eventually corrected through the identification of this genetically induced hormone antibody imbalances, the *Plechner Syndrome*. A simple hormone antibody test should be done on the prospective parents before the actual breeding is performed.

There are too many cavalier King Charles spaniels owners who are now dealing with the deadly effects of "gene bending". It is far better to discern the cause of the problem before the effects ravage the innocent sufferers. A proper blood test should be done on both parents before they are allowed to even get close, let alone, breed. You may find that you need to breed to a different mate to dilute out any possible genetic problems.

Have your CKCSs tested. If a problem is detected, a protocol of proper hormone balancing has been developed which will deal directly with the source of the imbalance and not just treat the effects. There is a way to create a breed for the future, free of these deadly health problems. If you are interested, you may want to check out... http://**www.drplechner.com**

Healthfully Yours,
Dr. Al Plechner & David Spangenburg

Nutritional Needs for your Pregnant Pet and her Offspring

Beginning the 5th week of your dog or cat's pregnancy, you should add a third meal, at midday, to your pet's diet. If they're not interested you shouldn't force the matter. Personally, I believe you should keep the protein, carbohydrate and fat in the same ratio, however, your vet may not agree. The most important thing to remember is that you need to increase your pet's nutritional intake without needlessly increasing their weight. This augmentation to their diet is designed to help the embryos to develop to their maximum potential, in health and fitness.

It is advisable at this time, to supplement their regular diet with a calcium/magnesium compound which also includes montmorillinite mineral clay. This essential (trace) mineral supplement, which is readily available online and at health or whole food stores, should be given twice daily and continued two weeks past weaning. This should guarantee that the mother does not develop low blood calcium, which could lead to undue shaking and possibly even, seizures. This malady is typically found in dogs with excessively large litters no matter what the mother's size or stature.

If the litter is fairly large, it is wise to divide the newborns into two separate groups. This will allow them the opportunity to nurse at separate times thereby guaranteeing a more even distribution of nutrition for the offspring. You must realize that 90 % of fatalities that occur with normal offspring are due to lack of nutrition and a reduction of their body temperature. Proper bedding for mom and her offspring is also very important. They need to be cozy but they also need room to maneuver. Certain large breeds mistakenly lie on their offspring, which may end in death

Puppies' immune systems are not fully developed when they are born and so are susceptible to any and all infectious diseases and conditions. Nature has developed an answer to this dangerous and possibly fatal inequity It has devised a way for the mother dog to pass on immunities *her* immune system has created in response to diseases which she has been recently vaccinated against and/or exposed to. This "passive immunity" is passed on to the puppies through the "first milk" produced by their mother.

Colostrum, as it is called, is a highly concentrated mixture of large protein antibody molecules, nutrients, vitamins and electrolytes. It flows only the first 24 - 48 hours following the birth of the litter. These first feedings are extremely important because once the colostrum stops, they will receive no more of their mother's antibodies. Colostrum, however, can be bought commercially in Bovine (Cow) form and, thankfully, its medicinal effects are universal so the puppies will continue to benefit from its extended use.

Once the puppies or kittens have reached 2 to 2 ½ weeks of age, you should start helping the mother to meet their nutritional demands by supplementing her breast feedings with baby sized meats for the young ones. Follow that up soon by mixing in a nutritionally balanced and natural canned food. If you allow the offspring to nurse after 3 weeks of age, it may be very damaging to their mother and her overall health.

Once the young ones are on solid food you should inspect the mother's breasts. If they continue to fill up with milk, it may be necessary to either milk the glands manually, allow short term nursing's or have your veterinarian give the mother an injection to halt milk production.

If this is your pet's (and your) first litter, it is always a good idea to ask your veterinary for any and all helpful directions. Personally, I like to do an exploratory X-ray at 6 ½ weeks into the pregnancy. It's important to check the size of the pelvic outlet in relation to the head size of each of the offspring. It is also very important to know, approximately, how many offspring are present and if said offspring are in the normal position for a safe and easy delivery.

When the new mother nears the end of term it is good to occasionally check her temperature. Many times, one to three days before labor begins, the mother's temperature may drop to below 100 degrees. When this happens it's a good possibility that labor may soon start.

One more important note, if labor does begin, and an amnion (a small green bubble) presents itself with no offspring, the time has come to get your veterinarian involved.

Healthfully Yours,
Dr. Al Plechner DVM & David Spangenburg

The Gift That Keeps on Giving

I got genes, you got genes, even little puppies got genes. They are our inheritances. Passed down, through the ages, from generation to generation, they are the conduit of our heredity. Short or tall, black hair or blond, green eyes or blue, they predetermine many things about our existence. Dominant or recessive, active or passive they sometimes affect the following generation, sometimes they lay dormant until the next. The genetic information they convey can be a blessing or sometimes a curse.

When a genetic imbalance occurs in a bitch, a certain antibody may not pass through the placenta to her pups. This particular antibody, called IgA, is a blessing meant to protect all the mucous membranes in the puppy's body from disease. If this antibody is absent, it curses the affected pups with an ineffective immune system and places them at the mercy of many deadly invaders.

IgA protection covers the digestive, respiratory, and urogenital systems, all of the biological systems that contain mucosa membranes. If an IgA imbalance occurs, these delicate membranes have no defense against the myriad of toxic organisms that can invade the gut, including E. coli. This genetic inheritance "opens the gates" to allow all sorts of invading armies of germs to lay siege to the unprotected lungs, stomach, intestines, bowels, bladder etc. Sad to say, these occupying barbarians can prove to be deadly lethal to these innocent defenseless puppies.

The use of IV antibiotics is a fine "temporary fix" for the IgA antibody deficiency but once the IV antibiotic is discontinued and replaced with an oral form of antibiotic the symptoms (signs) will begin again. The immune deficiency will still be present and the IgA deficiency prevents the absorption of oral medications. You need to strike at these invaders at their stronghold, the minute hormonal imbalance in the endocrine system that has derailed the immune system to begin with, *Plechner Syndrome*.

If all antibiotics fail, have your veterinarian do a E1 blood panel test to determine the levels of cortisol, total estrogen and T3 and T4 (Thyroid) hormones on the puppy and begin the hormone replacement treatment (*Plechner Protocol*) immediately. Balancing these hormones will re-regulate the immune system including the B- Lymphocyte which will begin producing the needed proper IgA antibody.

This hormonal imbalance has been passed on, genetically, to the puppy. The simple E1 blood panel test will determine if the parents are deficient or not. If parents have hormonal imbalances in the same areas, the imbalance will be passive in them and will be concentrated and active in their offspring. If the parents have imbalances but in different areas of hormonal production, the imbalance will be diluted out and does not usually occur in the offspring. No matter what, the parents should definitely be tested if they are going to be bred again.

All of this pain can easily be avoided, merely by E1 testing, proposed parents, to determine if they are compatible or whether different mates should be used. Testing will help you identify the cause of many diseases, including; infertility, lost litters, allergies, autoimmunity and cancer.

This very simple blood test is currently being done only at **National Veterinary Diagnostic Services.** The blood sample info and mailing instructions can be found in the *E-I Blood Panel Instructions* section of this book. More information is available on my website; http://www.drplechner.com.

The "genetic hole" has already been dug. If you would like to find a better way to stop these unhappy genetics, it really is very simple and very effective and will allow you to breed healthy for the future. It is our duty to "protect the puppies".

Healthfully Yours,
Dr. Al Plechner DVM & David Spangenburg

Guaranteeing a Nutritionally Sound Bitch for Breeding

When it comes to healthy breeding the most important factor is having a healthy and nutritionally fit bitch. It is essential that the prospective mother have a complete, balanced, nutritional program that she can easily absorb and utilize. Increasing the protein, fat and carbohydrate is a good start but still may not be enough to prepare a bitch for pregnancy.

Many times a very moderate trypsin deficiency can be present which prevents the complete digestion of proteins, fats and carbohydrates. The "sludging effect" that occurs with this deficiency, will also bind all the fat soluble vitamins, A, D, and E. Whether they occur naturally in the food or are supplemented, this binding will prevent their absorption and further impair the bitch's ability to carry her embryos to a complete term.

Over the years I have found, while preparing a bitch for pregnancy, that even though you do your best to feed her better you cannot always feed her *healthy* because the ingredients of her foods are coming out of over worked and nutritionally depleted agricultural soils.

30 years ago I researched a premium calcium montmorillinite "living clay" deposit that was enriched hydrothermally by geological actions of nature. This edible nutraceutical clay contained (and still contains) all those dwindling micronutrients in a chelated form which means the body can easily absorb only what it actually needs. Another important feature of this specific clay is it contains a very strong negative ion. This element enhances the absorption of foods, supplements and vitamins through the cell wall into the mitochondria creating greater amounts of energy and oxygen to be produced.

In each instance of providing this "living clay" to a prospective bitch, they always seemed to carry better, definitely had more vigor and produced more offspring with considerably less infant mortality.

I also found that the mother and the puppy's coats were thicker and the colors more intense. Their bone growth was stronger and denser and since this "living clay" was chelated, there was no chance for over mineralization. More importantly, this particular premium calcium montmorillonite clay has been proven to neutralize pathogens, toxins, heavy metals and radiation.

Another important note is that I've found this same phenomenon not only in dogs, but also in cats, horses, birds, fish, wildlife and...humans. In this day and age when so many of our pet foods contain contaminated ingredients from foreign countries, I use this natural product for all of my family animals and members including myself. I also strongly suggest its use for all of the patients I treat and their parents and family members. You can find out more about this remarkable living clay at **Earth's Living™** Calcium Bentonite Green Clay Their website, **http://earthslivingclay.com/** explains all you need to know about calcium montmorillonite for animals and humans.

Before the breeding is to occur, it is also critical that you make sure that there are no intestinal parasites and merely testing the feces of the bitch will not guarantee that she is parasite free. Many times, a female with balanced endocrine and immune systems will produce anti parasite antibodies which will allow the bitch to shed most parasite infestations. However if there happens to be an endocrine-immune imbalance (*Plechner Syndrome*), the fecal test of this bitch may be devoid of parasite eggs, and still all her puppies can still be born with intestinal parasites. If this is the case, the bitch should be wormed prior to breeding.

I firmly believe that before you do *any* breeding, it is important to have your veterinarian do an E-I animal blood test to determine if either of the proposed parents has *Plechner Syndrome*. If allergy, autoimmunity and/or cancer occur in either of the dog's family history, it is a sure way of preventing any of these, possibly catastrophic, problems from being passed on to their offspring.

My studies have proven that if these various hormone antibody imbalances can be identified in the parents then a straight forward treatment protocol will put things right.

More importantly, this simple hormonal replacement therapy can assure that these defects will not be passed on to their offspring. For more information, please go to **http://www.drplechner.com** .

These are just some of my thoughts after 50 years of clinical veterinary practice.

Healthfully Yours,
Dr. Al Plechner DVM & David Spangenburg

Pet Allergies

What Your Pet's Body is Trying to Tell You

Food allergies affect many pets and determining their presence is not always easy because they may manifest themselves in numerous ways. Most commonly, a food allergy occurs in the digestive system of your pet. The clinical signs may vary; from excess gas production and mucous coating the stool, to vomiting and diarrhea with blood.

Blood is often a common clinical sign with frequent vomiting and diarrhea in your dog and cat due to the fact that the blood supply to the digestive tract is very close to the surface and bleeding can occur easily because of food allergy inflammation. If the food allergy goes unnoticed for an extended period, often the reaction will spread into the pancreas and liver.

It's important for you to remember if you change to a new food too quickly; the production of digestive enzymes in your pet's pancreas may be affected. If the nutrient change is a ratio overload, the pancreas may not be able to respond quickly enough with the needed extra enzymes. Your pet will be unable to breakdown the new food, causing a slugging affect to occur, resulting in diarrhea.

Quite often you can read the signs of food allergy on the second most commonly affected system, the integumentary system, better known as the skin. The regions of the skin most often affected (the impact areas) usually are the skin of; the ears, the face, the feet and the abdomen.

I became aware of this many years ago but was curious *why* the inflammation primarily occurred at these locations? I knew there were certain cells called mast cells which contain granules of histamine. I was also aware that when a pet has an allergic reaction, the mast cells release their histamine and inflammation occurs. These facts do not explain why the allergy signs are so selective in their areas of display.

230

Research autopsies gave me an opportunity to study mass cell distribution in dogs and cats who had suffered from severe food allergies. What I found was that mast cells were *concentrated* in the skin of the; ears, face, feet, abdomen, and also in the skin just above the base of the tail. I also found that the mast cell concentration might vary from the skin of one ear to the other as well as the skin around the eyes. This explains why one ear or the skin around one eye will be more inflamed than the other.

An easy way for you to decide if a food is allergenic for your pet is to have your health care professional inject a steroid into your pets system, which will last 5 to 7 days. Often, what will be used will be Vetalog, Kenalog or Triamcinolone.

If in 3 to 5 days there is *no improvement*, than the food is the problem and should be changed. If this is the case, you can go to my website; http://www.drplechner.com and look at an article on FOOD ELIMINATION.

Hypoallergenic diets are being replicated now by many pet food manufactures and are available in duck, fish, rabbit, lamb and venison all with white potatoes. You should try to avoid any of the manufactured pet foods that contain sweet potatoes. Sweet potatoes are high in estrogen and can cause increased inflammation which might aggravate the allergenic effects.

If the allergic reaction *improves* with the injection, an inhaled airborne mold or pollen may be the problem. In any event when allergies are present, whether foods or inhalants, it is a good bet that your pet has a hormone antibody imbalance that is easily identified with a simple blood test.

This brings us to the urinary system, the third most common system adversely affected by a food allergy. For this to occur *Plechner Syndrome* must be present. This cortisol imbalance is caused by a deficient or defective (lacking or inadequate) cortisol (disease fighting hormone) leading to an elevated adrenal estrogen that binds (blocks) the availability of thyroid hormone and reduces antibody production and protection.

The main antibody deficiency occurs in all the mucous membranes of the body, including the kidneys and bladder. This deficient antibody is called IgA, which stands for immunoglobulin

A. Food allergies occur when the IgA is deficient. The impact areas will usually show where ever this deficiency is present and you need to realize that certain foods can be damaging to any of the systems that need to be protected with normal IgA. When this imbalance is present, the kidneys and bladder may develop chronic disorders.

Cats are well known for having ongoing bladder problems due to this imbalance. Almost always, the medical effects are treated. They may even resort to removing the tip of the penis in a male cat. Even though, this may allow the passage of all end products created by the imbalance, the problem will remain until the imbalance is corrected. The female cat with her short, wide urethra will also pass the end products without surgery but will still have bladder infections or inflammations until the imbalance is corrected.

Adding further misery for the pet is the fact, that the low IgA in the gut also causes malabsorption. This prevents the oral medications from being absorbed into the bloodstream in the proper amounts to help treat the problem. The imbalance also allows carbohydrates to be absorbed more easily than proteins. Proteins help with acidifying the urine, while carbohydrates cause the urine to be alkaline.

Once this imbalance is in place, the urine may remain alkaline. This in turn allows the minerals contained in the urine, to separate and solidify out in alkaline urine in the kidneys and bladder. This reaction may be the basis for bladder and kidney stones.

Creating further concern for the imbalanced patient is the presence of elevated estrogen. This excessive estrogen causes inflammation of the cells that line all the arteries in the body, the endothelial cells. When this occurs, the inflammation causes an increased production of a mucous like secretion that originates from the medulla of the kidney. This increased mucous, plus the precipitation (solidifying) of minerals in the alkaline urine, can combine to produce a material, which has a tooth paste like consistency, which often causes a urinary obstruction in male cats.

Another system that can be adversely affected by food allergies is the central nervous system. With low IgA allowing adverse reactions *and* the high estrogen causing an inflammation in the endothelial cells of the cerebral arteries, migraine headaches and even seizures are possible complications the patient may experience.

You should be aware that certain foods contain high levels of *natural* estrogens and should be avoided. It has come to light, that people should not feed an allergy or estrogen dominant animal typical snacks made out of apples, carrots or dehydrated sweet potatoes because these snacks are high in estrogen. A list of other estrogen laden foods can be seen on the website I listed earlier. This warning extends to dogs, cats and even people. Cases have been well documented in menstruating women, that when their ovaries are creating more estrogen and they also have prominent amounts of estrogen secreted from their adrenal glands, this state of *hyperestrogenism* is known to cause either migraine headaches and or epileptic seizures.

Hopefully you can see how important it is to make sure that this hormone immune imbalance does not affect you or your pet. After nearly 50 years of clinical practice and research my findings have led to the successful diagnosing and treatment of over 200,000 dogs, cats, horses and humans. Time after time, I assisted beloved pets that were given up for dead by my confused, disbelieving peers who told the owners that there was no hope, that nothing could be done. E-I testing and the *Protocol* proved them wrong

Still the corporate medical establishment refuses to accept my findings. They state that since there were no blind studies run, no placebos used, my findings are suspect, no matter what the documented outcome shows. I respectfully request they interview all of the owners I have helped. I did my research through my clinical practice *on my own time and my own dime.* My record of successes stands for everyone to see. If they have doubts about my findings let *them* run their *blind tests* and prove me wrong.

The time will come when *Plechner Syndrome* is proven to be the cause of many cancers, and auto-immunities including allergies whether food or inhalant induced. The danger of excessive estrogen is just now coming to light, even though I've been treating its maladies successfully for years. Perhaps now they'll become aware that excess estrogen in people, causing inflammation of arteries, just might be the cause of atherosclerosis, arteriosclerosis, coronary and carotid artery occlusion?

It seems that the modern corporate medicine paradigm for people and animals involves treating the medical signs, symptoms and effects rather than finding and curing the cause. I have always felt it is best to treat both the cause and the effect of the disease. My studies have allowed me to design an early identification test to determine a definite cause and a treatment *Protocol* that not only treats but quite possibly prevents a disease before it actually gets a chance to get a foothold.

If your pet, or yourself is suffering from food allergies it is your duty to check and see if this imbalance is the cause. If you do not correct this hormone antibody imbalance, your pet can reach a point of no return, meaning that almost all foods on earth eaten by your pet may cause an allergic reaction.

Healthfully Yours,
Dr. Al Plechner, DVM & David Spangenburg

Allergies are Seldom Just Skin Deep

There are a number of different types of skin sensitivities in dogs and cats and almost as many causes. Some come from external sources while others are generated from deep within the afflicted animal. To better determine the sensitivity, we need to be able to read the signs.

I hear you asking, "What are, signs?" Well, unlike human patients who can describe the symptoms they're experiencing, animals can't put those feelings into words. We have to able to interpret the signs their bodies are displaying. Is it a rash, an inflammation or an eruption? Is it Dry and scaly or moist and runny? By reading the signs, we can determine the cause of the reaction.

Let's take a brief look at some possible external causes that could affect your pet.

- **External parasites** that feed on our pets include fleas, flies, ticks, mange mites, spiders and stinging insects. Snake bites are entirely a different and possibly far more dangerous problem. It is important for you to able to determine whether your pet has been stung by a bee or bitten by a poisonous snake, especially if poisonous snakes are indigenous in your area. A stinging insect may cause a swelling with increased redness on the skin at the point where the sting occurred, however, if a snake bites the skin, the area will begin to turn red, then black and blue. If you are unable to tell, seek the help of a health care professional immediately.
- **Contact products** like flea deterrents, soaps and other applied chemicals, fertilizers, cleaning compounds, and perfumes can all cause skin sensitivity. Note if your dog or cat shows sensitivity to certain things, always spot check them, before you apply any new lotions, sprays or any other additive. You do this by drawing a quarter sized circle on the skin of the abdomen and applying the new product

in the center of the circle with a Q tip. Let the product sit for 15 minutes and then wash it off with warm water. Thoroughly check the center of the circle under a bright light. If the skin appears normal, it is probably safe to use the tested product on your pet, however, if any redness appears on the skin in the circle, or your pet begins to itch or scratch the circle during those 15 minutes, immediately rewash the area. Keep a list of products that cause reactions on your pet.

- **Excessive sunlight exposure.** Similar to humans wearing dark clothing, dark coated animals will feel the effects of the hot sun more because their darker color absorbs the heat more than light colors, which reflect it away. Even so, lighter colored animals are much more susceptible to sunburn and skin cancer than their darker coated brothers and sisters. Light colored animals or those lacking the black pigment around the eyes, ears, and nose, that spend a lot of time in the sun can get sunburned.

Now, let's take a look at some internal causes of skin sensitivity.

- **Sensitivity to certain foods** will manifest itself as inflamed skin; around the eyes, on the ears, the face, the feet and the abdomen. My own studies have shown me that a type of cell (called a mast cell) contains granules of histamine. This histamine, when released, causes inflammation in the areas these cells are concentrated in which happens to be the aforementioned areas and over the base of the tail. If the mast cell concentration is greater in one area than another, you may see more of a reaction in that ear than the other. This can occur around the eyes also.
- **Inhalant allergies** can also cause skin sensitivities, sometimes called Atopy. The respiratory tract may also be affected by these allergies.

- **If you and your pet both have** inhalant allergies, watch closely when you are affected because your pet may develop allergies at the same time.
- **Certain liver diseases** can produce metabolic products (phototoxic porphyrins) that cause photo sensitive skin, which may lead to sun burn.
- **Some antibiotics** like Tetracycline may also cause a photo sensitization which may lead to sun burn. You should be able to obtain a list of drugs and supplements that might cause these reactions from your health care professional.
- **Hormone antibody imbalances** are the main reasons that allergies, auto immunities and cancer may occur.

Healthfully Yours,
Dr. Al Plechner, DVM & David Spangenburg

Allergies, What Causes the Effect?

Your eyes are red, your nose is runny; you're sneezing and sniffling, a sad victim of all too familiar symptoms. There seems to be more and more out there suffering the signs and symptoms of allergies and most don't even know what is really causing it. Just what is an allergy?

The word allergy was coined by Austrian pediatrician, Clemens von Pirquet back in 1906, from the Ancient Greek words, allos which means "other" and ergon meaning "reaction". Pirquet noticed that some patients, upon receiving a second_injection of horse serum or smallpox vaccine had quicker, more severe reactions than they had with the first injection.

An allergy is an overreaction of the immune system when it feels threatened by a protein of a food, a bee sting, a drug (like penicillin), or an airborne mold or pollen. If the body views this environmental input as an invader it releases an overload of histamines in response. This can create symptoms as simple as a runny nose, itchy eyes, hives and general swelling to more severe reactions such as vomiting, diarrhea, quickened heart rate and trouble breathing and even possibly a loss of consciousness due to a drop in the patient's blood pressure. This is called anaphylaxis shock.

Even though, there are different ways to identify the culprits. Skin testing appears to be the favorite form of analysis, primarily because several allergens can be tested at the same time. Small amounts of specific allergens are administered to the skin usually on the forearm, upper arm, or the back. The skin is pricked so the allergen goes underneath the skin surface.

The site is closely watched for signs of a reaction on the skin. These signs are usually seen within 15-20 minutes and are typically, a swelling and redness on the site. The reaction time and the size of the reaction will determine the amount of sensitivity that the patient has to that particular allergen.

Skin testing for food allergens can also be done, however, the test can appear negative even if you or your pets are actually allergic to egg white. This is due to a partial protein called a hapten. When you ingest any food allergen, a hapten can join that food and cause a severe reaction,

Unlike a true antigen, it does not induce the formation of antibodies by itself alone. A hapten needs to bond to a carrier protein before it can induce an immune response that is a different from the allergy protein that is being tested for. Sometimes the hapten can even block immune response to the hapten-carrier adduct by preventing said adduct from binding to the antibody.

Once these allergens are identified, a specific serum is created and given in subcutaneous injections on a strict time table. The idea is to create blocking antibodies within the patient which prevent an overreaction to those certain allergens.

If this works for you or your pet, great, however, don't just stop there. How are you going to keep your systems from developing sensitivities to other allergens when you are actually only treating the signs or symptoms (the effects) and not the actual cause of these over-reactions? First and foremost, you need to determine just what causes the immune system to overreact in the first place.

Some people don't realize it but food allergies are very common in animals just as they are in people. You may be able to find a new food that does not cause problems but this is usually a temporary fix. So what do you do? You can keep trying different foods but this will prove quite expensive. Some people must keep experimenting until eventually the day comes when it seems that there's nothing at all that their pet can eat, without health problems.

People ask why their animals react to some dog foods and not others. Food reactions in a normal patient can occur with bad formulations. Possibly, they got a batch with infectious bacteria or some other toxic matter present or it could be as simple as the commercial food product had too much fat or too much seasoning present which can also cause a bad reaction.

What about all those animals (and people) that have actual food sensitivities? I've had people ask me, why does my one dog have a bad reaction to the food I feed and my other dog doesn't? Is there a basic reason why this occurs? Allergies often are genetically passed down but they can also be acquired.

These patients have a hormonal-antibody imbalance that causes the protective "mucous membrane antibody" (IgA antibody) in the stomach and intestines to be deficient. When this antibody is lacking, it creates other adverse reactions in this "imbalanced" patient. Many times you'll find that the reaction to the food is much less severe than their reaction to an insect bite or a vaccine reaction.

Why is the IgA antibody deficient? What causes this imbalance? The imbalance is due to deficient and/or defective natural cortisol that causes the pituitary gland to produce more Adrenocorticotropic hormone (ACTH) then necessary. When this occurs, it causes a sudden and excessive increase in adrenal estrogen. This extra estrogen not only causes the binding (blocking) of the thyroid hormones, but it also causes the immune cells to attack and make anti-antibodies to any foods that are given to the patient, whether they are animal or human. If you do not correct this imbalance, eventually any and all foods will create bad reactions and cause serious damage to the patient's system.

Are allergies just an inconvenience, or can they be lethal? A hormone antibody imbalance allergy can definitely worsen and possibly turn into a life threatening disease. How can you be completely sure that stress, environmental toxins, genetic defects or other such factors, will not further damage the body and allow autoimmunity or possibly even cancer to occur? That answer is simple, you can't! You need to take a closer look. One way to find out is to have your pet take a determining blood test and possibly have hormone replacement administered to avoid a possible health catastrophe.

Many years ago Dr. Jeff Chung and I developed a very accurate cytotoxic (toxic to cells) food test. The procedure was to place, on a warm culturing slide, smears of 40 different foods. The patient's blood was taken and spun down. The top coat from the spin down contained the white blood cells. These cells were then placed on the various food smears on the warm slide, and if a patient were reactant (allergic), the cytoplasm of the cells would contain vacuoles. I remember a male Doberman that was horribly allergic to tomatoes. When we placed his white cells on the plate with tomato, the white cells literally blew up.

Even though the test proved to be very accurate, the FDA decided that it should not be done in people and animals until they gave it their official approval. It was very frustrating to me because I knew from experience; they were not qualified to do this. Being basically, barely mediocre bureaucrats, they lacked not only the science but also the experience. Their seal of approval would take forever. Ah, well. Let's continue.

We've already talked about the recognized signs of an allergic reaction in part of this ongoing epic and how the medical profession for both people and animals, has merely identified the medical effects while the pharmaceutical companies continue to provide medications merely to treat these effects. I think the time has come to take a look at what actually causes these allergies to occur.

It seems to me you should not be content with just calming the effects of the disorder. I have always felt that it is our duty as medical professionals to uncover and remove the actual root of the disorder so that it ceases to exist altogether. I am a healer and will only be satisfied with giving my patients all that I have to give.

I know that most of you are aware of inhalants containing cortisone, such as Medrol packs for your asthma and all those steroids that are prescribed to you and your pet when you're suffering from allergies or even worse diseases. Most medical professionals say that even though these steroids supposedly have these great, short term effects, they cannot be used long term. In some cases they are correct because the professionals, for the most part, are not aware of how to safely use a cortisol replacement.

Cortisol replacement should only be given in physiologically small dosages as opposed to higher pharmacological dosages. Once the imbalance has been corrected, oral dosing should be continued on a regular basis, however, to keep the level physiological in a dog the cortisol needs to be used with one thyroid hormone = T4. In humans, the steroid needs to be used with two thyroid hormones, T3 and T4. This is of utmost importance when administering ongoing steroid replacement.

In *Plechner Syndrome,* a cortisol defect causes excessive adrenal estrogen production. This triggers the production of a reverse T3 which means that thyroid hormone is bound and cannot be accepted by the receptor sites in the body.

It also deregulates the immune cells (disease fighting cells) instructing them to <u>not</u> protect you from viruses, fungi and other outside invaders. This deregulation also causes these immune cells to not recognize the body's own tissue prompting them to make antibodies which can destroy red cells, white blood cells, muscle tissue etc. This deregulation could also allow uncontrolled tissue growth (cancer) and is the major defect which initiates all the auto-immune diseases that are plaguing the planet.

Get to the root of the problem and live a life free from the discomforts and possible dangers of allergies. *Plechner Syndrome,* can be easily measured in both humans and animals. Once your medical professional has the results they can initiate the proper hormone replacement. There is no reason your animal (or yourself) needs to suffer from allergenic effects.

Healthfully Yours,
Dr. Al Plechner, DVM & David Spangenburg

Are Vaccines, Too Much of a Good Thing?

There is no doubt that there is an over use of vaccines in our country in dogs and cats and, as quite a few people believe, even humans. Our *"vaccination nation"* has decided why depend on our bodies natural defenses when there's money to be made. The medical and pharmaceutical industries have found vaccinations to be a very lucrative revenue stream.

Many years ago, pediatricians would do a scratch test on an infant, at one year of age, to see if that infant had created protective antibodies. This quick and simple test is no longer done, even though the corporate medical establishment's so-called miracle shots might actually be damaging the immune systems of healthy human beings and animals and possibly even creating new diseases.

The April 29, 1995 issue of **Lancet** states that...

"...findings suggest that measles virus may play a part in the development not only of Crohn's disease but also of ulcerative colitis."

There is also a large portion of public opinion that is saying the excessive use of vaccines parallels the rise of autism.

Still, according to Barbara Loe Fisher, the co-founder and president of **National Vaccine Information Center,** and the author of *"The Consumer's Guide to Childhood Vaccines"* and *"Vaccines, Autism & Chronic Inflammation...*

"Many state governments now require nearly three dozen doses of more than a dozen vaccines to attend school. Medical and religious exemptions are becoming harder to get and exemptions for reasons of conscience are under attack by proponents of forced vaccination."

Pets too are legally required to have proper immunization in order to be licensed and legal in municipalities across our country. It seems you just can't escape the needle, but you can oversee the procedures and limit the amounts of vaccine given to your pets.

Many veterinary hospitals recommend dogs and cat vaccines to be given every three years, though recent findings have shown that after the first vaccines are given to a puppy or kitten, the protective antibodies created may last up to 5 to 7 years. I suggest that before you allow the vet to revaccinate your pet have them run an antibody titer blood test to check for the presence of the protective antibody. If it's present wait another year.

You need to understand, the way vaccine manufactures set the dosing it is "one dose fits all". That is not correct. You have to make sure the dosing is measured by the weight of the pet. If you have a 3 - 10 lb. dog you need to be sure it isn't given the same amount of vaccine that is given to an 80 - 100 lb. dog.

Small dogs have a reaction when given too much vaccine. Can you imagine the possible effects when a small dog is given three different vaccines at one time and each of those doses are the maximum doses for even the largest dog? Be sure to ask your veterinarian if he is dosing by the weight of the dog. If he will not reduce the amount of the vaccines according to weight for a very small dog, find a veterinarian that knows better. I personally believe that less vaccine is better as long as the patient develops protective antibodies. An antibody titer will tell for sure.

In animals, if multiple vaccines are given, they need to be placed in different areas of the body. If the vaccines are all injected into the same area they can create a type of cancer called a vaccine fibrosarcoma, which is usually fatal. Though this is seen most often in cats, it has been rarely observed in dogs.

According to Wikipedia, *"Vaccine Associated Sarcomas were first recognized at the* **University of Pennsylvania, School of Veterinary Medicine** *in 1991.*

I encountered my first case of fibrosarcoma over twenty years ago. The patient was a cat that supposedly had a cat bite abscess on its right hip area. Two different veterinarians had intervened surgically but the wound just would not heal. The patient was brought to me for a 3rd opinion. I observed that the opening had a rubbery type tissue lining the cavity. This was not consistent with an abscess so I decided to a do a biopsy. The results returned as a fibrosarcoma.

It's interesting to note that around this same time period, a friend of mine (veterinary oncologist, Dr. Alice Villalobos) had just published an article in a local journal describing vaccine related fibrosarcoma. This proved to be, just the beginning. Since then, numerous vaccines have been incriminated. The ongoing studies also led to the determination that multiple vaccines could be given at the same time as long as each vaccine is injected into different areas of the body.

Recently I have been working with a wonderful cat named Violetta. She was referred to me with a lump in her left thigh. It had been diagnosed as a nickel sized fibrosarcoma and amputation of the left rear leg was suggested. As I've mentioned before in this volume, all cancers that I have been encountered in my practice have had *Plechner Syndrome* present. I tested Violetta and, sure enough, the *Syndrome* was indeed, present.

Following replacement therapy I suggested removing the mass only and not the leg. Subsequent to the surgery, chemotherapy was initiated and the follow up EI test indicated that the chemo had put Violetta back in to the hormone antibody imbalance, which often happens.

Violetta's hormone replacement therapy was increased and now she is perfectly normal, four legged and will continue to live out a full life as long as the hormone replacement is continued. There have been no signs of the tumor reoccurring.

An endocrine/immune system imbalance can also affect the potency of the vaccine, causing a normal dose to become in effect, an overdose. It is wise to have your puppy or kitten, horse (or even your infant) tested for this imbalance. Have your healthcare professional run the **EI** blood test, if a hormonal imbalance is present than hormonal replacement therapy (*Plechner Protocol*) is called for.

One final thought. If your pet has come from a family of dogs or cats that have developed diseases even though they've been vaccinated.

You need to follow up the 12 week injections, with an antibody titer test to make sure your pet has actually produced the protective antibodies. Remember that you are your pets advocate, they cannot speak for themselves. It is your duty, not only to protect them but you must also make sure that you protect their rights also.

Healthfully Yours,
Dr. Al Plechner, DVM & David Spangenburg

Pet Health

Idiopathic Epilepsy

Idiopathic Epilepsy, like a tree, has many roots and these roots usually remain hidden, deep within your pet's unique physiology. As with essential tremors in humans, often, the true *cause* of idiopathic epilepsy may never be determined. Even if the cause remains concealed, the type of epilepsy can be determined by the degree of severity in which it manifests itself.

If the seizure is mild, (minor tremor or shaking of the head) it is referred to as a "Petite Mal". If the signs are more rigorous (patient is rendered helpless by uncontrollable muscle spasms), it is considered to be a full out, tonic, clonic, "Grand Mal". Even though the duration of the seizure usually lasts for only a few minutes it can go on for several hours, although this is, thankfully, very rare.

Just what is a seizure? Imagine, if you will, an electrical storm in the brain. We all know that neurons (normal brain cells) use chemical signals and electrical impulses to communicate with each other. These "lightening flash" communications can either, *activate* the next neuron (excitatory), or can turn the next neuron off (inhibitory).

The "messages" that travel along the neural highway contain the "directions" that a brain sends out to every nerve, muscle, joint, etc. throughout the body to keep it functioning and thriving. When the excitation or inhibition of these individual neurons in the brain is disrupted it can generate a seizure. The area of the brain, where the seizure activity occurs, will decide the effect it has on the body.

Even though, detecting a seizure before it happens is not always easy, a certain "aura" can alert an owner of an imminent "brain storm". Just as there are some dogs that can sense when their epileptic owner is going to have a seizure, some owners can *also* detect when their dog is going to have an epileptic episode. In many cases a certain set of symptoms or activities (a prodrome)

247

can precede a seizure. This "aura" is a recognizable change in the pet's usual behavior that warns the owner of an approaching seizure. Often an epileptic dog will sense something is coming and seek out its owner, in the hopes that nestling by their side might cause the signs of the seizure to diminish. Some epileptic humans "hear" a certain musical strain prior to a seizure episode that forewarns them to prepare for the upcoming event.

Causes for seizures include head trauma, brain tumors, and even low blood sugar whether due to insulin shock, genetic hypoglycemia or just a general inability of the liver to store and release glycogen in a timely manner. My clinical research studies have uncovered another possible cause. It involves a syndrome, which is activated by elevated adrenal estrogen, which creates an inflammation of all the endothelial cells that line the arteries of the body. When this elevated adrenal estrogen level combines with an increased level of ovarian estrogen, the concentration of *total estrogen* causes inflammation of the cerebral arteries, possibly leading to a migraine headache and/or an epileptic seizure episode.

Even though this is a recognized syndrome in females who are estrogen prominent, my clinical research has shown that in female animals, who have had their ovaries removed, and in males, who obviously have no ovaries, this elevated adrenal estrogen can still occur, becoming the major cause of epileptic seizures and other catastrophic diseases in the aforementioned animals

What is the primary reason for this harmful condition of adrenal estrogen dominance to occur? It is simply the continued use of unsound breeding practices such as structured breeding as opposed to functional breeding, which has allowed gene pools to stagnate and weaken. Any time a breeder tries to "create" a new color or "breed", or affect a more unique head or body shape or "fashion" a different gait, it is most often accomplished through line breeding. While it *is* possible to "fix" a desired trait through line breeding it is also more likely to "taint' the line by introducing defects by reducing the genetic diversity through line breeding.

Many breeders fool themselves into thinking they are doing an out cross because they are mating to a sire or a dame of the same breed "but" from a different country. The truth is, that the world of breeding has become smaller and smaller and it's, more than likely, that "line" was crossed many times before. There's a good possibility the breeders in that country, have created the same inbreeding problems that you are trying to avoid. Their supposedly clever "select over-breeding" has caused an endocrine immune imbalance that not only may allow epilepsy to occur, but has also created a defect that may also allow allergy, autoimmunity and possibly even cancer and other catastrophic diseases to occur within the affected litter.

I know you are asking yourself; just what it is this endocrine immune imbalance? It is, *Plechner Syndrome* a genetic imbalance that is causing the cortisol hormone, that is naturally produced by the <u>middle layer</u> adrenal cortex, to not be sufficient, bound (not recognized by the pituitary gland) or possibly just defective. This causes, false negative feedback to the pituitary, causing the pituitary to keep releasing its hormone ACTH, to encourage the middle layer_adrenal cortex to produce more cortisol, which it can't. So the inner layer_adrenal cortex responds by producing excess total estrogen and a male hormone called androgen.

(NOTE: This is why many female dogs will lift their leg like a male to urinate, and will hump other animals, including their owners. Also with this condition, female cats may spray the wall, marking their territory.)

The production of the excess estrogen does three things...

- First, it will bind the thyroid hormone and make normal thyroid hormone production not available for use in the body. In people, the mechanism that allows for this is the production of a reverse T3 hormone.
- Second, the excess estrogen will cause the B lymphocyte to reduce its production of antibody, and when the antibody in the mucous membranes of the gut is below 58 units, mal-absorption (non-absorption) will occur, including, Irritable Bowel Syndrome food allergies, vaccine reactions and stinging insect sensitivity.

- Third, the excess estrogen deregulates both the B and T lymphocytes, which causes them to lose recognition of self-tissue, which will lead to autoimmunity.

It has already been recognized, that if normal cells are exposed to elevated amounts of estrogen, increased cellular growth occurs, and is probably the cause of cancer in people and animals.

If you prefer to breed, rather than rescue, I have created a simple blood test, which will not only help you decide which Sire and Dame should (or shouldn't) be bred , but will also let you know if any of your pets have *Plechner Syndrome* and allow you to heal the actual cause rather than to just relieve the effects. Hopefully one day, this simple blood test will be a part of the standard birthing procedure, to insure the health and wellness of every puppy, kitten or human child.

Healthfully Yours,
Dr. Al Plechner DVM & David Spangenburg

Hyperestrogenism

An article from the University of Tennessee signals that my esteem fellow professionals are finally beginning to understand what this old Vet's been saying for many years now. They are beginning to realize the dangers of excessive adrenal estrogen. They are close, but alas...no cigar.

It seems they are attempting to reduce the production of adrenal estrogen by using various chemicals to affect its source, the adrenal gland. This approach at least shows someone's been listening to what this Animal Doctor has been saying for quite a while.

However, they still are off track. They keep trying to affect the middle layer of the adrenal cortex but they're barking up the wrong layer. They need to be studying the inner layer. That's where the problem lies. Even so, when they finally get there they're going to find that it's not going to be affected by their chemical assault.

I can understand their dilemma. The middle layer adrenal production of cortisol hormone appears quite normal in their eyes. The problem is that they need to understand that the cortisol being produced is defective and is not being recognized by the pituitary gland which keeps churning out the ACTH hormone which can cause an increase in the production of estrogen and androgen (which can be converted into estrogen) due to an enzyme in the fatty tissue called aromatase.

Since the elevated estrogen binds (blocks) the receiver sites of thyroid. The bound thyroid reduces the activity of the liver and kidneys which further guarantees less breakdown and elimination of the estrogen and androgen. This allows the estrogen and androgen to remain excessive. The patient, unavoidably, is also bound to gain weight, which at the same time produces more aromatase due to the increase of fatty tissue which inadvertently increases the amount of estrogen present...and so, round we go, in a vicious cycle.

It's just our luck! The corporate medical industry is finally realizing what I've been trying to tell them for years. That excess estrogen can cause real problems. Still it seems that they haven't listened to all of what this old Vet's been saying (they must've dozed off in the middle of the lecture).

The capper is that certain hormones like cortisol can be defective or bound (unable to get to the right receptors). The decreased or defective cortisol and the increased estrogen throws the immune system out of balance. When the immune system is imbalanced it may fall victim to a number of problems including; Aids, Multiple Sclerosis, Muscular Dystrophy, coronary occlusion, all types of auto-immunity, and even cancer.

Now, I understand that I am but a healer of 'animals'. However, I think we can all agree that all the creatures on this planet are very similar on the inside. What's good for the Goose...well, I think you understand. I just hope that those learned professionals at the University of Tennessee can rise above the status quo and maybe listen to alternative sources in their 'quest for the cures'. They should at least heed Shakespeare...

"There are more things in heaven and earth, Horatio, than are dreamt of in your philosophy."

Healthfully Yours,
Dr. Al Plechner DVM & David Spangenburg

Immune Mediated Chronic Bladder Infections

Has your dog or cat ever suffered from chronic bladder infections? You take them to the vet and when their urine is tested 'in office' with a dip strip, and inflammatory cells or white blood cells (WBCs) are present, you're told that your pet has a urinary tract infection. The vet prescribes a general antibiotic and the bladder infection seems to subside, only to return at a later date. So, back to your vet you go.

This time your vet decides to get a closer look. He takes another urine sample and sends it out to a laboratory to see if any unusual bacteria are present. If they discover any bacterial growth, the colony of bacteria will be exposed to several other different kinds of bacteria to see if any of those many antibiotics applied will kill this specific unusual bacterium.

Often a bladder x-ray and/or an ultra sound will be done to make sure there are no bladder stones or bladder tumors present. If the bladder scans show no complications, they turn their focus to the results of the urine culture and sensitivity to decide which specific antibiotic they'll be using to kill this unusual bacterium.

This is the chain of events that occurs in most instances of UTIs. If this is the case, the bladder infection should subside and not reoccur, Still, there are many cases where the urine culture and sensitivity may show no bacterial growth whatsoever, even though inflammatory cells or WBCs were found in the original urinalysis.

What does this indicate?

This indicates that your dog or cat may have an endocrine immune imbalance which has allowed for an immune mediated, chronic bladder infection to be recurring. If this is the case, it is easy to have your healthcare professional do an endocrine immune blood test and send it to a special laboratory that is qualified to do this type of testing.

This specific Laboratory is listed on my website*. I am in no way associated with this laboratory but at this time, it is the only veterinary laboratory that has the ability to provide credible laboratory results.

The test results, in all probability, will reveal that your pet has, the *Plechner Syndrome*, a hormone antibody imbalance, indicating imbalanced cortisol and elevated adrenal estrogen. It will also expose either a primary T3 T4 deficiency or normal thyroid hormones that are "bound" (elevated estrogen will bind the receptor sites rendering the Thyroid hormones unavailable for use in the body).

While the B and T lymphocytes (a type of WBCs generated to fight infection and inflammation) don't appear to be deficient they are actually deregulated. Not only have they lost their ability to protect your pet, they have also lost recognition of self-tissue and can begin to attack the normal tissue inside your pet creating an autoimmune disease. My findings have shown me that this Syndrome may also be the cause of allergies and even cancer.

It is easy to see why all those products that are touted to stimulate your pet's immune system, are actually furthering the deregulation and, in all reality, are turning off their natural immune defenses leaving them exposed and vulnerable to a myriad of diseases and disorders. Please, make sure you measure this endocrine immune deficiency before initiating any use of immune stimulants!

When a lack of antibody production by the B lymphocyte occurs in animals, all the immunoglobulins will be deficient including the mucous membrane antibody IgA whether secretory or circulatory.* When the IgA level is deficient, your pet may be subject to food allergies, vaccine reactions and insect sensitivities.

Impact areas are often genetically predetermined and the bladder seems to be one of those genetically targeted. This is why an immune mediated bladder infection due to the IgA imbalance can be triggered by a food allergy, a vaccine reaction or a simple insect bite.

*Also in Chapter 2 of this book.

Even if you feed your pet the most unprocessed, organic, natural food diet available you may have innocently introduced them to a food allergy that has initiated an immune mediated, chronic bladder infection. If that's not bad enough, food sensitivities may also cause a primary upset in the stomach and intestines.

The reaction in the bladder may be so subtle that a urine sample might need to be tested for occult blood (unseen by the naked eye) as opposed to copious amounts of visible blood including constant urination because the bladder is inflamed.

The IgA imbalance may also cause a secondary effect which may lead to itching of the face, feet and skin of the ventral abdomen where mast cells, that contain histamine, will degranulate the skin and cause inflammation.

If your pet is suffering from this endocrine immune imbalance, *Plechner Syndrome* can be determined by a simple blood test and applying the *Plechner Protocol* (hormonal replacement therapy) is the only way you will be able to control this condition. Please feel free to come to my website and look at the article on elimination diets. It will help you find the proper food to feed your pet in order to help avoid immune mediated chronic bladder infections.

Healthfully Yours,
Dr. Al Plechner DVM & David Spangenburg

* People apparently have subgroups of B cells and show different variations in levels of IgA, IgG IgM, IgD and IgE.

Alternative Cancer Treatments for Animals

One out of every four dogs in our environmentally challenged world of today will die of cancer and approximately 50% of dogs over 10 years of age will die from some cancer related death. With odds like that, we'd better discuss just what do you do if your animal is struck with cancer; especially if you don't want to put them through the costly, invasive, painful, and (far too many times) useless modern medical cancer treatments? There are definite alternatives that are much less distressing and costly.

Over the last forty years in almost every case of cancer that I have treated, the *Plechner Syndrome* has been present. So obviously, the first thing you need to determine is, does my pet have the *Syndrome?* First and foremost, have your veterinarian do the E/I blood test. (Details for the test and use of the proper laboratory are listed in this book and on my website).Once the test has identified the causative hormone/antibody imbalance, the *Plechner Protocol* can be initiated and the needed supplemental hormones can be given to control the imbalance which will slow done or possibly even stop the growth of the tumor.

Shark cartilage (available at most health food groceries and nutritional pharmacies) can be given twice daily to decrease the blood supply to any fast growing soft tissue tumor which is referred to as an anti-angiogenesis factor. Dosage is usually 500 mgs per 10 lbs. of body weight twice daily, up to a maximum of 2500 mgs twice daily for a very large dog.

Premium "living clay" such as calcium montmorillinite should be given orally and if the tumor is visible externally, a poultice of this same material can also be applied directly to the tumor site daily and left in place. The Gerson Institute in southern California has been using this premium calcium montmorillinite to treat human cancer patients with internal tumors successfully for many years and Mahatma Gandhi was also a loyal devotee.

Research studies indicate that rapidly growing tumors require a high <u>acid</u> based environment. The ingestion of premium calcium montmorillinite clay creates an alkaline environment with a PH of 8.3. Not only does this high alkaline PH slow down tumor growth, but it actually stops colonies of malignant cells breaking off from the primary tumor and prevents them from establishing another tumor. Therefore, metastasis of the primary tumor is stopped which is vital for cancer treatment. There is further information about this premium calcium montmorillinite clay throughout this book and at my website http://www.drplechner.com - under the articles button.

For many years, the Chinese have found asparagine (readily available in asparagus) to definitely help stop soft tissue tumor growth. I have found it best to give 5 to 7 steamed asparagus spears twice daily in your animal's food. Often it seemed to work best to blend the steamed asparagus spears and mix small amounts into the animal's food at a time to eventually be able to decide just how much of the asparagus blend the animal will eat before turning up their nose to the food completely.

When dealing with cancer, as with other diseases, it is always best to identify the cause rather than just treating the effects. Always remember the rhyme...

Treating the signs or symptoms may,
often hold the disease at bay.
But, alas, I have to say.
The cancer will not go away.

Healthfully yours,
Dr. Al Plechner DVM & David Spangenburg

Spaying and Neutering are more than just Population Control

We all know that the domestic dog and cat population has exploded in the past several decades. The rescue centers and animal pounds and shelters are filled to the max and still hungry and homeless strays haunt our city streets. All because humans have been reckless and irresponsible, that's right, we're to blame.

Our animals may be smart as can be, when it comes to getting treats but they can't run down to the Drugstore and purchase protection every time some cutie wags their tail. It's up to us to see that they aren't going to be filling up the streets with their offspring. It's up to each of us to make sure that our pets are not contributing to the population explosion

We really have no room to complain. The planet's entire human population was one billion in the early 1800's and guess what, just two hundred years later in 2011 we're almost at seven billion. That's quite a jump and we're gobbling up the earth's natural resources like piggies at an all you can eat buffet. Did we forget that we're supposed to be the planet's stewards?

Though we all know the good reasons for spaying and neutering, we also need to understand the possible health problems that might occur due to these procedures. You need to know the scientific facts, so you can see the pros and cons to spaying and neutering from a health stand point and not just from a sterility issue. We'll begin with female dogs.

The positive aspects of spaying are;

- If spayed before 3 years of age it reduces possible development of mammary glands tumors and tumors in other female organs.
- If an unsprayed female has false pregnancies, she is probably producing a cyst on an ovary, following ovulation. This cyst causes production of progesterone which is meant to prepare the dog for birth.

- If the cyst remains and the female goes back into heat, her ovaries will again produce estrogen. The combination of increased estrogen and progesterone will cause a pyometra, a toxic bacterial infection of the uterus, which can lead to death if not surgically treated immediately.
- Spaying reduces the dangers of fistulas and perianal gland tumors.

The negative aspects of spaying are;

- Vaccine reactions.
- Triples the risk for hypothyroidism.
- If spayed before reaching full maturity it will increase the possibilities of malignant bone tumors, particularly in the large breeds
- Excessive weight gain.
- Weakened bladder control especially when sleeping.
- If spayed before puberty, some bitches may have an inverted vagina which prevents the release of urine causing a urine scald which may cause continuing vaginitis and irritation and inflammation of the immediate area.
- Increased orthopedic problems and ongoing danger of Increases the risk factor of cardiac and splenic cancer.
- Spaying doubles the risk of cancer of the bladder and increases the threat of urinary tract infections.

How about the neutering of male dogs?
The positive aspects of neutering are;

- Obviously it eliminates the small risk of testicular cancer. Of the 3 types of testicular tumors only one is malignant. It is called a Sertoli cell tumor and it produces estrogen which in the early stages will cause the male dog to have enlarged nipples referred to as gynecomastia. This nipple enlargement may occur before the tumor spreads to other parts of the body (metastasis).

- Reduces the risk of benign (non-cancerous) tumors.
- Reduces the risk of fistulas and perianal gland tumors.

The negative aspects of neutering are;

- Excessive weight gain.
- Triples the risk of hypothyroidism.
- Doubles the risk of urinary tract tumors.
- Increases the risk of bone cancer if neutering is performed before the dog matures, especially in the larger breeds.
- Increased danger of hemangiosarcoma, a cardiac and splenic cancer.
- Increases the risk for senility on older dogs.
- Quadruples the possibility of prostate cancer.
- Increased orthopedic problems, and ongoing danger of vaccine reactions.

So what is the answer? How can you protect your pet from possible 'medical procedure induced' diseases and still remove the risk of unwanted reproduction?

Female dogs should probably not be spayed before they reach sexual maturity.

As for male dogs, I realized many years ago the possible dangers of neutering or desexing (castration). At that time, when I was still doing surgery, I would perform a very simple vasectomy which not only solved the overpopulation problem, but at the same time allowed the male dog to produce testosterone and remain hormonally healthy.

This procedure is less invasive and quicker to do then the standard neuter. All it took was making a small incision, identifying the spermatic cord, and cauterizing the cord with an electrocautery or laser unit. The procedure was completed in no time at all. It is less expensive and can be done with a local anesthetic so there's no risk from a general anesthesia.

MD's do this procedure for men as an office procedure. There is no reason why vets can't offer the same simple, safe, service. I was hoping the animal shelters and animal rights groups might advocate for this easier and safer procedure which accomplishes both purposes at the same time. I'm sure that it's been considered, but who knows why it's not in everyday practice.

No pun intended, but the ball is now in your court! It's totally up *to* you to decide if sterility is more important than risking possible health issues for your dog. To have the best of both worlds you may want to further explore vasectomies for male dogs and post puberty spays for female dogs.

Healthfully Yours,
Dr. Al Plechner DVM & David Spangenburg

Is Your Pack of Puppies,
Pooping Prodigiously?

You've heard me talk about the nutritional benefits of "Living clay" supplements such as *Nutramin* and *Terramin*. These amazing edible nutritive products are the only natural sources of the mighty trace mineral elements that have been stripped out of our once fertile agricultural soils by catastrophic, factory farming methods. The few remaining veins of these golden nutrients lay in rare deposits scattered few and far between, across this abused planet of ours.

Trace minerals are nature's multi-taskers, besides their remarkable nutritive value they are also natural medicinals. The calcium montmorillinite clay will soothe the intestinal lining of these poopy puppy patients due to its natural chelated kaolin. Its soothing action is much quicker and the coverage more complete than its impersonator, the "manmade chemical" kaolin, that resides in many anti-diarrheal medications for people and animals. The simple reason for this is that calcium montmorillinite raises the bowel's normally acidic PH value of 6 to 6.5PH to a more alkaline PH value of 8.3 which buffers and soothes the poor puppies inflamed bowel linings.

A fact that I have found, that is of even greater interest, is that the majority of intestinal parasites thrive in an acidic environment with the PH value of 6 to 6.5. So, when your pups ingest the living clay supplements and their internal environment of their bowels rise to a PH value of 8.3, many of the intestinal parasites present will not be able to survive such a high alkaline PH and so will die and will be naturally shed with the stools of the pups.

It has been proven that MRSA, the rapidly spreading, deadly flesh eating bacteria which causes catastrophic tissue and muscle damage and eventually death has grown resistant to most of the antibiotics in the modern medical arsenal. It has also been proven that when exposed to high alkaline 8.3 PH environment created by this calcium montmorillinite clay, the vicious bacteria, MRSA, will die. Amazingly, the deadly, antibiotic resistant bacteria cannot exist in this high alkaline environment.

Along with its power packed "catalog" of trace mineral elements, this 100% natural product is geothermally charged with an essential negative ion. It's called ION-MIN®, and it neutralizes the toxins, poisons and heavy metals which pollute our everyday environment. Similar "living clay" was used to cleanup and to bury the nuclear damage and radiation residue in Chernobyl, Russia. It was also taken orally by survivors and the cleanup workers and was administered to farm animals for miles around the meltdown damaged reactor. It is also an effective cleanup product for oil and chemical spills at sea as well as on land.

For more info, check out Calcium Bentonite Green Clay at http://earthslivingclay.com/. No, I don't own any stock but I am their consultant and I know what great supplements they offer.

Healthfully Yours,
Dr. Al Plechner DVM & David Spangenburg

Steroids, a Powerful Medical Remedy, so Feared, Misused and Misunderstood

Even though steroid supplementation in animals and humans is very common, their usage carries an unwarranted stigma. This is due to the serious side effects if these needed hormones are misused and misdosed.

Many feel that this great fear took root in 1948 when a famous clinic began giving mega doses of a steroid over prolonged periods of time. Their actions created a history of serious side effects that still overshadows the valuable potential of the synthetic hormone's proper usage today.

It began at the Mayo Clinic in Rochester, Minnesota. The doctors began a regime of daily injections of their "X Substance", a corticosteroid. The injections were given to a large number of arthritic patients for an extended period of time. Their results showed such dramatic improvements that all caution appears to be "thrown to the wind!" Needless to say as usage of steroids expanded, serious side effects began to rear their ugly heads and as **About.Com** shows in *The Facts of Corticosteroids*

"...it was realized that high doses given over prolonged periods of time turned steroids into "scare-oids".

http://arthritis.about.com/cs/steroids/a/corticostero ids.htm

This synthetic hormone proved to be a wonder drug but like any medication that is used inappropriately it caused many severe side effects. As patients were made aware of the possible problems, dosages dropt rapidly, treatment courses became shorter and some patients became so afraid of the possible side effects they refused any kind of steroidal treatment. Even today, almost 70 years later; in some circles it is still considered to be a hazardous substance.

The interesting thing is that the general public is ignorant of the fact that normal dogs, cats and human beings need to generate 30 to 35 units of natural cortisol every day of their life if they intend to maintain normal health.

As you expect though, if the cortisol production of a patient is normal and a steroid is introduced into that patients system, certain bad side effects will occur.

Even so, I personally have seen, thousands of times, that the proper use of a steroid in a patient with a cortisol imbalance is the replacement of cortisol to remedy (top off) that deficient cortisol.

The next question you'll probably ask is when a steroid is given and the patient becomes normal, could that steroid merely be filling an imbalance in the natural cortisol which is not being produced correctly in that patient to begin with?

Absolutely! Correct'o'mundo!

Now you're wondering if most of the contraindication of steroid use in patients is based upon giving a steroid to a patient that has normal cortisol production as opposed to a patient that has a cortisol imbalance.

Presently, in animals today, it is very common to see elevated cortisol levels that are defective, bound and inactive.

Huh?

They don't work.

This is commonly referred to as an *Atypical Cushing* or *Addison's Syndrome* however they should really be referred to as an *Atypical Cortisol Imbalance Syndrome,* more commonly known as *Plechner Syndrome.*

A health care professional does not need to subject patients to stimulation and depression tests. They can easily determine the working ability of the elevated cortisol level with a simple white blood cell differential test. This is because the *amount* of the cortisol has very little to do with its effectiveness.

From an educational stand point, it has been taught that if a cortisol level is elevated and active, the white cell differential will reflect a lack of lymphocytes and eosinophils. However, if these two cells are present, then the *elevated* cortisol is actually bound or defective and cannot be used by the body.

How hard is that to understand?

Active or in-active cortisol can also be determined by doing my endocrine immune (E-I) blood test which you can read about throughout this book and on my website.

When natural cortisol is deficient, bound or defective, the negative feedback to the pituitary gland is damaged. When this occurs, the pituitary will over stimulate the inner layer adrenal cortex to produce excess adrenal estrogen which will bind the receptor sites for active thyroid hormone T3 and it cannot be utilized by the body. When this occurs, any steroid replacement will become an overdose because the metabolism (action) of the liver and kidney are reduced.

Not only can the liver not breakdown the steroid in 24 hours but whatever is broken down by the liver cannot be excreted efficiently by the kidneys. Therefore the patient may experience an overdose of a vital hormone that has been innocently prescribed without prescribing a (needed) accompanying thyroid supplement. This is very prevalent in dogs and humans. Dogs normally will need a T4 supplement to guarantee the steroid replacement does not become an overdose.

A normal amount of steroid is *necessary* for transference of T4 to active T3.

This is very common in dogs.

In people the same condition may exist however if it does not, then the use of a T4 supplement may cause further problems. In humans, if a cortisol imbalance exists causing an elevated total estrogen, a Reverse T3 is often produced which binds the receptor sites of the T3. When this occurs, prescribing a T3 supplement will usually help however if a T4 supplement is included, the excess adrenal estrogen will cause the T4 supplement to turn into a Reverse T3 which will cause a further imbalance.

Elevated adrenal estrogen can raise havoc with the absorption of steroids. In fact if a steroid imbalance has been identified in a patient, there is no guarantee that the patient can absorb oral steroids without measuring IgA (immunoglobulin A) levels first. Correct IgA levels protect all the mucous membranes in the body including the gut.

It is vital for the patient to absorb most oral medications. This is often why a patient in the hospital seems to do well on and IV or an IM antibiotic and when sent home on the sane oral medication they again fall ill to the original disease. The patient is again at step one, all because no one checked their IgA levels.

This should be a standard procedure with any general blood test. When this IgA deficiency has been identified, an injectable steroid may be the only way to bypass the gut, reduce the pituitary ACTH including the adrenal estrogen and increase the IgA so that oral steroids can be absorbed. If you need help in discovering the correct injectable steroids to be used and the proper dosages to be given you can contact me at my website address under the Consulting button.

http://www.drplechner.com

Last but certainly not least, pertains to the handling of the blood. If you have a blood sample drawn to send to the lab for testing keep the sample refrigerated. If the blood sample is not kept cool the entire time, from draw to testing, all the hormones and antibodies will be erroneously elevated. This is why **a temperature strip must accompany every refrigerated blood sample to indicate that the sample has not been exposed to heat and the results are not erroneous.**

I sincerely hope that someday very soon national standards are set for hormone antibody testing. Standards need to be the same no matter what laboratory the blood test is sent to. I have established national levels in animals including total estrogen, cortisol, T3 T4 and IgA, IgG and IgM. Why can't this be done for humans?

Please, visit my website and take a look at the lectures I presented to the Broda Barnes MD Research Foundation. You'll find it under my Article buttons involving the 3rd lecture. It will explain to you why national standards are a necessity when you can actually see all the different values that come from different laboratories for the exact same test.

As a health care professional, where you send your serum sample will determine whether your patient is normal or diseased. The wrong values from a blood test are really confusing for the health care professional and quite possibly dangerous for the patient. This deficiency within the healthcare industry really needs to be corrected. Standardized lab testing is essential for you and your pet to lead a more normal healthy life.

Healthfully Yours,
Dr. AL Plechner DVM & David Spangenburg

Miscellaneous

Choose Your Friends Well

Choosing a dog can prove to be quite a process or it can happen with just one look. You know what I mean. It can involve plenty of research at the library or on the 'net' or it can be like love at first sight. It all depends on who's looking and if you're looking for a definite breed or you're just looking for your next best friend.

Before you do choose a special pet, FIRST, check out available dogs through local rescues and shelters. There are far too many great animals just chillin' at your local pounds and rescues waiting for someone just like you to give them a happy home. What they offer you is...priceless! While you're there pick two, so your new friend has a friend to keep them company when you're away. Whether you decide, big or little (or one of each) pick a breed or a size that seems to fit the personality of the household.

Are you the jogging type and want your new dog to hit the streets with you? Well, most dogs can *run* but certain breeds are more adaptable for jogging. What you need is a more laid back dog who can adjust its gait to match your jogging comfort level speed. If you have arthritis you should choose a dog that prefers to travel slowly, like you. A hunting or working breed would likely feel stifled or too constrained.

It's tough to walk any dog in a busy city but it's even more difficult with a "field trial" breed. They usually have been trained to run long, and controlled, only with a whistle. This is a dangerous practice on a busy city street, no matter how smart or fleet the dog. If you live in the city and must have such a dog, for their protection, walk them with a collar and leash or (better yet) take them to a good dog park, if available.

How about a dog for security? Often people will choose a large or, what they feel is, a vicious breed that they think most criminals fear. This is a good start but most people that rescue or buy these animals don't go to the trouble to learn how to deal with these dogs correctly. This is why you hear so many horrible stories about attacks on children, people and other animals and the main reason Pit bulls, Doberman Pinchers, and Rottweillers have been singled out as dangerous pets!   Actually, the truly dangerous animal happens to be the uneducated, owner.

Many men try to live their egos through their "macho" pets. You know the ones I'm talking about, the ones whose own macho, is "not so, much so". They want everyone to think their dog is a real "Bad Ass". This is usually accomplished by negative training and intimidation and will, in most cases, result in creating an animal that is dangerous to everyone including its owner. Your dogs are what you make them. An important fact to remember, "There are no bad dogs, only bad owners".

While we are being so philosophical, here's another good precept to live by...

"All those times in your life when you feel like doing something, you just know is wrong. Stop, and be the good person, that your pets think you are."

Rule one, of Dr. Plechner's rules for training your pets...

You must be smarter than your pet.

Most people fail.

If you really don't want to get involved in training your pets, there are plenty of trained professionals who'll be happy to help you. If that's not in the family budget there are plenty of helpful books and DVDs at your local library branch for free. Take all the good advice you gather and combine it with personal observations about your dog's individual personality that you've gleaned during your day to day exchanges. Mix all that up with patience, persistence and a whole lot of love and you should do quite fine.

Some dogs are easier to train than others, which reminds me about another good rule to follow...

You may want to avoid Terriers.

They are outstanding, but definitely have a mind of their own and sometimes can be difficult to house break, particularly if you failed my rule one.

You must be smarter than your pet.

Often you pick a puppy with great eyes, a unique color, or just a great look and personality. I remember a classic mismatch that did occur when a wonderful family picked a wonderful puppy that was so cute and cuddly they didn't even think to research into the puppy's breed's history. The family had just lost an older pet and decided that they needed to fill their house with happiness... the sooner the better.

So, home comes, Mabel. She was an 8 week old Queensland Healer, so cute you just could not believe it. Everything was great. She settled in with the family, filling that void of their recent loss. The family decided to hold a major party at their home in Malibu, to celebrate their joy. They invited 300 guests.

Uh, ohh!

She was an 8 week old Queensland Healer, bred to guide and drive herd animals by nipping at their heels and through Mabel's eyes, this was an entire "herd of people". You can just imagine what happened next.

Mabel lay under the couch and to the horror of her owners, the hosts of this grand party, she'd race out and bite the back of each guest's shoes, if they made the fatal mistake of even getting <u>near</u> her couch.

After the party the owners ask me to check Mabel, to see if elevated total estrogen was causing her bad behavior. It sounded to me like Mabel was doing a good job of exactly what she had been bred to do and upon testing, Mabel was found to be perfectly normal.

It was apparent, that Mabel didn't quite understand the family's needs and the family in turn, didn't quite understand Mabel's innate drives. All's well that ends well though, after a little behavior modification, for all concerned, everyone involved lived happily ever after.

Hopefully, some of the above will make it easier for you to pick a wonderful pet. Research is the key. Be aware of the kind of pet that suits you and your household's lifestyle then go out and find that special one that meets your heart. You'll know the one, when you see them. Then study up so you can fulfill their needs and let them know how they can fulfill your needs so you can have a happy, long life together.

You also need to accept the fact that you have taken on a major responsibility. Your new pet needs to be cared for in a manner which allows you both, to flourish to a ripe old age. I have had a cat patient live to 28 years and a dog patient live to 27. Parrots can live even longer at 50 to 100 years in captivity and pet Turtles live 100-150 years, so you may have to set up a trust fund. A pet/care giver arrangement is a long term, happy investment for both you and your pet and its rewards and responsibilities are boundless.

For those of you out there who would like a pet but don't want a major responsibility, there's always Goldfish and small reptiles but don't forget to clean the bowls and to feed them.

Healthfully Yours,
Dr. Al Plechner & David Spangenburg

Out of the Frying Pan, Into the Fire

Using easily cleaned, nonstick, cookware sure does make doing the dishes a whole lot easier but is that worth endangering your health? The **Environmental Protection Agency (EPA)** has been taking a real close look at Teflon coated cookware and has found that if the Teflon cookware becomes too overheated, up to fifteen different toxins are released into your food. Not only that, over heated Teflon cookware releases polytetrafluoroethylene (PTFE) and other toxic gases directly into the air in your house at a rate which will kill your pet birds, if they're housed anywhere close to your kitchen.

Birds of all kinds, that reside too close to the cooking area, and are exposed to PTFE, are generally found dead on the bottom of their cage. If the birds are only moderately exposed to PTFE, they may experience difficult breathing, possible wheezing, a loss of coordination, weakness, depression and seizures. It's important to note that boiling vinegar, which is often used in home canning, can also cause death for the birds that are caged nearby.

Obviously if you keep birds in your home, keep them far away from the kitchen and in a well-ventilated area. Often by the time we vets see these birds, the damage is so extensive, that treatment is hopeless. At the time of autopsy, the entire respiratory tract is found to be damaged beyond repair.

This cookware, when used properly and not allowed to overheat, is perfectly safe to use. Even so, I think we've all experienced a major distraction while we were preparing food and had the misfortune to burn dinner to a crisp. Breathing in the toxins released into the air has been known to cause ill effects in humans similar to the flu, so much so that scientists have dubbed it the "Teflon Flu".

This "flu" may manifest itself as a headache, nausea, fever, muscle aches and a general state of malaise where you just don't feel well at all. Unfortunately our pets can't talk, so we can only imagine how they feel when exposed to this toxic cocktail released into the air and into their lungs? Considering their smaller size and more sensitive systems these toxins can possibly be downright deadly!

The EPA labeled PFOA as a <u>probable</u> carcinogen. PFOA has been linked to cancer and birth defects in laboratory animals and PFOA may be linked to birth defects in two families that had family members working in a factory that produces Teflon cookware. And, to put the icing on the cake, once PFOA is absorbed by the body or released into the environment, there's no breakdown just a <u>buildup</u>. That's right; it just gets better and better.

Recent blood studies amongst a cross section of California women show a definite increase in 12 types of these damaging chemicals. PFC (perfluorooctase) is number one chemical found in the blood samples from these women and (PFOA) perfluorooctanoic acid is the second most common chemical found in their blood stream.

The studies further indicate that from 1960 to 2009, the PFC has increased 10 fold. During the years 1960 to 1980 PFOA had also increased but, oddly enough, had slightly decreased by 2009. Both these chemicals stay in the body for many years, but even if their exposure is reduced to zero, their 'half-life' still remains in the body for at least 4 years.

The DuPont Corporation, which happens to be one of the larger producers of Teflon cookware, has assured the EPA, that PFOA will be taken out of their product by 2015. One wonders though, how many people and animals may get ill and possibly even develop catastrophic diseases from PFOA, while we wait another 4 years.

According to the **Environmental Working Group**...

"PFCs have been found in nearly all Americans tested by federal public health officials. Chemicals from this family are associated with smaller birth weight and size in newborn babies, elevated cholesterol, abnormal thyroid hormone levels, liver inflammation and weakened immune defense against disease." *The toxic effects of PFC include...*

- *Cancer*
- *Reproductive disorders*
- *Birth defects*
- *Hypothyroidism*
- *Immune system disorders*
- *Organ damage*

Even the act of manufacturing these Teflon coated pans, contributes to environmental pollution. Drinking water contaminated with PFC has been detected near each of the manufacturing facilities which make these cook wares Check out the **Environmental Working Group**, on the 'Net'...

http://www.ewg.org/

...or at your local library. It's just plain healthy to make yourselves aware of the toxic substances that threaten our world. Are there other dangerous products to avoid?

- Nonstick cookware (use glass, stainless steel, cast iron and ceramic cookware)
- Stain proof clothing and carpeting
- Carpet and carpet stain protectors
- Flame retardants with PFC
- Paper and cardboard packaging of greasy foods.
- Microwave popcorn

My final thought is that...

The world of convenience that man has created for himself, in essence, is actually leading to our demise. Progress shouldn't just make things easier. It should make our world and everything on it healthier, so we can all live to enjoy it.

Maybe Grandma was wiser than we thought; always using her heavy cast iron pots and pans around the kitchen. She knew, way back then, she just needed a little olive oil in her skillet to make it a nonstick frying pan. And, you know what?

I do miss my Grandma.

Healthfully Yours,
Dr. Al Plechner DVM & David Spangenburg

Picking a Healthy Pet

People always ask me, what should I look for to make sure that I'm picking a healthy pet that's going to fit right in with my family? Most rescue organizations and city shelters do thorough health checks on the animals before they put them up for adoption. However there are certain clinical signs to look for that point out possibly hidden immune system imbalances that can cause health problems for your pet later on.

Let's begin with dogs.

What is the first and most important consideration you need to think about, their personality. Is he or she going to fit *your* family's lifestyle? - You need to pick a dog that has an energy level that fits your lifestyle. If you're a hearth and home type family pick a dog that is mellow and doesn't need a lot of action and adventure. If you're an active household keep an eye out for that playful pooch who can't sit still.

It is very important to realize many of these adoptees have not had the best care before they got to the shelter or rescue center. Pay attention to their initial response to you. Does the adoptee seem shy, aggressive or fearful upon first contact? If so they may need extra attention the first weeks at home.

One great way to help determine the personality of a puppy is to hold them in your cupped hands lying on their back. If the puppy struggles to turn over and doesn't just lie there, that may be a sign of an aggressive personality and possibly a good candidate for obedience class.

I love all my animals and it can be difficult adding a new member to your family. Make sure you bring in your other furry family members to see if the proposed adoptee is accepted and accepting.

As far as health is concerned, there are clinical signs to be aware of. The condition of their coat and skin is always a good Look at the hair. Is it sparse with areas of no hair? Look at the skin of the stomach. Is the skin, red (inflamed)? or are sores present? Are there any spots that appear as light gray to a black pigmented skin? I am not talking about piebald type markings similar to a Dalmatian's spots. Look for irregular unhealthy looking areas and eruptions. The excess pigmentation often represents a hormonal imbalance involving excess estrogen from the adrenal gland and a nonfunctional thyroid gland.

I am not trying to scare you away from rescue animals. Almost all shelters and rescue organizations have medical professionals that thoroughly examine and care for their animals. I urge you to support your local Shelters and Rescues. As far as I am concerned they are the only way to go and even dogs from a reputable breeder can develop health problems. I just want you to know what to look for.

Let's talk about adopting a cat or kitten.

As with dogs both need to pass the personality test. Does the possible pet enjoy being held and petted? Do they pass the purr test when you cuddle and pet them? Are they aggressive with their claws or teeth?

It can be difficult picking out a healthy kitten they may carry a genetic flaw that cannot be detected by a visual examine. It is wise to have a blood test done to insure that the kitten does not already have feline leukemia, feline infectious anemia or feline infectious peritonitis. All three diseases come from an adrenal imbalance which weakens their natural defenses and makes them highly susceptible to these lethal diseases.

Again, I am not trying to scare you but you need to be aware of these lethal illnesses before you introduce the new adoptee into your home.

It is much easier to identify hormonal imbalances in older cats. The first sign of an imbalance is easy to see. It will be a gingival flare (a red line on the gums). Lift up the top lip of the cat and check the gum tissue as it meets the enamel of the tooth. If a red line is present it indicates an antibody deficiency in all the mucous membranes throughout the body. It is a strong indication that this cat may end up with major problems in the future involving the skin, the intestines, the lungs, the kidneys and/or the bladder.

Are there other signs to look for? Is there hair loss, often accompanied with scabs on the skin? Are there blackheads or pimples on the chin or a thickening of the bottom lip called a neuroma? Most rescue centers are affiliated with a Vet/Pet Health Clinic and so provide a guaranteed bill of health on their animals and some may even allow your own Vet an opportunity to give the adoptee a thorough exam and blood tests prior to adoption. It is always better to be safe than sorry.

Whatever clinical signs of possible imbalances that you see, it does not mean you should turn off the "This is the one!" feelings you have for this animal and not adopt it. Their problems can be controlled, but you need to realize that there will be some possible health expenses to correct these imbalances and to assure a long healthy life for your adoptee. Whether adopting animals or children or even having your own, you accept the responsibility to keep them healthy.

Healthfully Yours,
Dr. Al Plechner DVM & David Spangenburg

To Drive or to Fly, That is the Question

"My family will be traveling over the holidays, and we would like to take our 4-year-old Boston terrier with us. She is typically good in the car, but we are considering flying for the approximately 400-mile journey. Do you think flying would be quicker and less stressful for her than Driving would be, and, if so, can you recommend any non-narcotic ways of calming her for the duration of the flight?

This is a question that's often asked of vets. So, we thought it would be good to mention it here. A 400 mile trip, during the holidays, for me it's a no-brainer, like the Marshall Tucker Band, I'd "Take the Highway". Flying is more problematic, most airlines require a certificate of health. That means a trip to your veterinarian for a quick checkup. It's only good for 10 days. Going for a longer stay? You'll need one for the return trip.

Arrival time is 1 ½ to two hours before boarding. Your pet will need an airline approved carrier that fits under your seat. A 400 mile flight means about a 1 ½ - 2 hour flight time. That is of course, after the plane leaves the tarmac. *Tarmac Time* can be like the "Twilight Zone" and can range from 30 minutes (not during the holidays!) up to 1 to 2 hours and possibly higher.

With the best possible circumstances, your pet, will only have to lay in the carrier around 5 hours and that's not counting, delays or possible cancellation! A car trip, 65 MPH, is around 6 hours, not counting rest stops and eating. Flying time is pretty close to driving time and your pet will be happier, riding in the "pack's" car, sharing holiday tunes with the family.

Either way, your pet should receive a light amount of food and water at least an hour before travel. If she travels in the car, her potty breaks will coincide with the family's needs. Feed her a little dry food or treats, when the family has something to eat.

As for sedation, if needed, natural is the way to go. Her veterinarian should decide on a beginning test dose. Make sure you establish the proper dose before going on your trip.

Many people do not do this ahead of time and the results can be traumatic for both the family and the pet. Use **Rescue Remedy** or antihistamines instead of chemical or pharmaceutical tranquillizers. Again, have her vet decide the dosing. If your pet has ADHD and is totally out of control, I'd find a reputable (and bonded) pet sitter to look after them, at home.

Healthfully Yours,
Dr. Al Plechner DVM & David Spangenburg

In Closing

There is no closing to Dr. Al Plechner's work. While he is in his seventies, he still is in lively practice at **Center-Sinai Animal Hospital** in Los Angeles, California and, at the same time, through long distance consultations, he is healing other patients all over the world.

These other patients may be being ministered by thousands of other healer's hands but those hands, are being guided by Dr. Al's fruitful, clinical research findings and his, ever present, heartfelt encouragement and learned advice.

These distant healers are battling *Plechner's Syndrome,* in the many and varied deadly forms it assumes in each of the afflicted immune systems it inhabits. Their weapons are their individual skills, concern, commitment, and the *Plechner Protocol.*

******

Sent: Tuesday, December 13, 2011 2:25 PM
To: Dr.plechner@hughes.net
Subject: **Questions about your protocol: Cat with viral disease, Cat with Chronic Pancreatitis, and Chihuahua with aftermath of viper bite!**

Dear Dr. Plechner,

Greetings from Italy! I hate to trouble you again, but have some questions for you again regarding your protocol, and also want to share with you an amazing story of a 4.5 kg (9.92 lbs.) **Chihuahua surviving a viper bite, thanks to what you taught me about cortisone!**

Also I have some good news; I have finished both of my degrees--the one in naturopathy and the one in bio-nutrition and am now seeing patients as a nutritionist! Unfortunately, Italy is the only country in Europe which does not recognize naturopathic physicians!

Cat with viral infection:

The first question: is for a cat which has now been surviving leukemia and FIP (had ascites, etc.,) and perhaps another Corona virus, for some years, on your protocol, plus very strong anti-oxidant therapy, vitamins and minerals, etc. The original dose of cortisone was 17.5 mg of delta-cortene, later modified to 16 mg of Delta-cortene after checking the EI-1 panel.

About a year ago, the cat stopped eating well, had symptoms of gastritis, was given DGL (licorice) which was withdrawn after it started acting strangely, and now has been receiving injectable subcutaneous fluids, anti-oxidants, de-toxifiers, and therapy for gastritis at the vets. All the blood work is normal. The cat has seemed a little strange as if it is hallucinating occasionally, and with dilated pupils sometimes.

We want to put the cat on injectable Depo-medrol while it is not eating well.

** What dose of Depo-medrol should we try as the equivalent of 16 mg of Deltacortene orally?

Cat with chronic pancreatitis

The second question is for a cat with chronic pancreatitis. He has been on your protocol for some time now, and takes 17.5mg of Deltacortene a day, and 100 mcg of Eutirox (thyroxin, T 4) twice a day. His most recent blood tests, about a year ago, confirmed that these are correct dosages for him. He eats a hypo-allergenic diet of Hills ZD dry cat food plus defatted mutton and zucchini, millet, onions, or carrots.

The veterinarian insists, during his occasional episodes of pancreatitis, that the Deltacortene dose be lowered to 5 mg. because of the pancreatitis. However, if we are only replacing what cortisone his adrenals do not make, does this make sense? This cat also showed altered liver consistency on his last ultrasound.

** The vet blamed his cortisone therapy, but I wonder if it could be all the Ranitidine, and Plasil, and Baytril he has taken? Or could it be the fact that he has given him DGL (licorice) for his gastritis? Could the licorice make the cortisone circulate too long, and thus overdose him? Or could this liver problem be due to the LOWERED dose of Deltacortene?

Chihuahua with viper bite

The other question regards a Chihuahua (4 kg.). The history is interesting because the dog was bitten by a viper this summer. We thought it had caught a wasp in its mouth at first, and it is an allergic dog with food allergies and wheezes often. After the viper bite, it was having a respiratory crisis, so it was given an immediate injection of 20 mg. of Solu-medrol. It then walked strangely for a few minutes, then acted lethargic, but became totally normal within four or five hours!

The episode seemed resolved and we still did not realize that it was a viper bite not a wasp bite. But, early the next morning its whole body was swollen, and it was in a respiratory crisis again, so it was given another 20 mg. injection of Solu-medrol and rushed to the vet.

The dog has a strange breathing problem which seems to have an allergic trigger from some foods, and wood smoke or car exhaust. On arrival, the vet was screaming that the dog had been given too much cortisone, and that it surely should not have been given the second cortisone shot. At the vet's we did infusions of fluids with glutathione, Samyr, Rossovet, Vitamin C, & Essentiale N (I.V. Phosphatidyl choline) to try to lower the inflammation and detoxify the poisons in system. (The vet had no access to anti-venom.) We kept the dog on thyroid and the hypoallergenic diet.

The vet, then, against furious argument that the dog should be kept on INJECTIBLE cortisone, took out all but 5 mg of oral Deltacortene!!! By the second day, the dog was swollen and in breathing crisis, clearly at risk of dying, so with the vet screaming, the dog was taken away from that clinic to another vet for an ultrasound. That vet, also, was against maintaining the dog on injectable cortisone, so the dog was taken home. It was so lethargic-- that finally all of the vet's advice was ignored and it was given a shot of 10 mg of Solu-Medrol the next morning. In a half

284

an hour or less, the dog was no longer a lethargic dying dog; it was a nearly normal dog!!!

The dog was maintained on Depo-Medrol 10mg. every two weeks for about 6-8 weeks, because it would go into respiratory crises every time the dose was lowered-- even when we tried lowering the dose to 8 mg. of Depo-medrol.

After about six weeks, slowly the dog was weaned off the Depo-Medrol and put back on the oral therapy of 2.5 mg of natural oil-based cortisone (2X/day), 1.25 mg. Deltacortene (1 X/ day), and 12mcg of Eutirox (2 X/day). It seemed a bit too low, but given the fatty liver and the vet screaming "Cushing's" we gave the dog the dose we knew it had tolerated well before.

When the dog was given the ultrasound 3 days after the viper bite, the liver was quite swollen, and that there were ascites (abnormal accumulation of fluid in the abdomen), and also a heart problem which was possibly caused by excess fluid in the tissues around the heart, and there were tracts of malabsorptive bowel! In my opinion (from what I learned from you) this is why the dog was dying on 5 mg. of oral Deltacortene, it did not absorb enough of it in the viper bite situation!) The adrenals were basically normal in size (despite all the screaming the vet had done about Cushing's disease, though the vet doing the ultrasound thought one might be a shade smaller.

After two weeks of infusions and on injectable cortisone (10 mg Depo-Medrol) therapy, with 12 mg oral Eutirox twice a day, a second ultrasound was done, and everything had returned to normal, except the liver was still very swollen, and the intestine still showed the malabsorptive areas. The adrenals were NORMAL in size. The vet said that it was probably a fatty liver due to the cortisone treatment, but was quite amazed at otherwise how well the dog had recovered.

The blood work showed some loss of red cells, but far less than expected with a viper bite, and therefore also the kidney function was undamaged. The liver enzyme levels were quite high, but had come down about 25 percent.

Both vets seemed to blame the cortisone for WHATEVER was wrong, though the second vet did admit that the red cells were saved from the viper venom by the cortisone, and that the lack of destruction of the red cells had saved the kidneys. He thought that the cortisone had also saved the nervous system (when the dog walked funny, and then got better after the cortisone shot). He thought that the nervous system had been saved by the cortisone slowing down the entry of the poison.

Now, given the fatty liver problem, the dog has been on oral therapy again for a few months of 2.5 mg. Natural cortisone in oil, twice a day, Delta-cortene 1.25 mg. once a day, and 12 mcg. of Eutirox twice a day. An attempt was made to heavily curtail its searching for "windfall" in the garden. But then, the dog started losing its hair--especially on the extremities. The dog started urinating a lot.

Although the dog had been put on a low dose of oral cortisone--the same dose it took successfully for a few years with no fatty liver problem developing, the vet blamed HIGH cortisone for the loss of the hair and the swollen liver, and went on about Cushing's disease, which she also did during the viper episode even as she was almost killing the dog by switching to oral cortisone and by lowering the dose too fast! This was an inadequate cortisone dose situation and Cushing's disease was being blamed!

An EI-1 panel was run after the dog was on the oral therapy again for a while and here are the results. Again, it looks like LOW cortisone and thyroid, despite the vet blaming high cortisone, as usual:

Hormonal Studies
Total Estrogen 35.16 Hpg/dl (range 30-35)
Cortisol 0.56 L ug/dl (range 1-2.5)
Test re-checked and verified
Thyroid Studies
T-3 101.18   ng/dl (range 100-200)
T-4 2.00   ug/dl (range 2.00-4.00)
Immunology
IgA 53 L   mg/dl (range 70-170)
gG 710 L   mg/dl (range 1,000 - 2,000)
IgM 69 L   mg/dl (range 100-200)

The other blood tests reveal:
Eosinophils 7 percent   (range 2-10 percent)
BUN (mg/dl) 25   (range 20-40)
Total Bilirubin (mg/dl) 0.5   (range 0.07-0.71)
Creatinine (mg/dl)   0.9   (range 1.0-2.0)
Glucose (mg/dl)   65   (range 60-100
Cholesterol (mg/dl)   350   (range 125-250)
AST (IU/L)   149
ALT (IU/L)   310

Right after the viper bite the liver enzyme levels were about four times this high, and two weeks later they came down to about three times this high. The vets all blame the cortisone; Dr. Ali blames the inflammation and toxicity of the viper bite.

The dog eats a hypo-allergenic diet, Hill's ZD Ultra-hypoallergenic dry dog food, plus fresh de-fatted mutton (defatted with boiling water) and cooked zucchini, millet, onions or carrots.

One thing is for sure, WHATEVER happens the vets ALWAYS blame the cortisone therapy! It gets tiresome, as they don't seem to focus on the fact that the animals are surmounting otherwise insurmountable problems--and that on the long term therapy we are only trying to put into the system the amount of cortisone it lacks--instead they just keep damning the cortisone for anything, and everything!

You would think that they would notice that a 4.5 kg. Chihuahua surviving a viper bite is pretty amazing...

** Given the above tests, to put this dog into a more precise balance, what type and dose of cortisone would you try? What dose of Eutirox would you try? We will give the doses you recommend, and then check the E I-1 panel again in two weeks.

** Is there anything else you could recommend for the liver? (She is getting Silymarin, phosphatidyl choline, broad spectrum anti-oxidants (co q10, germanium, vitamin c, vitamin e). She is taking the digestive enzymes, mineral powders you recommended, and sometimes having castor oil rubs over the chest and liver area (recommended by Dr. Majid Ali).

As always, your help is much appreciated!!! The blindness of the establishment on the cortisone issue must be maddening for you; it certainly has been for me!!!

Thanks to you, Fiocco is still surviving and doing well!!!
Wishing you all the best, and for a very Merry Christmas,

Marta Nardi

******

From: Al Plechner [mailto:Dr.plechner@hughes.net]
Sent: Tuesday, December 13, 2011 3:52 PM
To: 'martanardi****@libero.it'
Subject: FW: Questions about your protocol: Cat with viral disease, Cat with Chronic Pancreatitis, and Chihuahua with aftermath of viper bite!

Congratulations on your degrees! I am very proud of you!
It is so unfortunate that most of the healers do not understand the need and significance use for cortisol replacement. Your cat should go on 1.25 mgs of Depomedrol per pound of body weight IM. This should be repeated in 10 days. I use to use licorice but discovered that it usually changes into more estrogen. Be careful.
Please realize that Depomedrol is not as strong as it used to be, and if the cat has abdominal fluid that is straw colored, FIP is probably present.
With my own clinical studies I have found that.1 mgs of a T4 supplement AM and PM will help. If the pupils keep dilating and CNS problems continue, unfortunately the retro virus has penetrated the blood brain barrier and that definitely is not a good thing. The steroid did not cause the **pancreatitis**. It may have come from the other supplements.

As for the **viper bite**.

The enlarged liver was due to the viper bite and the imbalance it may have caused. Looking at the EI test results, the elevated estrogen is binding the T3 receptor sites and a T4 replacement is indicated at .1 mg per pound of body weight BID.

With an IGA of 53, until that level rises, oral steroids will not be absorbed. Best to give 2 IM injections of Depomedrol at a 10 day interval, and 10 days later begin the oral version. It seems like 1.25mgs per pound of body weight will work better.

Thank you for, as we say in America, "to sticking with your guns". Your input is so valuable and so necessary; people like yourself will shape the future health care of the world.

Please give Fiocco a hug for me, keep up your great direction and have Happy Holidays.

AL

******

Subject: Tigre the Maine Coon

Hi Dr. Plechner,

Hope everything is well with you. I need your expertise. My Maine Coon, Tigre is having his teeth x-rayed tomorrow; he is my cat with high cortisol levels. He is also on your protocol of .1 Vetalog and 35mg of Depomedrol. However, I am concerned because he is going to be anesthetized in order to do this procedure. Should my vet Dr. Poling be adding cortisol at any time during this procedure? I am on Cortef and I was told that if I were to be placed under anesthesia, I would be given added cortisol. Does it work this way with animals? He has tooth resorption issues. Also, I started all three cats on Nutramin. This is a great product. Thank you for introducing it to me. Get to bed early.

Thank you,
Carol-Ann and Boo

******

From: Al Plechner <dr.plechner@hughes.net>
Sent: Mon, Feb 27, 2012 9:33 pm
Subject: FW: Tigre the Maine Coon

His Depomedrol should give enough cortisol during the procedure but if your vet wants to do an IV catheter with a soluble cortisone drip that can be done also. Hopefully iso-fluorine gas can be used for the procedure.
Please let me know how things go.

Dr. P

******

Subject: Re: Tigre the Maine coon

Thanks Dr. P.

I really appreciate all the information you give to me. My husband has met 3 different people at Dr. Margo Roman's office that were following your protocol. [Dr. Roman takes care of Boo] Last week I gave my best friend your site info and she is having her Vet check her 28 year old horse, who is on thyroid med, for Plechner's Syndrome. You are a popular guy!!!

Gratefully,
Carol-Ann and Boo

******

Emails, phone calls, long distance healing, such has been a major part of Dr. Al Plechner's life. Even though his proven findings have not found their way into the curriculums being used by the mainstream veterinary schools, word has gotten out.

Mostly from clients whose pets have been given a new chance for life. "Mommies and Daddies", whose little ones have been brought back from the brink, grateful people who have experienced a "miracle" ...word, gets around.

Each case that Al consults with generates another set of talented, healing hands that are being guided by the curious brains and loving hearts of other medical professionals. These brave souls are driven by the amazingly simple, unreasonably controversial but obviously successful *Plechner Protocol*. Science and medicine have always been advanced by the intrepid curiosity and bold actions of concerned individuals who are not content to accept death as "the only humane answer". Those who chose to take the road less traveled.

There are, sad to say, other healers who Al has helped, to heal their patients as well as themselves, many of which are afraid to face ostracization by their peers and possible censure by the powers that be, because they did "step outside the box" even though their courageous efforts saved lives. At many chapter meetings, Al has asked some of them to pass the information on to their peers and the general response is...

"Are you crazy? I love your work but doing it, could cost me my license"!

What a sad commentary when, saving lives takes a back seat to, maintaining the status quo. Still, the good word is passed along. That's why Al and I wrote this book. We're reaching out to all of you, to tell you, never give up hope. If your pet is ill and the vet doesn't have an answer except...euthanasia.

Get a second opinion.

You can find more answers at Dr. Plechner's website ...

http://www.Drplechner.com.

Medical professionals who are interested in reading about the *Plechner Protocol* in relation to human health, "*Endocrine - Immune Mechanisms in Animals and Human Health Implications, A Compendium of Articles by Dr. Alfred J. Plechner*" is also available at Amazon.com.

I'd like to close my work, with an introduction. Actually, a series of quotes from William Shatner's Introduction to Dr. Al's first book *Pet Allergies, Remedies for an Epidemic*", published back in 1986.

"*...a crisis in health and survival has developed that envelopes not just Dobermans but many breeds of dogs and cats. As the results of improper breeding become more and more evident in the growing incidence of disease, the work of dedicated people like Al Plechner becomes all that more important... someone not content to merely treat the symptoms of diseases. He looks for their causes. What Plechner practices, I believe, is the cutting edge of veterinary medicine...Al Plechner's innovative research into food, allergies and hormonal relationships has had a big impact...*"

- William Shatner

Acknowledgements

I'd like to thank all of Dr. Al's people, who took the time to share their own personal and genuine accounts, about their very intense struggles to maintain their pet's good health in the environmentally challenged world that we live in today. You are all to be commended for your love and commitment.

I'd also like to thank my family, for their patience and confidence, especially my dogs, Skipper, Scout and Merle'n. It wasn't easy for them to lie in their beds by my computer every day, toys close at hand, waiting for Dad to take a break so we could all play.

A standing ovation goes to my wife Kate, (the family's chief bread winner) who endures living with a "writer" whose attention span is easily distracted and whose brain is always "shuffling through the files" looking for a "tasty turn of the phrase".

Very special thanks are also due to...

Ken Collier for his courage and strength, he refused to accept the status quo and went above and beyond to prove his commitment and love for Jazzy.

Al's granddaughter Jayden and loyal dog Jack; for their patience, talent and the "just right" dramatic pose that we used for our cover photo and to Jayden's mom Shelley for taking all of the great photos.

Roz Wheelock, for her thoughtful insight about Dr. Al and his work and her "beyond the call of duty" aid in attaining access to the great "Shatner".

William Shatner's Personal Assistant, Chris Carr, for his incredibly able organization and assistance.

William Shatner for sharing a portion of his ever busy life, to take part in this project and for his patience and good humor during my hesitant, somewhat star struck and digitally challenged interview.

And, of course, my sincere thanks to my dear friend and partner, Dr. Al Plechner. Though we've never met "face to face", his passion, love and complete commitment to all of the flora and fauna of our damaged planet; has sustained my intense dedication to this project for three years. We endured a few wrong turns along the way but our almost daily exchange of emails, kept us on track and truer to course than any GPS could possibly achieve.

We made it, Al!

About the Authors

David Spangenburg - is an actor, musician/songwriter, TV producer/ writer/director and an Arts documentarian/archivist. The creative constant throughout all these varied professions has been his writing. He is a Freelance Wordsmith, currently working in both the print world and cyberspace. His short fiction, essays, articles, poetry, blogs and Op-eds can be found in various magazines, newspapers and on numerous websites. A talented Playwright, he penned the Book and Lyrics to the cult classic musical comedy, "*Carhops, Lost in Time*" and the hilarious two act stage play "*Pirates of the Airwaves!*" which featured, legendary character actor and friend, Victor Wong ("*Last Emperor*", "*Big Trouble in Little China*", "*Golden Child*", *"Joy Luck Club"*). He wrote, produced and directed; "*caught between heaven & hell and no tomorrow*", "*Tapestry*" and "*Stream of Being*" a series of critically acclaimed, Multi-Medium Performance Theatre Productions staged throughout Northern California. He lives in the Gulf Coast Beach Town, St Petersburg, FL with his wife Kate and their three dogs, Rat Terrier - Skipper, Wire Haired Dachshund - Scout and 16 year old Double Sable Merle Sheltie - Merle'n.

Dr. Al Plechner DVM – a 1966 graduate of the University of California, Davis, School of Veterinary Medicine, practiced in West Los Angeles for close to fifty years. Developing a special interest in nutrition and food allergies, his clinical research led him to discover their relationship to hormone-immune imbalances in dogs, cats and horses. Doctor Plechner formulated the first hypoallergenic foods for pets, the first lamb and rice diet, the first vegetarian diet and is the co-creator of *Nature's Recipes*. He also identified endocrine-immune imbalances caused by defective adrenals as well as estrogen dominance in both male and female animals. His clinical findings have been published in veterinary and human medical journals as well as popular animal magazines. He published *Pet Allergies, Remedies for an Epidemic* in 1986,

295

Pets at Risk, From Allergies to Cancer and a Compendium of Medical articles, *Endocrine-Immune Mechanisms in Animal and Human Health Implications* in 2003 and *"Fifty Years of Healing"* in 2012. Though still in active practice in Los Angeles, CA, His home is in the middle of one million acres of state forest, 15 miles from Orofino Idaho. where he lives with his son Jay, daughter in law Shelly, granddaughter Jayden and Big Jack, a Fila, Magnum, an Irish Wolf Hound, their 2 cats, Bert and Ernie and GoGo, a Yorkshire Terrier that was dropped off for a short "baby sit" whose owner never returned.

Made in the USA
Lexington, KY
14 March 2013